ESCAPE INTO DANGER

ESCAPE INTO DANGER

The True Story of a
Kievan Girl in World War II

SOPHIA ORLOVSKY WILLIAMS

ROWMAN & LITTLEFIELD PUBLISHERS, INC.
Lanham • Boulder • New York • Toronto • Plymouth, UK

Published by Rowman & Littlefield Publishers, Inc.
A wholly owned subsidary of The Rowman & Littlefield Publishing Group, Inc.
4501 Forbes Boulevard, Suite 200, Lanham, Maryland 20706
www.rowmanlittlefield.com

Estover Road, Plymouth PL6 7PY, United Kingdom

British Library Cataloguing in Publication Information Available

Library of Congress Cataloging-in-Publication Data
Williams, Sophia, 1923–
  Escape into danger : the true story of a Kievan girl in World War II / Sophia
Orlovsky Williams.
    p. cm.
  ISBN 978-1-4422-1468-2 (cloth : alk. paper) — ISBN 978-1-4422-1470-5
(electronic)
  1. Williams, Sophia, 1923– 2. World War, 1939–1945—Personal narratives,
Ukrainian. 3. World War, 1939–1945—Ukraine. 4. Ukraine—History—German
occupation, 1941–1944. 5. Ukraine—Biography. 6. Ukrainian Americans—
Biography. I. Title.
  D811.5.W4937 2012
  940.53'4777092—dc23
[B]
                                                                        2011036163

∞™ The paper used in this publication meets the minimum requirements of
American National Standard for Information Sciences—Permanence of Paper
for Printed Library Materials, ANSI/NISO Z39.48-1992.

Printed in the United States of America

Dedicated to the memory of the 100,000 Kievans of various ethnic groups, mostly Jews, killed by the Nazis at Babi Yar

CONTENTS

PART III: GERMAN OCCUPATION

PART IV: EYE OF THE HURRICANE

PART V: INSIDE NAZI GERMANY

PART VI: POSTWAR GERMANY

ACKNOWLEDGMENTS

For the constructive criticism from my caring friends and readers of the book-in-the-making, I am deeply grateful.

Thank you to Patricia Golemon for editorial comments and valuable suggestions.

Lou Bilter and Carol Sue Finkelstein, my dear friends, you have been helpful and supportive, and I thank you.

Thank you to Mark Zaltsberg and Vladimir Sukholutsky for contagious enthusiasm and encouragement.

Thank you to Rhoda Clamen for wise counsel and openhearted hospitality.

Thank you to Carolyn Murphy for unflagging support since China days.

Special thanks to Susan McEachern, Janice Braunstein, Grace Baumgartner, and Catherine Bielitz, the wonderful editorial staff at Rowman & Littlefield who brought the finished book into the world.

AUTHOR'S NOTE

I changed a few names to protect the guilty in some lands—innocent in the USA—and to protect the privacy of an extended family.

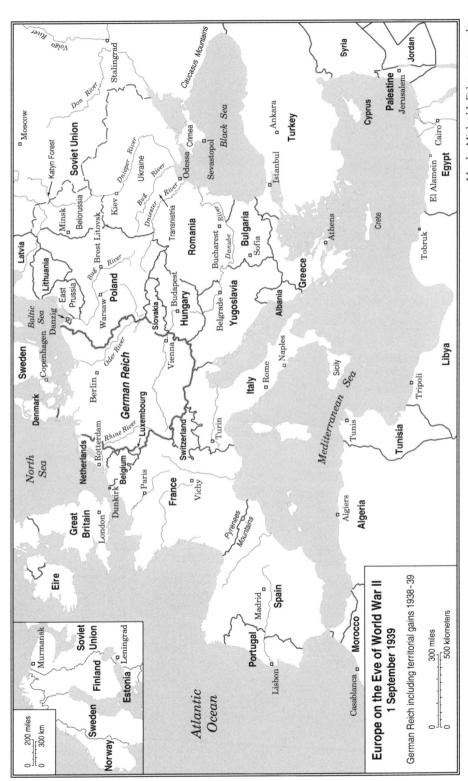

Map by Michael J. Fisher, cartographer

Europe on the Eve of World War II
1 September 1939

German Reich including territorial gains 1938–39

300 miles

500 kilometers

ESCAPE INTO DANGER

Part I

SPRING OF YOUTH

1

FULL OF SPUNK

My mother never wavered in her assertion that the Soviet Union and I were born by accident. She never wanted to have any children, and she pined for the czar. My father, eight years younger than my mother, welcomed both of us—his only daughter and the Soviet regime.

My mother and her family were Roman Catholics of Polish and German ancestry. My father was Jewish—never mind my mother's claim that he had converted to Catholicism. When in time I became aware of such things, I understood that my father could not have converted because he was a Bolshevik inclined to atheism. I was born on December 29, 1923. They named me Sophia and a priest baptized me, but I was not reared a Catholic.

We lived with my Jewish grandparents and Uncle Lazar in Podol, a low-lying district of Kiev, where my small life was steady and secure.

Chestnut trees were in bloom when in 1928 we moved up the hill to Vladimirskaya Street No. 45, in the very navel of the city and diagonally across from the opera house. This location delighted my mother, a former singer with the opera. My father was quite satisfied: he found two large rooms for us in an eight-room apartment occupied by seven families. In those days, that was a feat.

My delight was the courtyard, large and alive with noisy children playing games of hopscotch, hide-and-seek, and tag. Boys were kicking a ball and running madly after it. Even while the movers were unloading our furniture and trying to get me out of their way, I met my future playmates, classmates, and friends.

The movers struggled with our old grand piano up the 109 steps to the top floor. As soon as they left, I ran upstairs. My mother was singing an aria from *The Barber of Seville.* She surveyed the unfurled Oriental rugs and set out to decorate the creamy walls with paintings, a stuffed baby crocodile, and a Caucasian dagger. She hung her portrait over the marble fireplace where logs would burn in winter.

These were the final days of the New Economic Policy, the brief period after the Russian Revolution when private enterprise was permitted. The firewood to keep our rooms warm was still plentiful, and the water to flush our communal toilet was still running.

Every summer we spent at our dacha in the forest of Pushcha Voditsa. Wild strawberries and mushrooms grew in the woods in profusion; a heavenly scent hung in the air when the jasmine and wild cherry trees were in bloom. Aunts and cousins and both grandmothers often spent the day with us, and we went on picnics in the meadows alive with butterflies. We carried blankets and baskets filled with food and drink. Many visitors flocked to the dacha for joyful social evenings. They drank vodka from cucumbers cut in half and scooped out—one of my mother's inventions. She claimed vodka tasted better that way.

My father usually arrived at the dacha after work. I'd always be there, waiting for him at the streetcar stop. "How are things, Sonyechka?" he'd ask me, his Sonya, lifting me on his shoulders and carrying me home. I felt proud of my father; he was tall and lean, and his full head of hair was dark and wavy. I loved to watch his long fingers dance across the piano keys or strum the mandolin. Unlike my mischievous mother, he was serious most of the time, but even then his big brown eyes seemed to smile. Surely he was the smartest, the best-looking papa of them all.

Sometimes he did not come, and I would go home feeling sad. The summer of 1929 was the saddest. One early July day, as I returned from romping in the meadows, our summer furniture and bedding were on the porch. A horse-drawn dray was waiting to be loaded.

With tears in her eyes, my mother said, "We're going home." I asked her why, and she cried. "Your papa found someone else, my little dove."

I had never seen my mother cry before, and it frightened me. "Mamochka"—I touched her face—"don't cry."

She hugged me closely to her and sobbed.

Soon after, my parents were divorced. My mother was inconsolable. Bitterly she complained about her lot in life, blaming the Revolution for everything, cursing Stalin and the Bolsheviks. I was four-and-a-half years old and couldn't understand what Stalin and the Revolution had to do with my father leaving us, but I too was hurt. I missed my papa.

★ ★ ★

My mother, a well-groomed, green-eyed beauty with a sweep of reddish-blond hair, easily attracted the opposite sex. Yet she never remarried. Two months after the divorce she met the proprietor of a bookstore she said would be my new papa. I remembered him only because the world map on the wall beside my bed and many of the books on the shelves above my desk came from him: *Gulliver's Travels*, a well-worn collection of poems by Pushkin, *Pinocchio*, exquisitely illustrated old Russian fairy tales, *Twenty Thousand Leagues under the Sea*, and more. The man died that summer from fish poisoning, and my mother grieved.

The gloomy summer had faded into a golden October when a man I called Uncle Otari appeared in my mother's romantic sanctuary. He was from Georgia, a handsome man with blazing dark eyes, tall and wiry. Mother's eyes sparkled when he arrived. Both loved company, and on many nights a jovial group gathered around our table, eating, drinking, and singing Russian romances and Gypsy songs. On my fifth birthday I ate with the grown-ups. Then I danced *Lesginka*, Uncle Otari's native dance, which I had learned from him. I grabbed our dagger from the wall and brandished it as I moved my feet in the fiery rhythm of the Caucasian Mountain dance. I loved to dance and would soon enroll myself for free ballet lessons at the opera.

The following spring, Mama took me into the woods where the trees were immense and it smelled of pinesap. She seemed deep in thought for long moments as she watched a bird soaring in the sky. Then she leaned against a tree, tilted her head up, and in a full voice began to sing a poignant Ukrainian ballad: "Why wasn't I born a falcon? Why can't I fly? Had God given me wings, I would've abandoned the earth. I'd have flown to the skies." I wanted to know why she wanted to fly away, but she did not answer. Instead, she told me that Uncle Otari had been sent far away. She prayed for his return. But he never came back. He perished in Siberia.

After Uncle Otari, men came and went, ringing our doorbell whenever the notion struck them. I didn't like these "uncles," but I did like the cheese and sausages they brought.

One day I returned home from an errand empty-handed. "I'm hungry, Mamochka."

"I gave you money to buy something to eat."

"I gave it to a beggar woman in the street." With her wispy white hair she looked like Babushka, my darling granny.

Mother made a sound of frustration. "There's some bread in the kitchen. Have that and I'll make you a nice cup of tea."

Each family in our communal kitchen had a table with shelves above and a Primus (a one-flame kerosene burner). The tantalizing aroma of Ukrainian borscht hovered in the air. Other times it smelled of fried potatoes, meat dumplings, fried or gefilte fish, chickens. Mama ignited our Primus and put a kettle on. As usual, the kitchen faucet was dripping. I ate quickly and ran downstairs to play. In the evening, I asked for another piece of bread.

Mother sighed. "You finished all we had, Zosik. There's nothing in the house . . . and no money. Maybe somebody will come."

My mother's men friends gave her money or brought food wrapped in newspapers. I understood nothing about sexual politics at that time, but I knew we depended on these men. I hoped, as Mama did, that our doorbell would ring.

The bell did not ring. "I don't know what to do." Mama's eyes began to overflow. "You can thank your papa for leaving us destitute."

"Can't you sell something?"

"I have nothing left to sell." She had already parted with some jewelry, also an Oriental rug. "What about the other rugs and paintings?" I asked. My mother was horrified. "I would rather starve."

"Why can't I see my papa? He won't let me starve."

Aunt Yulia, my mother's sweet-natured sister who loved to cook and bake, was concerned about my growing up without a father. She admonished my mother, "You can't let the child run around unattended, Mimi. She's barely six years old! What will become of her? Send her to her father, let him take care of her." My mother would have none of that. "Don't you worry about my Zosik. She's a bright girl and full of spunk. She'll be all right."

"Your papa doesn't love you anymore, Zosik," my mother told me. "Why must you insist on seeing him? He's no good. He and that—that witch with shaggy hair he married."

"Then why don't you go to work?" I exploded. I did feel mean. Papa had stopped paying alimony to make Mama go to work because he *did* love me. Uncle Vanya had said so to Aunt Yulia.

Mother didn't like what I said and became hysterical. Father had destroyed her singing career, she sobbed, and then he deserted her. After a time she calmed down, as I knew she would. She dragged her fur coat from the wardrobe—a luxurious otter lined with emerald green silk—shook off the mothballs, and declared in a dramatic soprano voice, "This is the last thing I'm going to sacrifice."

Mother's wardrobe from previous years was substantial; she was always well dressed, bucking the trend toward the drab attire of the day. It pained her to part with the coat, while I gloated when it was sold and we went shopping for food at the Bessarabka farmers market.

The market was colorful with berries, melons, ropes of onions, and flowers. It swarmed with plump women bargainers and farmers hawking their own produce.

A peasant called out: "Chickens! Young, fat chickens!"

Mother stopped with regal poise, inspected a chicken, and sniffed and pinched it. "Fat, you dare say? I see nothing but bones wrapped in skin. *Blue* skin!"

The shrewd peasant answered, "Wouldn't you be blue if everybody pinched you all the time?"

"Well, at least I wouldn't smell like that," Mama fired back, and she shot away to avoid hearing the reply.

That day we ate beef roasted with potatoes, sweet corn on the cob, and a huge watermelon. What a feast!

My old shoes were flopping out their last days. Our expedition to buy a new pair was a fiasco. We combed the stores and, finally, found a pair that fit. The cashier took the money from my mother and then coolly claimed she had not been paid. We had been robbed in the most blatant way possible. My mother stormed out of the store like all three Furies in one. I grabbed my old shoes and trailed barefoot behind her.

Mother finally had no choice but to go to work at the arms-producing plant, called Bolshevik. She hated the job, but her lack of qualifications made it impossible to find anything better.

My father found out that Mother had started working. To get me off the street, he somehow managed to enroll me in School No. 54 on Lenin Street. Children in the Soviet Union did not start school until age eight. I was not yet seven. I set off for school on September 1, 1930, wearing brand-new ankle-high shoes with laces. Mama strapped my brown satchel across my shoulders and kissed me good-bye.

Mother worked long hours and rarely cooked. I fended for myself, spending my daily allowance gleefully on ice cream and seltzer water sweetened with fruit syrup. Or I'd buy a long string of tiny bagels, hang it around my neck like a necklace, and munch on the go. My friends had no money of their own—their mothers were at home and cooked for them—so I was the richest little girl on our block but also the hungriest.

Yet, I did not feel deprived. I was a happy, active child. Each day was a new beginning, and I accepted cheerfully what each day brought.

2

"LET IT ROT!"

Our neighbors' pots were soon as empty as ours. Famine, as well as epidemics of scarlet fever, diphtheria, meningitis, and typhus, hit Kiev with brutal force soon after Stalin's forced collectivization began in 1930. Rationing was introduced, and overnight, lines began to form for meager supplies of bread fortified with sawdust, mildewed millet, and potatoes, either rotten or frozen, depending on the time of year. The endless lines became a way of life.

In August 1931, Mama and I escaped from Kiev to eat and drink milk to our hearts' content in the country. The whitewashed peasant cottages with sloped roofs of straw were surrounded by greenery: fruit trees, raspberry bushes, patches of pumpkins, tall sunflowers, and dill weeds. On Sunday the village lads brought out their accordions, and the maidens gathered around them to sing and dance. As I watched them, the sky turned black. The sudden downpour accompanied by fierce thunder and lightning was spectacular; I was sorry, almost resentful, when it was over.

Farms were still privately owned in this prosperous nook of the Ukraine, and food was plentiful. I couldn't understand why it was forbidden to bring any of it back home: the police boarded the trains and confiscated food carried by passengers returning to the starving city. And when after the storm I started gathering the fruit that had been knocked off the trees, the farmer told me angrily, "Let it rot!" I skipped away, puzzled.

The peasants bitterly resented collectivization and revolted against it. Many had abandoned the farms; others slaughtered and poisoned cattle and burned their crops rather than surrender them to the collectives. Before the revolt was crushed, cities in the fertile Ukraine suffered extreme shortages of food. Coal production had also declined, which led to acute shortages of

fuel. Hardships were frightful. Millions of people died in the Ukraine during the famine, which reached its peak in the winter of 1933.

The bout of scarlet fever I had in 1932 was a blessing. The uniformed
paramedics and the siren-screaming ambulance that took me to a hospital
for treatment and forty-two days in isolation had so impressed my mother
that she quit the arms-producing plant, joined the ambulance corps, and
became a paramedic.

I returned home in an ambulance! My mother picked me up. She
looked well and content, her voice now stronger and more confident. She
told me that the people standing in endless lines for their share of bread let
the ambulance attendants go to the front of the line. "Not only that," she
added, "the families of the sick who live on the outskirts and have garden
plots give us apples, a few potatoes, now and then a head of cabbage or an
egg. So, my little one"—her lips curled in a smile—"you no longer have to
stand in line for scraps of food. Happy?" Yes, and relieved to see my mother
in a good, optimistic mood for a change.

"Come after school sometime, and we'll give you a ride," she said.
"It'll help your immune system resist infections."

I did just as my heterodox mother advised, and there was nothing
more exciting. I loved the speed and the sirens of the ambulance, and the
feeling of being important when all traffic stopped to let us through.

To curb the epidemics, the government ordered that all persons with
a communicable disease be treated in isolation hospitals. The ambulances
were constantly on the move, transporting the ill to the hospitals. But not
all were willing to leave their homes. My mother was bribed with gifts of
food, had doors slammed in her face, was verbally abused, was terrorized
and bitten by dogs.

One wintry night she came home greatly disturbed. "We had to pick
up a typhoid-stricken man in Lukyanovka today. But we couldn't find
him. We searched and searched the house, and there in the basement was
a corpse."

"What's so special about that?" I shrugged my shoulders. Many horse-
drawn drays transported corpses to cemeteries every day.

"Not just a corpse, Sophia. A corpse with its buttocks and thighs sliced
off! Listen to me. Don't you dare buy sausages from a peddler—not even if
he insists they're made from pure horsemeat."

"Disgusting!" It made me want to throw up.

★　★　★

Housing was getting more and more scarce in the city, and most people had
to live one family of three and four to a singe room. Mother outwitted the

system by selling the smaller of our two rooms before the authorities could take it away from us. We also sold our prized possession, the grand piano, to our new neighbor, a prominent actor.

Mother created a lovely home for us in the midst of the drab proletarian realism. She arranged our large room into three separate areas: sitting-dining area, her "boudoir," and my bedroom-study. The round dining table with brass-trimmed pedestal stood near the entry door. At the far end of the room, spanning the left corner near the fireplace, a low divan was covered with an Oriental rug and piled with soft cushions. The rug continued on down, covering some of the intricately inlaid parquet floor. Behind the divan, a Chinese bowl on a pedestal was filled with fresh flowers, brilliant autumn leaves, or dried sunflowers. We had an aquarium, a tall, narrow cylinder with a domed lid. To keep the fish happy, Mother placed a lightbulb inside the lid.

An ebony bust of a grinning Mephistopheles—with red lights inserted into his eyes (one of my mother's macabre creations)—guarded the entrance to my hideaway. I had a daybed, a narrow wardrobe, and a desk with bookshelves above. The desk and the wardrobe placed against the back of Mother's mirrored triple armoire separated her area from mine. We each had a folding silk screen and a French window with access to the terrace. I closed my screen only when my mother entertained. Her boudoir was a symphony in terra-cotta satin and white lace.

To camouflage the unsightly door to our new neighbor, the actor, my mother had a floor-to-ceiling canvas painted by an artist. In her passion for the unusual, she requested the design to be abstract—at a time when modern abstract art was denounced as bourgeois decadence.

What I always loved about our home was the view from our rooftop terrace: we looked down on the tall chestnut trees that lined Vladimirskaya Street, the opera and ballet theater to the left, and to the right the golden cupolas of the Saint Sophia Cathedral. Directly across the street, the ancient Golden Gates held court over the city in the park with its cascading fountain.

Mother's small circle of friends continued to frequent our house. When food was scarce, they joyfully shared whatever they could glean.

★　★　★

On Sunday, January 1, 1933, a few days after Mother and I celebrated my ninth birthday, I set out for Irininskaya Street to see my father, breaking the promise I had made to my mother never to seek him out. An icy wind howled and blew into my face that day. I pulled my wool beret down over my ears and plowed on, fighting against the fierce wind like a bull charging a red cape.

Valentina Sergeyevna, my father's second wife, opened the door when I arrived. I remembered meeting her on a boat with my father before my parents were divorced. I called her Tetya (Aunt) Valya. She was twenty-nine now, much younger than my mother. Her chestnut curls were tight. She crinkled her soft-gray eyes when she smiled. "Well, look who's here!"

She took me by the hand and led the way through a dark and drafty corridor into their warm room. Books and newspapers were scattered about. Fire roared in the potbellied stove set up in the middle of the room for extra warmth.

And there, sitting at the table and reading, was my papa. I wrapped my arms around his neck, and he kissed me on the cheek. All at once he unwrapped my arms. "A nine-year-old should be able to keep her nose clean." He frowned. "Where's your handkerchief?"

Tears of humiliation sprang to my eyes, but I fought them back. "I lost it, Papa." He gave me his handkerchief.

"How she has grown," Tetya Valya intervened. "Look at her deep dimples and rosy cheeks." She took a pinch of my cheek.

"She's beginning to look like her mother," Papa said, and I cringed inwardly. I wanted to look like him.

"There's a lot of you in her, Misha. Sonya's beautiful green eyes may be her mother's, but the determination in them is yours. She also has your stubborn chin. Just look at it. She's your child, my love, there's no mistaking that."

I gave Tetya Valya a grateful smile. I leaned against the tall tile stove and watched her place a breadbasket on the table, also cherry preserves and a slab of margarine in a crystal bowl. She poured tea into china cups, and we sat down to eat.

"What do you do with yourself all day?" Father was sipping tea and swallowing cherries from a teaspoon.

Eagerly I named my friends and enumerated the games we played. I told him that I wanted to be a ballerina and was attending ballet classes at the opera. I wanted my father to be proud of me, but he didn't seem impressed. It dampened my spirits somewhat, but it did not detract from the joy I felt at having Papa in my life again.

"How are you doing at school? Learning anything? More than our lovable nitwit Svyatoslav, I hope."

Who is Svyatoslav? I wondered, when Tetya Valya picked up a pillow and threatened to throw it at my father.

"I warn you, Misha. You say that once more about my son, and I'll put rat poison in your food."

"Hmm . . . that's what I've been eating anyhow. Can't you think of anything more powerful?"

Tetya Valya threw the pillow at him. Imitating Charlie Chaplin's walk, Father shuffled across the room and got a feather pillow from the bed. They got into a pillow fight, laughing and carrying on like two silly children. I kept giggling into the palm of my hand, enjoying the fight.

Father returned to the table. "Let me see, where was I? Ah yes, Svetik." And he proceeded to tell me that the boy, named Svyatoslav after his illustrious grandfather, was in his fourth year at school and still unable to spell his name.

Could Svetik be that stupid? I was two years younger, a third grader, and could already read and write, and sometimes I could even read what I wrote. I was good at arithmetic and tried to show off to Papa by manipulating some numbers. He patted me on the head, picked up a newspaper from the floor, and resumed reading. Tetya Valya busied herself clearing the table. It was time for me to go, but I wasn't sure how to make an exit, so I lingered.

At last Papa dropped the paper and looked at me, fidgeting. "Ready to run? Well, go on. Be good, Sonyechka, and do come again, will you? And remember, you must study harder if you want to amount to anything."

Oh yes, I will come again, I thought on my way home. There was nothing I wanted more than to win my father's approval, and as I joyfully skidded on the ice I resolved to study harder and try to impress him with what I had learned.

It was my father's interest in my education and the pressure I felt to keep up with my classmates and the studious Inna Bregman, my best friend, that kept me on the right path.

When my mother found out about my visit—Sergei, the boy next door, squealed on me—she cried and called me a willful child, disobedient and disloyal. I felt bad about it but not bad enough to stay away from Irininskaya Street. For several years I sneaked around corners like a thief to see my father occasionally.

My father had a wry sense of humor; he was distant at first and difficult to please. Tetya Valya treated me the same as she treated her son and stood up for me when I erred. Her first husband had died when he plummeted down the bluff skiing in the riverside park. She was eighteen at the time and Svetik only a baby. I felt sorry for the skinny boy with spiky straw-blond hair, because my father called him Nitwit and because he had no father at all.

My father and Tetya Valya were happy together. Both loved classical music, read a great deal, and played the piano. The top of their upright was piled with musical scores; a glass-fronted bookcase was crammed with novels and poetry by French, German, and Russian authors and poets.

Father was a mandolin virtuoso; as a young man he had played the mandolin in the Red Army orchestra. Tetya Valya drew ink sketches of old people's faces and hands. The lovable Nitwit didn't do well at school, but he had great talent for painting and sculpture. His sculptures later brought him many accolades.

After joining the Kiev Scientific Film Studio in 1936, Father traveled a great deal. When he was out of town, mostly in Moscow or on location, I visited with Tetya Valya, who practiced cosmetology at home.

The loveliest afternoons were when Papa was home and in the mood to play the mandolin or amuse us with his rubber-faced impersonations of characters from Chekhov's plays. Or when Papa and I huddled next to the potbellied stove and played chess. But those afternoons were oh, so rare!

Not content with occasional visits, I began to take advantage of a disagreement with Mother to stay at Father's overnight. I also began visiting Uncles Lazar, Yasha, and Boris and their families. Mama finally gave up the battle, and after several years of tears and arguments there were no more scenes.

3

POLITICS

I joined the Young Pioneers when our entire class was pledged to follow the teachings of Ilyich, as we affectionately called Lenin. Like all my friends, I was an avid Soviet patriot. Our leaders were my heroes. I had faith in Stalin, blind faith in his leadership. I firmly believed that had it not been for the October Revolution, Mother Russia would have remained backward and insignificant, its people poor, illiterate, and oppressed.

My mother had no use for any of my heroes. She never had a good word to say about the Soviet regime. Our talks usually turned into arguments.

She often recalled the days when she was young. She brought to life the banquets and soirees she had attended with gallant officers and dapper cavaliers who kissed her hand and showered her with perfume and flowers. "Nowadays, men shower me with firewood and bottles of kerosene." She laughed, and I laughed with her. "Ekh, Zosik, Zosik, those were the days." Her voice was soft, melodious. "What a wonderful life we had under the czar."

My amusement instantly cooled. "Maybe *you* had. Most people, the masses, were illiterate, downtrodden, and destitute."

"That's what *they* tell you. You believe them and repeat everything like a parrot." *They* and *them* in the parlance of the day were usually the Soviet authorities. "People are starving today. And this in the fertile Ukraine."

"Well," I drawled, "that may be so. But it's only because our peasants are lazy, that's why."

"Stop wagging your tongue. The peasants refuse to work because Stalin forced them into collectives. And the kulaks who really knew how to make the land produce were all eliminated."

"What do you mean by that?" I demanded.

"Never mind. The less you know about it the better. With your mouth, you could get us in trouble."

"I'm not a blabbermouth. I'm twelve years old."

"Ah, when I was twelve . . ."

Mother hated our communal apartment existence and grumbled at intervals. Some time later, it was: "This living in one room and waiting in line to use the toilet, it's abominable."

"It doesn't bother me one bit." Everybody lived like us.

"But it bothers me. We're all forced to sleep in the same room with our children. My family had a large house. It belonged to us. Do you understand?"

"What's so great about owning a house? Everything on Soviet soil belongs to us today, not just the house."

This exasperated my mother. "You're almost fourteen and silly as ever. You're like the rest of them who don't know what it's like to own property, to be well off. Everybody lives in poverty today in this proletarian society of equal misery for all."

Another time, another year, Mother said, "They took everything away from us. My family lost their shoe factory—nationalized! But what did they give us in return? Nothing. Nothing but promises."

"They freed us from the czarist yoke and made us equal."

"For God's sake, don't annoy me with all that chatter about freedom and equality." She flared up. "I'm sick of listening to you defend this new way of life. I'll *never* get used to it, so let me be."

"Not so loud, Mama," I whispered through my teeth.

"You can't chain up an old house dog and expect him not to yelp."

"Mama, please! The walls have ears."

"So let them hear me and denounce me." She raised her voice still higher. "Let them come and get me too."

"Please, Mamochka," I begged, frightened now.

She sobbed, and then she said, "No, I must be careful, for your sake, Zosik. If they took me away, what would happen to you?"

Nothing, I thought, silently watching her cry for a time. *I can look after myself just fine.* But I did not want her arrested. She was my mama. I felt protective toward her, almost as if I were the mother and she the child. She no longer cared where I went or how long I stayed away from home, obviously grateful not to have me underfoot. But I knew even then, though I could not have formulated the thought, that it was the child in her who trusted me to stay out of trouble. I also knew that she liked me better now;

she had recently begun to dress me nicely and to seek my company. Now she claimed to care, to care about what would happen to me if she were arrested. And I thought that perhaps, after all, she had always cared about me in her own obscure way. And I cared, and I could not allow her to be taken away.

"Please, Mama, don't cry. When I finish college, I'll work hard. I'll help you then, and someday I'll take care of you."

She clasped my hand. I looked closely at her and marveled at how lovely she looked. Nearly fifty and not a wrinkle on her skin, her complexion flawless. And very few gray hairs—I knew exactly how many, for I had pulled them for a kopeck each.

"You are the prettiest woman in Kiev," I said with conviction and a big smile, knowing this would cheer her up.

She examined herself in front of the mirror, raised and lowered her eyebrows, and wiped her tears. Then she powdered her nose, touched up her eye makeup, and put on lipstick.

"No grease, no smooth ride," she said, and she smiled.

★   ★   ★

After years of hunger, meat and potatoes sizzled again in our neighbors' frying pans. The peasants' revolt had been crushed. Rationing had been abolished. Stalin proclaimed, "Life has become better, life has become more joyful." And the sea of gray quilted jackets seemed to have vanished overnight. Kievans began to wear colorful attire and a smile.

The tenants congregated in the kitchen.

"Look at these beautiful plump herrings I got at the Gastronome yesterday. I stood in line only one hour."

"They were giving out milk and crawfish yesterday. Yes, yes, it is getting better," Madame Arendarev, wearing a brightly colored shift, agreed. The Arendarevs were a congenial couple. He was a professor at the university. Their son Sergei was my pal.

"The fools," my mother muttered in the privacy of our room. "Give them a drop of milk, and they think they're getting a bucketful. Why, under the czar I could've bought enough to fill a bathtub."

"That's the trouble with you. You want milk to bathe in."

"Why not?" she said in a silken voice. "You think I can do that when we achieve Communism?"

The next morning Madame Arendarev was sobbing in the kitchen. They had come for her husband in the night, and we all knew what that meant: five years, perhaps forever, in Siberia. Our neighbors moved about with their heads bent, as if at a funeral. No one said a word nor tried to console Madame Arendarev—except my mother.

Two days after the arrest, Sergei and I were looking at my picture album when Leonid Charny, a high-ranking man with the terror-inspiring NKVD (later known as the KGB) came to visit my mother. He was a friendly man, so open it was impossible to imagine a drop of malice in his soul. Mother also knew he still had some sentimentality in the depths of his heart, despite the spine-chilling routines of his job as an interrogator of political prisoners. She was going to play on that.

After some conversation between Charny and Mother, we heard her say in a sonorous voice, "Aren't these two a pleasure to look at? The pride and backbone of the Soviet Union—its future! I'm proud of my Sophia." She turned to me, smiling. "You do want to join the Komsomol, don't you? And you, Sergei?"

Mother and I exchanged glances. I knew she was expecting a positive reply. I didn't know about Sergei, but I fully intended to join, eventually. *But what does it matter to Mama? Where did this patriotism suddenly come from? Does she want to impress Comrade Charny?* Another split second and I knew, and I answered, "Yes, yes!" with appropriate enthusiasm. Sergei's yes was more subdued.

Mama's smile faded. She cocked her head and with sadness in her voice continued, "Too bad, though—Sergei's future is a bit grim."

"How is that?" Charny wanted to know.

"They took his father away."

"When?"

"Two nights ago."

Sergei and I did not get to hear the rest. What was left of the mission to be accomplished must have come to my mother with great ease when she winked at me to run along.

Arendarev was cleared of all charges, and he returned home a few days later a free man, which was something of a miracle. The families of convicts did not normally hear from them until they had reached their destinations. Until Arendarev, we had not seen or heard of a single release.

Mother's daring was notorious, but this act topped them all. Had they convicted Arendarev instead of clearing his name, Charny might have felt compelled to order Mother's arrest, if only to place himself above suspicion or to protect himself from a possible trap.

I was dying to find out why Arendarev had been arrested in the first place. Everybody was so secretive.

"Maybe he was caught smearing Stalin's face with shit?" Mother suggested.

Newspapers were what we used for toilet paper. Since our papers often carried pictures of our wise leader, his image was put to good use. If the evidence could not be flushed (our water was rarely running—the pressure was too low), the culprit could be caught and reported by a neighbor. Five years, minimum.

After five years of hard labor in Siberia, Uncle Yosif, Mother's brother, was released. He returned a frightened man who minded his own business and spoke to no strangers, afraid they would twist his words. He was gentle and considerate of everyone. We loved him dearly and found it hard to bear when in the summer of 1939 he was again arrested as an enemy of the people and again condemned—this time to *ten* years in Siberia, where he died some years later.

I had never been so angry in my life. It was then that my hero image of Stalin crumbled. *All these terrible, unfair arrests—just like under the czars! To condemn innocent men to suffer in Siberia is cruel!* I fumed with adolescent righteousness. *Could Stalin actually know about them? Whether he knows or not,* I decided, *he can't be wise. He rushed collectivization and made a mess of it, trying to accomplish in five years what Lenin said would take fifty.*

"I wish Lenin were still alive," I said in a whisper to Aunt Yulia and her husband, Uncle Vanya, on a subsequent visit with them. "Things would have been different if—"

"Shhh," they silenced me.

The three-story brick house where they lived with their son used to belong to Uncle Vanya. The three-room apartment that the family was allowed to keep after the state had appropriated the building was modest enough. They did not have to share it with strangers, and they were content. Recently, though, they had had to surrender half of the larger room to another family. They had installed a plywood partition, and you could hear the new tenants breathe on the other side of it. Without privacy, my aunt and uncle had to think before they spoke.

Uncle Vanya was a fine man, a gentleman with a trim mustache and a warm smile. That evening he escorted me to the streetcar stop so he could talk without fear of being overheard. He had never talked to me like this before. *This,* I thought with my chest puffed up, *is because he now looks on me as an adult, a trustworthy adult.* I sensed he was a deeply disillusioned man. While he cared about his son and wife, he no longer cared about himself. He expected a war to break out, and when it happened, he said, he would not be there to look after his vulnerable family. Nor would he be called to serve the Mother Russia that he loved. For years he had been waiting for the NKVD to come for him at night. For years he had lived in fear.

"How awful!" I cried.

"Yes, it's been weighing heavily upon my soul. Now the waiting period is nearly over. I feel relieved."

"How do you know? How could you be relieved about *that*?"

"I know I will be arrested. Yes . . . I know ahead of time. A friend of my colleague saw my name on the list."

Yet he was calm about it. He even smiled when I urged him to run away and hide somewhere. Somehow he looked forward to the arrest, as if he had lived in hiding all these years and was anxious to get it over with. It was incomprehensible to me.

"You believe in people and our glorious leadership," he had said to me. "You are an idealist."

The NKVD did come for him—in broad daylight.

When they took him away, declared an enemy of the people just because he had owned property, I didn't know who or what to believe in anymore.

4

INTERNATIONALKA

On September 1, 1939, one week after Stalin signed a nonaggression pact with Hitler, the German Army attacked Poland. The Red Army attacked from the east, and the two friendly nations divided Poland between them. The Soviet Union gained Western Ukraine and Western Belorussia. And we rejoiced: suddenly, ready-made dresses and swimsuits became available.

The following January, when I reached the required age of sixteen, I applied at the police station for a passport. These were domestic passports with a photograph, introduced in 1930 as a device to control the lives and movement of the population and issued only to city and town dwellers. Without this key document, it was impossible to get the mandatory residency permit or a job in the city. Thus the peasants were tied to the land.

I presented my birth certificate and was asked my full name: surname, first name, and patronymic.

"Orlovskaya, Sophia Mikhailovna."

The policeman wrote that down. "Nationality?"

"*Internationalka.*"

The policeman lifted his eyes and inspected my face for signs of idiocy. "This is no place to play the fool," he said testily. "International, indeed."

That made me mad, and I argued indignantly. "Only *internationalka* correctly describes my mixed ethnic origin: Jewish, Polish, and German. Not only that, the official anthem of the Soviet Union is the International, so to call myself *internationalka* [a word I had coined] is most appropriate. And patriotic besides."

The man still insisted I must have a specific nationality. "Your father's, normally. Or your mother's. Make up your mind."

My mind was made up, but it irritated me. Given the choice, I could have picked *any* nationality. *What is the point? What purpose does it serve, anyway? All the forms we have to fill out. Each one has a space for us to write in our nationality—even at the library! Ridiculous*, I thought disgustedly. But to argue with a minor bureaucrat was futile.

"Jewish," I said, glad to have the matter settled once and for all.

It was an easy choice to make. I felt close to my mother's family and I loved them, but I adored my father and I admired and felt close to my Jewish family too. Papa's three brothers were intellectuals. I gravitated toward them. Uncle Boris was a lawyer, Uncle Yasha an engineer. Uncle Lazar, my favorite since early childhood, was a mathematician and an Anglophile; he made me laugh because he slept on a cot, paced the room reading Shakespeare aloud, and ate standing up.

I was proud of my father and wanted to identify with him. Papa's conversion to Catholicism meant absolutely nothing to me. In my mind, Papa was Jewish, as he had been before he married my mother.

Mother's reaction to my choice was earthshaking—or at least, floor-shaking. She stamped her foot so hard a picture fell from the wall. "You told them you're Jewish? You've lost your mind! You're a Catholic, Sophia, a Roman Catholic."

"Religion has nothing to do with it. My passport clearly says: 'Nationality: Jewish.' See? Not 'Religion.' "

Indeed, in the land where religion was derided as the opiate of the masses, where children were brainwashed to deny God, "Jewish" was regarded by Soviet authorities not as a religion but as a distinct nationality, one of more than a hundred ethnic groups, or nationalities, populating the Soviet Union.

Mother's sentiment on the subject was predictable. But I had expected Father to approve my choice. Instead, he seemed disturbed and merely shook his head, as if to say, "What's done is done."

Still, I could tell Father was pleased I had thought of his and not Mother's family when deciding on a nationality. At least Papa, unlike Mama, appreciated my argument with the police. He laughed uproariously and remarked, "Only in the Soviet Union is it possible to be a Roman Catholic Jew."

And I, unenlightened that I was, said to myself, *What's so funny about that? I am a Roman Catholic Jew.* I saw no contradiction in that. One was a religion, the other an ethnic identity.

My father had a short-wave radio, and he listened to the forbidden foreign broadcasts. He probably knew about the rampant anti-Semitism inside the Third Reich and in Nazi-occupied Poland. Certainly our lofty leadership knew. But Father never talked to me about it or expressed his fear that anti-Semitism lay dormant in our midst and could surface again. This, in addition to his open skepticism that Hitler would abide by the so-called friendship pact signed in August 1939, must have troubled him when he saw my passport—the sort of passport that helped the Nazis identify Soviet Jews.

But how many other Jews were troubled? There was no overt anti-Semitism in the Soviet Union at the time, least of all in multiethnic cities like Kiev. How many felt threatened by events outside the heavily guarded Soviet borders? Instead of short-wave radios, most of us had a black concave disk the size of a large dinner plate, plugged into a specially installed outlet in our homes. The contraption had no volume control and no choice of stations. We listened to and relied on the unreliable news reports broadcast all over Russia from Radio Moscow. One can safely assume that the majority of Jews, who could have left Kiev when the Germans invaded Russia, chose to stay because they were uninformed and unafraid, as I was.

★   ★   ★

Club Medsantrud, a trade union club for workers of medical professions, occupied the stately old mansion in our courtyard. As youngsters, we had to sneak in to "our" club to see a film, or to attend a concert or a variety show—and we stayed, whispering and giggling, until we were thrown out.

I remember the day the dancing group of eight girls I had organized in my preteens performed folkloric dances on the stage of the Club Medsantrud. As a sign of their appreciation, the management honored me with a large buttercream torte after the show.

Mother had seen me in *The Nutcracker* at the opera when I danced the part of the little mouse, and later when I performed national dances of the USSR under the great dance master and choreographer Chestyakov. But she had never attended any of the amateur shows or festivals in which I had appeared. This time she came, and it was a joy to see her beaming face in the audience.

"I was so proud of you," she said, as we sat down to enjoy the torte. "You were wonderful! I particularly liked your exuberant arrangement of the *Gopak*" (a Ukrainian folk dance).

"I'm glad you enjoyed the performance, Mama. This was my last one," I said. "I'm giving up dancing."

"Surely you're not serious. You mustn't give it up."

"I'm too busy with school work." We attended school six days a week. "And swimming takes up the rest of my time."

"Swimming!" Mother scoffed. "You can't make a living by wriggling in the water."

"I don't intend to. I want to be an engineer. Our country needs engineers, Mama. You yourself have told me that many thousands of engineers were eliminated. Killed, you meant."

"I wouldn't give up ballet for that, if I were you."

"That's where we're different."

★   ★   ★

The water sports club Vodnik boasted a top-notch polo team and several champion swimmers of the USSR and the Ukrainian SSR. The club's summer swimming pool was on the river, inside a rectangular raft anchored offshore, with a ten-meter diving board. Floating in the river, connected to the raft by gangplanks, was the clubhouse. Most club members were working people who belonged to the inland waterway trade unions.

"They're a wonderful lot," I said to my best friend Inna, trying to entice her to join the club. "Like a big family, and so funny. They laugh all the time."

My studious classmate declined. "I don't know where you find time for all that. But I'll tell you what—I'll attend the next meet and root for you. If you don't win, I'll never speak to you again." Her amber eyes were smiling.

"Then you'll miss out on meeting Shura Prudnik, my teammate. She's a champion swimmer of the USSR and a record holder." Shura was a sturdy girl, her eyes quick and dark, her brows straight and narrow as if painted on with India ink. I had grown attached to this quiet, sensitive eighteen-year-old. "You'd like her."

Inna tossed her headful of beautiful red hair and laughed. "Not if she's anything like you."

Volodya Vertinsky, my coach, was a handsome man whom many women found irresistible. Under his expert coaching I became good in the 100-meter crawl and the 200-meter backstroke. My goal was to win the Ukrainian championship. I swam daily, rain or shine, to reach that goal.

5

AN OMEN FULFILLED

German troops were marching into Paris in June when finally, after ten grueling years, the class of 1940 celebrated high school graduation with a costume ball.

Mother's opera connections allowed my chums and me to be the best dressed. Inna Bregman and Anya Kogan, both redheads, were smashing as gypsies from *Carmen*. Sergei Arendarev and his pal looked impressive as toreadors. I chose a pale blue satin gown over a billowing crinoline, à la Catherine the Great, and was amazed that this elaborate costume could make me feel and look so good.

I had no idea how others felt about my looks. I didn't crave attention and had yet to hear a single compliment about my looks. I probably was a pretty girl. Yet all I knew was that while I resembled my father, I was blessed to have inherited my mother's flawless complexion, her green eyes, and her soft tone of voice. A year earlier I had been short, my chest was flat, and I envied the girls who had full bosoms. Now it seemed I had grown up overnight. Much to my delight, when I looked at myself in the mirror, a slender girl with well-developed breasts was smiling at me. I felt like Cinderella on her way to the ball.

"What a grand time we had," I told my mother after the ball. "We hid behind our masks and poked fun at our esteemed educators with impunity. We fox-trotted with them."

"Did you dance with Sergei? He's a nice-looking boy."

"Sure I did. Sergei is a good dancer but . . . he's turning into a pest. He follows me around all the time. It's lucky I run faster than he does."

Now that I had started dancing with boys, and as if I hadn't already learned about sex by osmosis, Mother decided it was time for me to know about it. Her lecture was simple. "Don't let any man reach above your knees," she said matter-of-factly.

Desperately trying not to laugh, I asked, "What should I do if a man does?"

"Scream."

Following graduation, I applied at the Institute of Aeronautics, but I flunked French during the entrance exam.

"You're still only sixteen. Go back to dancing," Mother pleaded with me once again. "Ballet is art, it's grace, it's beauty! As a ballerina you would be everyone's darling, have admirers in the highest circles, go to Moscow and Leningrad. Maybe even to Paris one day," she added wistfully. Travel abroad was the most coveted privilege in the Soviet Union.

"No, Mama. I have my heart set on being an engineer. I will apply again next year. I'll make it then. I'm well grounded in algebra, trigonometry, solid geometry, and physics," I explained. "Nor did I do too badly in chemistry. Of course, geography has always been my favorite," I added. "Why? Because I can travel the world with my fingertips."

"That's all you'll ever do, travel vicariously under *Batiushka* [Gentle Father] Stalin," Mother observed.

★   ★   ★

Thank God Papa never expected me to amount to anything, so he won't be disappointed, I thought on my way to see him. But he was disappointed, though he reacted reasonably.

"It's a good thing you started school much earlier than most. You can afford to waste one year," he said, and he offered to pay for private French lessons, which I would start taking in the fall.

Father's attitude toward me had changed. *Maybe he thinks I might someday amount to something after all.*

That summer, for the first time, he asked me to go fishing with him and Tetya Valya. We walked to Natalka, far beyond Podol, carrying bread, potatoes, sunflower oil, and fishing rods. While Papa fished from the riverbank, Tetya Valya and I collected twigs, built a fire, and baked the potatoes; then we fried the fish Papa caught. Natalka meadows were carpeted with wildflowers. I braided daisies, pink carnations, and blue cornflowers into a wreath and wore it on the way home.

Father began to check up on my activities, and I had to ask permission to go out in the evenings when I stayed overnight with them. I laughed inwardly at the irony. For years I had been striving for exactly such a response. Delighted with his sudden attention, I could not bring myself to remind him of all those years when I was far less able to take care of myself but had all the freedom in the world.

"What have you done with your hair?" Papa asked one day upon his return from Moscow.

"It's a permanent." I felt good about my shoulder-length hair, golden blond now from constant exposure to the sun and the chlorine in the winter swimming pool. The curls were loose and looked natural.

He knit his brows together. "You're too young for this sort of thing."

Tetya Valya came to my defense, as usual. "Everybody is getting permanents these days. There's nothing wrong with it."

"I don't care what others do. It is my daughter we're discussing now."

It made me happy, very happy to hear him say that. I had grown up with the feeling that he thought of me only as my mother's child. At last he admitted that I was also his.

Inna Bregman telephoned one mid-October afternoon, a trivial incident with huge consequences. "Anya and I are going dancing at the Medsantrud tonight. Will you join us?"

I had a French lesson that night, but I said yes. And for Papa's benefit, "See you tomorrow."

"Not tomorrow. Tonight, I said."

"No problem. I'll meet you there." I made a smiling sound into the receiver, cut her off with a short *"Au revoir,"* hung up, and faded into the semiprivate corner of the room to dress. I shined my high heels, I put a few drops of the emerald cologne Chypre behind my ears, and I was gone, swinging my briefcase, to "study French."

The band was playing a rumba, probably the carioca. The dance floor was crowded. A group of men in Red Army uniforms leaned nonchalantly against the wall. They whistled softly when we approached and asked us to dance. I didn't like the peculiar odor of their boots or the way my pockmarked partner shuffled his feet. I decided then and there that as much as I loved watching soldiers marching during the May Day parades, I didn't care to dance with them.

I was glad to see Sergei that night. We were dancing to "Tango Nocturno" and having a wild time, dipping, gliding, and making fancy turns, when my glance was drawn to the door.

There, his gaze fixed on me, stood Father.

My heart skipped a beat. Papa hadn't laid his hand on me since I was four, but he would give it to me now! Father motioned me to follow. He was seething, but he controlled himself—admirably, I thought. Not a sound passed his lips until we reached a pharmacy. "Go ahead," he snapped. I must have given him at least a two-aspirin headache.

Tetya Valya was ironing when I burst in, eager to have a word with her. *"Tu as commis un faux pas,"* she said. "You dressed in your best and put on perfume. Papa suspected you were up to something, so he followed you. No telling what he might do. But don't worry. Get in there." Thoroughly mortified, I pressed myself into the corner of the room with the round dining table pushed against it.

Father entered the room. He took one look at me cowering behind the barricade and at Tetya Valya with an iron filled with glowing coal poised in her hand, and he broke into a smile. But the smile was brief, his punishment severe.

"If you know what's best for you, you'll continue learning French. But," he said decisively, "from now on you pay for it yourself."

I wondered what I could do to earn money for my French lessons, when an opportunity presented itself later that fall. But I did not, even in the depth of my dazzled mind, expect my life to change so drastically as a result.

★ ★ ★

After the partition of Poland, the Vodnik swimming team attended competitions in Lvov, in the Western Ukraine, which I still considered to be abroad. Most of us did, I think.

Shura, the champion swimmer, had wanted very badly to go abroad with the team, but she was not asked because her brother-in-law, a polo player, was sitting out a term in Siberia. And why was he arrested? Because he had traveled to France—summoned to represent the USSR at sporting games!

In November 1940, Shura quit her job to pursue a career as a swimming coach. Thanks to the recommendation of my coach, the irresistible Vertinsky, I promptly took over Shura's job as a switchboard operator for DURP, the Dnieper River Fleet Administration. The Vodnik Club was under the auspices of DURP.

★ ★ ★

I was climbing Mikhailovsky Lane on a mid-February afternoon. A thin sheet of ice covered the steep lane, and it was slippery. Dark clouds were gathering overhead. *It's going to snow again.* I grimaced at the thought, when suddenly a bolt of lightning crisscrossed the sky. I stopped, spellbound. *A thunderstorm in winter?*

The other pedestrians had also stopped, and all were looking at the brooding sky.

An old woman clucked her tongue. "The war will come."

"War," another woman echoed. "Holy Mother of God." She shivered and crossed herself.

Superstitious old women. I frowned. All the same, I shivered, too.

★   ★   ★

Spring came, and I forgot the lightning. The city was alive with flowers shooting up from the soil. The branches of the massive chestnut trees were lit with pale pink, candle-like blossoms. The fragrant bird cherry trees and jasmine were in bloom.

It was a Sunday afternoon in May. Shura Prudnik and I left the Dynamo Stadium after a soccer game, crossed a pedestrian bridge above the linden-tree-lined Petrovskaya Lane, and proceeded through the park that edged the cliff above the river, past couples promenading arm-in-arm, past gaily dressed little girls rolling hoops, dodging children on tricycles. A boy in a sailor suit was trying to retrieve his paper boat floating in the fountain. Two babushkas with white kerchiefs tied under their chins gossiped on a bench, two baby carriages between them in the shade. Men played chess with intent expressions; onlookers stood silently around them.

"Inna sends her greetings," I said. "We hoped you'd come with us to the parade. You missed a good one. The display of our military might was powerful, spectacular!"

Shura shrugged sheepishly. "I overslept."

"Shame on you! May Day is not for sleeping."

"Nor is it for looking on. If anything, we should join the procession ourselves next year."

"And miss the military parade? Not I."

We crossed the street and climbed the green slopes of Vladimirskaya Hill. Shura's mother was expecting us for supper. All the same, we stopped at the vista point with the bird's-eye view of Podol, the Dnieper River, and the flatlands beyond. At the uppermost pavilion we each ordered a dish of two scoops of ice cream, one chocolate and one vanilla.

"There's nothing like ice cream for an appetizer!" Shura said. We broke into peals of laughter and couldn't help ourselves. It was a wonderful time in the spring of youth for both of us. Life was good, and we looked into the future full of confidence.

The opening of the new soccer stadium was scheduled for the first Sunday of summer. Shura and I had both received invitations to the long-awaited event—such an honor—and we talked excitedly about it.

In love with our town, we kept interrupting ourselves. "Just look at it." We admired the panorama below, the beauty and tranquility that surrounded us.

"Just listen to the chorus of birds." We heard a nightingale. The stimulating scent of spring was everywhere.

★   ★   ★

It's the first Sunday of summer! With a burst of joy I leaped from bed the moment I woke. I put on a colorful cotton dress with spaghetti straps, slipped into sandals, and was ready to start the day with a swim in the river. The sky was crystalline blue.

And I, just seventeen, was carefree.

Mother stirred in her boudoir. "Leaving already, Zosik?" Her voice was as soft as a summer breeze. "I was hoping you'd spend the day with me in Pushcha Voditsa."

"Today?" *Of all days,* I thought to myself and laughed out loud for the happiness I felt. "I'm invited to the opening ceremony and soccer games at the stadium—the new one! *Au revoir,* Mama."

I rushed out of the room, ran down the six flights of white marble stairs and out of the building, slammed the door behind me, and hurried up Vladimirskaya Street. At the Saint Sophia Cathedral I slowed down, but I was still out of breath when I reached the funicular at the top of the steep Vladimirskaya Hill.

Shura was waiting at the ferry terminal in a state of utter perplexity. The ferry was not running, and there was not a soul in sight. Most unusual—every sunny Sunday Kievans swarmed to the beaches on Trukhanov Island. Now the waterfront was deserted. It was quiet and unreal. Gentle waves lapped against the embankment, boats bobbed in the water. We stood at the shoreline, stunned.

Shura broke the silence. "What the devil's going on?"

"Who knows? I heard women talking on the funicular about explosions. 'Unearthly explosions,' they said. I thought nothing of it. Now I wonder . . ." The superstitious old women and Uncle Vanya's predictions on the eve of his arrest popped into my head, and I said, "Maybe war has started."

"Don't be silly."

I picked up a pebble and tossed it into the river. "I have a strange feeling."

We watched the ripples disappear.

"I do too. But war? There was nothing on the news. Let's go and find out what's wrong," she said, "and stop guessing at what might be."

We could find no one who knew.

At noon, some six hours after an outlying district of Kiev was bombed, Foreign Minister Molotov made an announcement. At dawn, the Germans had attacked Russia. We were at war.

It was June 22, 1941.

Part II

THE STEPPES AFLAME

6

PARTINGS

The glorious summer came suddenly to an end when Fascist Germany attacked Russia. Although Sunday, June 22, was a bright, sunny day, no sun could brighten the gloom that hung over the city. Tension was in the streets; people walked grim-faced, preoccupied. Others gathered solemnly around loudspeakers, waiting for more news. No one spoke. No one smiled, and no one cried.

Mother was not surprised to see me home so soon. "I guess you heard . . ." She was obviously distraught.

"Yes, Mama. But don't you worry, the Fascists will be beaten in no time at all."

"Fascists, Communists, they're all the same to me. No, Zosik, it isn't that. It's the war itself."

"It won't last. Our borders are so well protected, they'll never get across." I wished she had seen the May Day parade and the most popular, inspiring film *If War Breaks Out Tomorrow* so she'd know how well prepared we were.

"Then you think we can stop the Germans?"

"Oh yes," I said resolutely. "We can. And we will. Hitler hasn't got a chance. He will be crushed, as was Napoleon when he invaded Russia in 1812." I was parroting phrases from Foreign Minister Molotov's speech broadcast from Radio Moscow at noon that day. "As Molotov says," I added, "the enemy will be smashed! Victory will be ours."

"Oh, Zosik, Zosik. Why did it have to come? God knows Russia has suffered long enough." She sighed. "It's going to be a long, terrible war."

"It won't," I said with all the confidence of a seventeen-year-old.

All that day I felt a sense of excitement, a deep-down anticipation of the historic events about to unfold. *Only why, may the devil get them, did the*

Germans have to choose this Sunday to attack? The opening of the stadium had been postponed.

I put on a poppy-red shift and went to see my father. He was preparing to leave when I breezed in.

"Where are you going this time, Papa?"

"To play soldier, of course."

"At your age?" My father was forty-three.

His mouth melted into an oblique smile. "I may be old, but don't make me sound ancient."

"I thought only young men would be called up."

"Ah, yes. But it takes old men to put the Germans on the run." He was a reserve Red Army officer, but I hadn't known it.

Father reported for active duty the next day. Tetya Valya and I saw him off at the compound where troops were being dispatched to the front. The men were kissing and embracing wives, mothers, sweethearts. The women wiped their tears one moment, smiled and waved with damp handkerchiefs the next.

Standing beside my father in a long line of men waiting their turn to report for duty, I forced myself to keep quiet, although I had a sudden urge to tell him how much I loved him, how much I had missed not having him around when I was growing up. *Papa looks more handsome than ever,* I thought proudly. His dark wavy forelock fluttered in the breeze, and in his eyes I saw intelligence and determination.

Tetya Valya held his hand in both of hers. "How long . . . before I see you again?" Her voice quavered with emotion.

"Who can tell? The only thing I'm sure of is that we'll fight to win."

The seriousness of the situation was beginning to sink in. I worried about Papa, but at the same time I rejected the thought that something could happen to him. And while I wondered how long these men would be separated from their loved ones, I refused to consider that many of them might never return.

Father's turn came. I hugged him hard. "I'm so proud of you, Papa."

He put his arm around me, a rare fatherly gesture, and I sensed that he was moved. "Remember, Sonya, the decisions you make as you mature will have far-reaching consequences. So choose wisely, and take good care of yourself."

"Sure. You do, too, Papa. I want to see you back real soon."

He embraced Tetya Valya, and they kissed good-bye.

"I'll fight for Kiev and our homeland to the last drop of my blood," he said. Then he was gone.

★   ★   ★

Within ten days, frightened of invasion, many of my friends and their families packed and left Kiev for Soviet Central Asia. All the young men I knew, including Svetik and Sergei, had departed for the front. Uncle Lazar was called up; his young wife and her mother, anxious to leave, asked if I could get passes for them to sail on a boat. I used my DURP connections to get the passes for them, though I could not understand their fear and did not appreciate the silent panic that drove them east.

★   ★   ★

Four months earlier, in February, I had been promoted to secretary of the DURP Communications Office. The former secretary had been arrested for political reasons, and the position had to be filled at once. I felt honored to be chosen as a replacement, to have a typist working under my supervision. Driven by my inner competitive spirit, I worked hard.

A scant week before the outbreak of the war, I was summoned to bring some files to the office of Aleksandr Mikhailovich Platonov, deputy chief of DURP. I sailed downstairs from my office, across the yard, and up two flights of stairs of the main building. His secretary, a gray-haired gentleman with a solemn countenance, escorted me from an outer office into an inner one and left me to face Comrade Platonov alone.

He sat behind his desk in a high-backed leather chair, a broad-shouldered man with ruggedly handsome features, obviously self-assured.

"Ah, Comrade Orlovskaya. You are prompt."

"I came as quickly as I could."

There was a silence then. He looked at me but didn't speak. I stood awkwardly near the door, thinking that I should give him the files and go. But I was glued to the spot, tongue-tied and staring at his serene, intense, slate-gray eyes. When I worked at the switchboard I had admired his deep voice over the telephone, and my image of him was that of an older, barrel-chested man. I was surprised to see how young he was, twenty-seven at the most, and good-looking. Suddenly aware that I was staring, I blushed profusely and made some asinine remark about how beautiful his office was. The high-ceilinged room with dark red drapes was spacious but hardly beautiful. Pictures of Marx, Lenin, and Stalin hung on a wall.

"It's functional." He made a sweeping gesture with his hand. "Be seated." I placed the files before him on the desk and sat facing him. "Now tell me, how do you like your new job?"

"It's absorbing and challenging. I like it very much."

"Glad to hear that. You were an efficient switchboard operator, and I have no doubt you'll make a competent secretary. Are you still interested in pursuing an engineering career?"

"Yes." *How would he know that?*

He either noticed my perplexed expression or guessed my thoughts, and he flashed a smile. "I know a few things about you. You're quite a swimmer, an asset to the Vodnik team, I hear. When did you join the club?"

"In 1938. But I started swimming long before then."

"What other sports do you like? Boating, sailing?"

"All water sports. And soccer."

"So do I," he said. "I used to sail in my student days. My only sport nowadays is fishing. No time for anything else."

"Sculling is my recent passion. Last Sunday we raced against Club Dynamo."

"And did your team win?"

"Not with me as an oarsman," I laughed. I didn't feel quite so awkward anymore. Again I had two hands instead of three, and I knew what to do with both of them.

Our talk came to an end. Comrade Platonov handed me the files he had asked for, never bothering to look at them.

Why did he ask me to come? I wondered.

★   ★   ★

On July 3, eleven days after the war started, Stalin broke his silence. In a calm tone of voice he told us over the radio that despite the Red Army's heroic efforts, German-Fascist troops had already captured Lithuania, parts of Latvia, Western Ukraine, and Western Belorussia. These territories had become part of the Soviet Union quite recently and in my mind did not belong to us. Still, the invasion came as a shock. Then Stalin explained that when Germany attacked, our troops had not been fully mobilized or assembled at the frontier. The loss didn't seem so tragic anymore. I thought that perhaps those new territories had been deliberately surrendered, to lure the enemy in, to make them spread their troops so we could wipe them out before they ever stepped on Russian soil. *It's a trap!* I said in my head. *And the Fascists will fall for it.*

Stalin urged us to unite, to fight fearlessly against a cruel enemy who was after our land and its resources, an enemy who would enslave us and obliterate our culture. He went on to say that our struggle must be merciless against all panic-mongers and deserters; spies must be annihilated. Should units of the Red Army be forced to retreat, all valuable property that could not be evacuated would have to be destroyed. "The enemy must not be left a single engine nor a railway truck . . . not a pound of bread nor a pint of oil." He concluded with "Onward, to victory!"

★   ★   ★

Within days of Stalin's address to the nation, my boss, Comrade Gorsky, asked me to stay after work to help him destroy some crucial office files and documents. The two of us burned papers in the furnace steadily through the evening and late into the night. I wondered but didn't dare ask why things were being destroyed. It seemed premature to worry that the documents might fall into the hands of the enemy. On the way home, Gorsky indicated it was a precautionary measure. "Don't say a word about it to anyone." Of course I wouldn't. I was not about to be declared a panic-monger. But why the secrecy? Anybody could see the smoke belching from the office chimneys into the warm midnight summer sky.

At the same time, plants, factories, and their workers with families began evacuating to the eastern regions of the Soviet Union, where they would switch to production of arms and war machinery. To forsake Kiev for any other reason seemed disloyal. I decided that I would not desert my town. I was needed right there.

A few days later Comrade Gorsky informed me that DURP had set aside two ships to transfer our core group to the area offices in Zaporozhye. The flagship *Stalin* was to sail first. "I'll be taking the second ship, and I suggest you do too." Though the chance of sailing some five hundred kilometers down the Dnieper, halfway to the Black Sea, was enticing, I remained staunch in my resolve to stay.

On July 10, Aleksandr Platonov summoned me to his office, and he said, "There is work to be done that cannot be carried out here in these uncertain circumstances." He was choosing his words with care. "There is the danger that Kiev might be severely bombed. Our working atmosphere might be disrupted. Come with us to Zaporozhye. We'll need your help." He added, "I will personally arrange for you and your mother to sail on the first ship with me."

What he implied had a profound effect on me. My answer was an immediate yes. I would go where I was needed. Apart from that, I felt an obscure urge to be near Aleksandr Platonov.

"We will be sailing tomorrow, around five in the afternoon," he said. "I'll be expecting you."

What could be more exciting than to sail downstream in the company of such an extraordinary man? I thought as I rushed home. I took the 109 marble steps two at a time.

"We're off to Zaporozhye, Mama!" I threw my arms around her.

She looked at me in disbelief. "What made you suddenly change your mind?"

"DURP needs me there," I said, and caught myself entertaining the idea that he, Comrade Platonov himself, wanted me to join his staff. To think that a man of such eminence might need my help made me feel three meters tall. "We're sailing tomorrow. From then on, Mamochka, I'll be taking care of you," I added, brimming with adolescent exuberance.

"Tomorrow? Dear God, Sophia! I need time to think, to—"

"There isn't time, Mama. Decide now and start packing. I'll help you." My decisions had always been made in a flash. I had discovered that when I took time to think things through, nothing happened. When I acted spontaneously, things fell neatly into place. I loved challenge and faced it head on.

"I hate being uprooted. My life has been hard enough without this upheaval."

"Uprooted! We won't be gone but a short time. It's not forever. Please, Mamochka, say yes."

Reluctantly, she agreed.

The next day, after dashing around to see Tetya Valya and the few remaining friends and members of my family, I went home to pick up Mother. She had already said farewell to Aunt Yulia, and the two sisters had had a good cry.

"What's all this?" I was stunned to see bundle upon bundle, as well as two rugs rolled up and stacked against the wall like stuffed soldiers.

"You asked me to pack, so I did," she said indignantly.

"Only what we're to take with us. Essentials, I told you."

"You don't expect me to leave all this behind? I won't."

"They won't let us board the ship with a load like that. Who's going to drag it all? One suitcase, two at the most, but the cushions, tapestry—and rugs?" *Ludicrous*, I thought. "It will all be here when we return."

"I refuse to leave without my things."

I knew it was hopeless. Mother clung to her possessions as relics of happy czarist days. I told her Kiev might be severely bombed, that soon there would be little left to eat in the city. All in vain.

"If that's how you feel." I heaved a sigh and started to pack my things. I stuffed one suitcase with several summer dresses, skirts, shirts, swimsuits, and a lightweight coat. I shoved all my shoes into a string bag. For sentimental reasons I crammed my briefcase with some souvenirs, a photo album, my French dictionary, and *War and Peace* to read en route. I changed into a pastel-colored cotton dress. Around my neck I wore a gold locket my Jewish grandmother had given me before she died; in it was a tiny photograph of my father.

Mama watched me dress in silence. Then she said, "You aren't really serious about going by yourself?" I said I was and asked her to reconsider. Once again she refused and became hysterical. "Don't go, Zosik. Don't leave me." Tears rolled down her powdered cheeks.

Why, really, is she crying? She was never there when I needed her, never looked after me, didn't care how much time I spent away from home, or where. Why this overwhelming concern for me now? Then I thought, *If she really cared about me she'd come with me. She would think of me for a change instead of her precious possessions. Mothers of my friends have all departed with their daughters. Why couldn't my mother, for once, be a mother to me?*

I kept my thoughts to myself. Mama would never know how sad I felt, and why. "There's no reason to cry. I'm not leaving you. I'll be back before the summer ends." To prove that I believed what I was saying, I opened up my suitcase. "See? I'm taking only summer things with me."

Mother calmed down somewhat.

"I know, Zosik, I know you feel you must go. You want to get ahead in life. Still, I wish you'd stay. God knows what might happen. It may be a long time before I see you again."

"Come with me."

Her answer was a deep sigh and still more tears.

She saw me off to the landing. "I'm afraid to lose you, Zosik. I love you, remember that."

I kissed her wet cheeks again and again, and then I left.

As I was walking down the stairs, a man was climbing up. From the ground floor I heard my mother greet him. She had stopped crying, and her beautiful, infectious laughter rang out, filling the stairwell.

★   ★   ★

Slowly, I walked along Vladimirskaya Street, seeing nothing and feeling no bitterness, no pain, nor the excitement I had felt earlier in anticipation of the trip. I tried to focus on Aleksandr Platonov. He would be on the same ship . . . *The journey will be exciting, yes. But I'll still be alone. If only Mama had refused yesterday. Now it's too late . . . Wait—maybe not!*

I started to run, the suitcase rubbing my right leg, the string bag and the briefcase pounding against my left. Breathless, I arrived on Irininskaya Street.

"Tetya Valya, will you come with me?"

"And your mother?"

"She changed her mind, so I hoped—"

"When?"

"Right now. The ship sails around five."

"I won't be long," she said, unbuttoning her flowered frock. Within an hour, she had dressed, packed two suitcases, and we were on our way.

Instead of taking the funicular railway, Tetya Valya suggested we proceed on foot along the route so dear and familiar to both of us, and I gladly agreed. "God knows when we'll be back," she said. From Irininskaya, we turned on to Vladimirskaya Street and walked past Saint Sophia Cathedral, past the monument to Bogdan Khmelnitsky, the legendary Cossack warrior who in 1654 forged an alliance with Moscow against Poland. And down we went along the winding footpaths of Vladimirskaya Hill, down the Vladimir Descent, and all the way to the docks.

The ship was not ready for boarding, which neither surprised nor annoyed any of us assembled at the docks. We were used to delays and inefficiency. Back at the offices of DURP, as we waited and wondered what was causing the delay, we heard several planes flying overhead. *Must be our planes*, we thought, for no air raid sirens had sounded.

We spent the night in the office. In the morning we learned that the Germans had tried to destroy a critical bridge over the Dnieper. The disaster was narrowly averted when a heroic Soviet pilot locked wingtips with a German. Both planes dived and soared, circling the bridge as one, until the enemy was finally chased away.

At noon the next day, July 12, about forty employees of DURP, predominantly male, were aboard the flagship *Stalin*.

I stood on deck and wanted to cry. There was no sign of Aleksandr Platonov. I knew that I would not have agreed to go to Zaporozhye if it hadn't been for him.

After what seemed a very long time, I saw him run up the ramp. He was the last to come aboard. Within moments, the ship blew its shrill whistle, puffed, blew the whistle again, and eased away from the dock.

I remained on deck to absorb the beautiful sight of Kiev on the Dnieper Heights. The cliff and parks above were swathed in lush greenery.

Protruding above the foliage, the golden cupolas crowning old churches sparkled in the sun. The colossal monument to Prince Vladimir, holding a cross in his hand, faced the river where under his reign in the tenth century Kievans were baptized. The Dnieper wound beside the cliff; across the river, on Trukhanov Island, sand lay like powdered gold. People were basking in the sun and swimming in the river.

The ship sailed past the ancient Pechersk Monastery, and Kiev—known as the mother of all Russian towns—was soon behind us.

A woman beside me was sobbing. Tetya Valya's eyes were moist. When the women cried out, "*Proshchai*, Kiev. Farewell!" I pulled out my handkerchief and waved my city good-bye.

★   ★   ★

If someone had told me "You will not see your beloved Kiev again for twenty years," I would not have left on the ship. Yet had I stayed, I would most likely have been among the hundred thousand Kievans of various ethnic groups, but mostly Jews, killed by the Nazis during their bloody occupation of Kiev, an occupation that lasted two years and is remembered as the most tragic period in Kiev's thousand-year history. In just two days, on September 29–30, 1941, only twelve weeks following our departure, *Einsatzgruppe C* (Special Action Group C) massacred 33,771 Jews at the infamous ravine in Kiev called Babi Yar.

7

FLAGSHIP *STALIN*

The sunlit sky was reflected on the dark blue waters of the broad Dnieper. We sailed by day past numerous river towns, docked at night with lights out, hiding from enemy planes that scouted the river and bombed everything in sight.

Before dawn the day after we left Kiev, German planes attacked us for the first time. We were startled from sleep by the ship's shrill whistle and the captain's order: "Vacate the ship!" Bombs splattered all around us. The sudden attack stunned the group into a momentary immobility but then caused havoc as everyone started to run ashore. They shook their fists. "The Fascists be damned to hell!" a booming voice cursed—it was a man running after his shrieking wife. Tetya Valya gripped my arm. "Run!" she yelled, propelling me off the ramp with such force I lost my footing and landed on the shore headfirst.

"That was a graceful swan dive you did," she said with a chuckle as we crouched among the reeds. "Glad you didn't hurt yourself."

We returned to the ship after the short but terrifying attack and soon sailed again, the parade of nature gently passing by.

Gazing at the churning wake, Tetya Valya and I watched a small boat cut across the current and an angler fishing from his tar-coated canoe lined with straw. We reminisced about our fishing expedition with my father.

"I'm so glad Papa married you," I said. "You have so much in common. It's wonderful."

"Yes, we do. We are happy together. And this," she added with emphasis, "despite his occasional trespasses."

"His what? Trespassing means unlawful crossing of Soviet borders." I was perplexed and intrigued at the same time.

Tetya Valya laughed. "Your papa is no angel, that's what I meant. He has, or rather had, a little black book where he kept addresses of the women he could visit while in Moscow. I found the book and obliterated certain entries. When my lovable Misha returned from his subsequent trip to the capital, the first thing he did when he stepped off the train was brandish his fist at me, saying with a grin, 'You spoiled my trip!' That's your papa." She shook her head with a little smile.

And I had thought my papa was a saint. What a revelation! The part of me that had learned to live with Mother's promiscuity now rationalized: *You have seen enough men pass through the portals of your mother's boudoir to not be shocked by your father's philandering.* Still, I was disappointed. Yet this did not in any way diminish the love I felt for him, a sentiment Tetya Valya and I shared.

Since early childhood I had been exposed to the most intimate games people played. I had vowed never to be like my mother and, like all my friends, resolved to remain "pure" until I married, until some frog somewhere persuaded me he was a prince. But, unlike my friends, I was tolerant of others, even when people's affairs were anything but private—a virgin willing to tolerate, not a saint ready to throw stones.

When the myriad of stars lit up the sky, the ship anchored for the night and we went ashore. Far away from river towns, in a cove carpeted by sweet-smelling grass, someone lit a bonfire. Even as a child I had delighted in the feel of soft grass beneath me, and now, as I felt it brush caressingly against my legs, I daydreamed of the man who would not join us in the cove. *How pleasant it would be to sit beside Aleksandr Platonov in the grass, to hold hands, to have him hold me . . .*

We sat around the smoldering brushwood, each immersed in our own thoughts and dreams. The hush was broken as deep male voices, one a powerful baritone, burst into song:

> The mighty Dnieper roars and moans,
> Angry winds are howling,
> Bending down tall willow trees,
> Raising waves the size of mountains.

Tears came to my eyes. I loved the song. The haunting, plaintive melody and the lyrics by the beloved Ukrainian poet Shevchenko stirred my very soul.

After a game of chess on deck, while the ship was anchored offshore, I plunged into the river with a splash and swam out a distance on my back.

When I saw Platonov watching me from his cabin, I reversed my stroke and twirled in the water like a trained seal, to show off.

He called to me: "If you stay in the water a minute longer, you'll turn to mush! Come to my cabin—we'll play chess."

I did a backward somersault and shot up out of the water, laughing. "I accept the challenge on one condition."

"What's that?"

"Don't be upset if I beat you."

"Come up and I'll show you who is going to beat whom."

I wanted to prove myself a worthy opponent but could not concentrate on the game. His nearness was disturbing. And his watching me rather than the chessboard didn't help.

We had been playing for an hour or so, both so conscious of each other that our chess moves were meaningless, when his secretary walked in. The somber-mannered gentleman studied the chessboard for some moments and then allowed himself the luxury of a smile. "What's the name of this game?"

I was about to say, "Chess, of course," when Aleksandr Platonov started laughing. I looked at the chessboard and reddened, then tried to hide my embarrassment behind a smile. White and black kings had been downed for heaven knows how long.

As the ship continued toward Zaporozhye, air raid sirens sounded, and the *Stalin*'s whistle blew to warn us of an imminent bomb attack at the river town of Cherkassy, then near Kremenchug, and in Dnepropetrovsk harbor. But the Nazi bombardiers had very poor aim. The piers and docks were hit but the *Stalin* remained afloat.

At Dnepropetrovsk, the river flowed into a man-made sea, built to flood the rapids that had caused so much trouble to Zaporozhye Cossacks in the past. The Cossacks once skimmed these formidable rapids in their lightweight *chaika* (seagull) canoes. New Zaporozhye, a modern town, had sprung up with the construction of the dam. DURP's offices were located in Old Zaporozhye, below the dam.

We disembarked and were directed to our accommodations. Aleksandr Platonov stayed in town, near DURP. Tetya Valya found a basement room.

I opted for a houseboat and was assigned a tiny compartment with a bunk bed. Sharing the facilities with some twenty men and two women aboard reminded me of our communal apartment, where twenty people of assorted ages shared two toilets. I easily adapted to this "cozy" arrangement and felt quite comfortable among the men. They called me *nasha dochenka* (our little girl) but treated me with the same respect accorded the older workers.

I loved living on the river and enjoyed commuting by motorboat, dangling my suntanned legs over the starboard and munching juicy local apricots.

Life was simple and carefree on the houseboat; at times I found it difficult to believe we were at war. Our "backyard" was heavily wooded and carpeted with moss, the air permeated with wonderful earthy fragrance and the songs of birds. I swam and tramped about the woods. The men kept their spirits high with a shot of vodka every night.

For some reason the second ship never sailed, and Comrade Gorsky hadn't shown up. In his absence I reported to Aleksandr Platonov. Though we were rarely alone, I felt happy just to be near him. He praised my enthusiasm for work and dedication to our cause. "It's our responsibility, our duty to be where we're needed most," he said. "I'm so glad you came with us."

One day he cornered me alone. "Stay in town after work. We'll go for a stroll," he said hurriedly. "I want to see you tonight."

I burst into Tetya Valya's room. "Do you mind sharing your bed with me tonight?" She had offered it before, but I thought I'd ask anyway. "Aleksandr Mikhailovich asked me for an evening stroll. Imagine that! I think he really likes me."

"You have a crush on him," she said, "that's what I think."

My friends and I danced with boys and flirted with them, but we did not date while in high school, and I for one hadn't yet met a boy who could hold my interest for very long. My crushes had all been short-lived. This was different. "I'm in love, Tetya Valya." *In love for the first time*, I added to myself, as I was getting ready for the date, my first.

Aleksandr Platonov met me on a street corner, away from DURP, so as not to be seen by coworkers. The secrecy of our tête-à-tête tickled me. *How terribly romantic!* We did not speak of the war. We talked instead of how it would be when we returned to Kiev to celebrate our victory.

I told Aleksandr Platonov how much I missed Kiev and was stunned to hear him say that he didn't. Then he added, "Not when I'm with you."

The blood came rushing to my cheeks, betraying me, and I looked away. He took my hand and squeezed it. "Look at the sky, Zoya. Have you ever seen this many stars so clearly? You don't mind if I call you Zoya, do you?"

"Not at all." My mother called me Zosik or Sophia, when she was angry with me. My father and his family called me Sonya. Others called me Zosia or Zoya, all variations of Sophia. "All my friends call me Zoya," I said.

"And do you consider me a friend?"

To avoid his probing gaze, I scanned the sky. "I wish I knew all of them by name."

"What, your friends?"

I threw back my head and laughed. "The stars, of course. Do you know how many stars there are in our galaxy?" I gave him a random number in the billions. "You don't believe me? Count them yourself."

The man who seemed preoccupied and rarely smiled these days, now laughed without restraint. And it didn't matter that he was nine years older than I was, or that he laughed at my juvenile and silly challenge. I was glad to hear him laugh.

In a quiet side street we stood staring wordlessly at each other. He cupped my face in both of his hands and studied it for long moments. "I can't stop looking at you. You little devil, you bewitched me." He kissed me then and in a barely audible voice said, "I love you."

8

NARROW ESCAPES

Comrade Gorsky arrived by train and brought letters from my parents, which had been sent to the DURP office in Kiev. Mama's said that all was well at home. Papa's was hastily scrawled on a torn piece of paper; soiled and water-stained, it had obviously been written at the front in pouring rain.

"Dear Sonya! You have been on my mind a great deal. I wonder how you are and whether you're still at home. If this letter reaches you, I urge you to leave Kiev. I'm feeling well for an old man. The German invaders are getting what they deserve. Be good and brave. Your papa embraces you."

Tetya Valya read the letter and, wringing her hands, cried out, "No return address! How do we let him know where we are?"

"He'll write again," said I. "Surely his next letter will tell us how to get in touch with him."

We kept hoping for more letters, but none ever came.

I was busy at work helping prepare classified lists of the entire river fleet, which was to be sunk should the Germans ever reach the Dnieper.

No sooner were the lists compiled than the captains were ordered: "Prepare to sink the river fleet!"

The captains cried like little boys, among them one who had grown up on his riverboat. Another confessed he was more attached to his steamer than to his wife.

We were sad but not discouraged. This was only an alert. Communications between Kiev and Zaporozhye remained intact. The front lines, somewhere along the old Russian-Polish frontier, were far away. No one dreamed how fast the Germans could reach the Dnieper or how bewildered we would be when they did.

★   ★   ★

August 1941 was hot and dry. The countryside was a golden sea of ripened wheat—dotted with crimson poppies and vivid blue cornflowers—and tall sunflowers stretching to the horizon. The harvest looked promising; there would be plenty of bread, sunflower oil, and potatoes for the winter.

After my usual evening swim, I was sitting alone by the shore. Except for insects singing and an owl hooting its mournful call somewhere out in the woods, there was nothing but silence.

Suddenly there was the faint sound of machine-gun fire, "Rat-tat-tat!" hurtling on the surface of the water. I tensed and listened. Another salvo, sharper than the first, made me jump. I ran for the houseboat. Panic raced through me.

"The Germans are coming!" I shouted.

"You must be out of your mind," Comrade Zhuk, a burly man, reprimanded me. "Don't say a thing like that."

"But I heard! I heard the shooting."

"Just keep it to yourself. Do you want to be arrested for causing mass hysteria and flight?" His slanted eyes narrowed to slits. "That's panic mongering."

I lay on my hardwood bench and fumed with righteous anger. *How dare Comrade Zhuk threaten me with arrest for shouting a warning? The Germans must be near. What the radio keeps announcing is not true. Conditions are not as normal as everyone pretends. So let the devil take them! Why should I care?*

The next morning, barely hiding my anxiety, I approached Nadya Dubenko at the switchboard, our main contact with the headquarters in Kiev and generally our best source of information. The local women operators were pleasant and accommodating, and I made a point of dropping in to see them every day. "What's happening, any news?"

Glued to her earphones and listening intently, Nadya motioned me to wait. And then, "You're to get ready for immediate evacuation. A ship will take you to New Zaporozhye, where you'll board a train. Better hurry, get packed."

With our suitcases, cartons, bundles, and baskets, we assembled at the river; we were mostly Kievans who had sailed together in July. Office machines, equipment, and crates with provisions were stacked at the dock. The ship had not yet arrived. But where was Aleksandr? I ran to the office and searched for him. He was not there. I raced back to the river, then to the switchboard room across the road. Nadya, however, had no idea. Comrade Gorsky, my former boss, had also disappeared.

As I was leaving, Nadya received a communication that she repeated to me in strict confidence: Should the Germans get any closer, the hydro-electric power station, the dam, and the bridges across the Dnieper were to be destroyed.

Why must everything be confidential! I groaned and ran back to the river, hoping that by now Aleksandr would be there. He was not. No doubt he had left. And he hadn't even said farewell.

A sense of loss, of being abandoned by the man I loved, engulfed my entire being. There was an intense pain in my throat. I wanted to say, "Tetya Valya, I've never felt so wretched in my life!" But I couldn't do it, lest the tears I had suppressed burst forth.

Everyone around me was tense, not a sound passing through tightly sealed lips. The silence was ominous.

What was that noise?

It was just a boy jumping into the river for a swim; he left his shirt and pants hanging from a rock jutting out from the embankment, well above the water line. My eyes wandered abstractedly from the rock to the horizon; Aleksandr absorbed my mind.

My idle glance fell on the rock again, and Aleksandr was instantly forgotten. The rock was under water. The boy's clothes were afloat. The floodgates had been opened, and I knew what that meant. My mouth fell open to shout a warning.

But all at once, deafening explosions ripped the air. The dam and the power plant, the mighty Dneproges, had been blown up. Yet there we stood, below the dam, as if paralyzed, too stunned to react. The water was rising and gaining momentum. Still we did not move, still we waited in silence for our steamboat to show up.

We looked on helplessly and in despair as our soldiers tried to cross the river in canoes and astride logs, paddling furiously with their bare hands. Several men on a log had almost reached the crest of a wave when a high wall of water curled up behind them. The men and the log were tossed about as the wave broke. For a time the men stayed afloat, splashing in the turbulence; then their boots and tunics dragged them down.

"Tetya Valya, we must help!"

She grabbed my arm so hard it hurt. "It would be suicide to try to help!" And I, who so proudly wore the now worthless medal of proficiency

in lifesaving and deep-river diving, seethed with frustration at our impo-
tence. *Why did we let the Germans get this far?*

All at once, the water came rushing at us with torrential speed. The
churning, foaming river filled with debris and capsized boats and rafts. A
soldier's boot was afloat.

Barefoot and stripped to the waist, a soldier crawled out of the water
and called to us with bitterness in his voice, "Everything's lost."

At last we saw our ship. Clearly the captain was desperately trying to
steer it toward the landing where we stood. But the raging flood was so
powerful that the battered vessel, listing and twisting like a nutshell, was
swept downstream toward the Black Sea.

Fear gripped us. We grabbed our belongings and started to run for
high ground, not once looking back or pausing for breath. We ran for our
lives, the unleashed fury of the Dnieper at our heels.

In a square in the center of town, we slumped to the ground. The
water had stopped rising somewhere below the square, now packed with
people. Of the original forty from Kiev, only eight remained: a married
couple, four men, Tetya Valya, and I. *What happened to the rest of our people?*

We had barely stopped panting when the whizzing sound of approaching planes pierced the air.

"Aha! Our planes have come at last," I said to no one in particular,
thinking they would stop the Fascist troops from advancing any further.
"Give it to them!" I cheered.

Then I saw the dreaded black crosses on their wings. *German planes!*
I cursed and hugged the ground, covering my head instinctively with my
hands like everybody else. A woman with two small children threw herself
protectively on top of them. There was no time to run for cover, no place
to hide.

Fear gripped my guts as I watched the German bombers, flying auda-
ciously low, unload their deadly cargo over the unprotected city in the vicinity of Zaporozhye Steel Plant. Luckily, the crowd in the square was spared.

Tetya Valya lifted her eyes, raised her hands heavenward, and said
aloud, "Thank you, O Lord." The prayer was so unexpected and sincere
that my coworkers turned to stare at her.

The bombing ceased, and we took to the road. The railroad station
at Zaporozhye was not an option, since a train might never come. Obviously, German troops were near. We had no idea which way to go: east or
northeast, or maybe southeast? Like lemmings, our group of eight Kievans
followed the stream of people ahead of us.

9

FLIGHT TO THE EAST

After the flood came an inferno. Before us, engulfed in flames, lay the steppes. The Germans were bombing escape routes and machine-gunning the fleeing crowds. Farther east, the Soviets—our own planes!—were dropping bombs and setting fire to the rich Ukrainian farmlands, ripe and ready for harvest.

I remembered what Stalin had said: "The enemy must not be left a pound of bread nor a pint of oil . . ." Scorched earth, he meant.

And our people were dying.

Has the world gone mad?

Frightened and bewildered, we walked in silence along the narrow stretch of land, fires raging on both sides of us.

Masses of people were on the road. A silent procession of town and country folk, several with everything they owned—chairs and tables and iron bedsteads—piled high on wagons drawn by skeletal old mares. Most horses had been sent to war, so a peasant who still had one was lucky. Many pulled and pushed *tachka* (wheelbarrows) or *tarataika* (two-wheeled carts). Others carried luggage by hand: bundles and bags and plywood cases filled to bursting and held together by rope. Some carried infants in their arms in addition to their burdens.

We trudged for many hours before we reached land untouched by flames, a flat countryside with vast fields of wheat, corn, sunflowers, and sugar beets. No woods, not even a single tree, provided relief from the sun or broke the monotony. No rivers, no lakes or streams would quench our thirst. And not a railroad track in sight.

"My back is about to give out," the solidly built wife of Comrade Zhuk complained.

"If you weren't so dumpy, I'd carry you," Zhuk guffawed.

Tetya Valya cast a sidelong wink at me. "I'm light as a feather. Do you think he'd carry me? My feet are killing me."

"I wouldn't want him to, even if I were dying." I had disliked the man ever since he had accused me of panic mongering.

Near sundown, a cluster of trees appeared off the road. Driven by thirst, we hurried toward it to find a hamlet set among pear and apple trees, overrun by hundreds of people. It was next to impossible to get near the well, the only source of water. Trying frantically to penetrate one circle after another, at least ten deep, everyone pushed and shoved and spat obscenities. Much water was wasted, spilled by the many hands grabbing for the pail before it could be steadied on the ledge of the well. Cups and tin cans were knocked from people's hands just as they were about to drink. People acted like animals. Surely, with all the waste the well would soon run dry.

A tin can gripped tightly in my hand, I stretched my arm through the throng before me toward the well, and waited. As I had hoped, a pail tipped by unseen hands filled my can with water. I retrieved it without spilling a drop and drank greedily. Tetya Valya also quenched her thirst. We rested a bit under an orchard tree and moved on.

Our group of eight Kievans, walking at various speeds, drifted apart. Tetya Valya and I ended up on our own. Night fell, and we lay down off the road on freshly raked hay. The cut grass dried in the sun gave off a tranquilizing scent. We slept soundly until dawn.

I woke up thinking about Aleksandr, and it hurt. *He was only teasing when he said he loved me. He couldn't possibly have meant it and then left without so much as a good-bye.*

We started early and walked briskly until heat and thirst forced us to slow down. By the end of the second day, we were dragging our feet.

All the while we kept looking for railroad tracks and straining our ears for the sound of a train. But all we could hear was the shuffling of many feet. Now and then a baby cried.

The procession consisted of mostly women. Many wore peasant-style blouses, long skirts, tunics, and sturdy shoes. Their heads were wrapped in white or colorful kerchiefs, some tied under their chins. They appeared protected from the sun. Tetya Valya and I had nothing we could use for a kerchief; our heads were bare. The straps on my sandals had broken, and my only spare shoes had high heels. We couldn't help but stand out in the crowd: Tetya Valya in a sleeveless, short, pink-patterned dress and sandals, and I in a pleated black skirt of Polish synthetic silk, a pale yellow short-sleeved jersey shirt, and high-heeled shoes.

I was afraid to ruin my high heels, so after a time I took them off and continued barefoot. "If only we had taken Papa's carpet slippers along," I thought aloud. The parched earth was rough under my bare feet.

"Slippers?" Tetya Valya turned to look at me and smiled suddenly. "They'd turn to rags in a minute. Let's find you a pair of boots the old men are dropping."

"I'd rather suffer than put on someone else's stinking boots."

The sun was blazing hot and our loads seemed heavier with each passing step. From time to time, we paused to rest or stopped to open our suitcases for yet another and another inspection—what could we throw away this time? Most people had taken with them what they valued most or considered essential, yet now they discarded things to lighten their loads. The roadside was littered with ragged coats and quilted jackets, tin kettles, rubber galoshes, cast-iron pots, one of Tetya Valya's suitcases, and now her sturdy overcoat. I ditched my French dictionary, *War and Peace*, and my photo album. But not the irreplaceable, cherished photographs.

No one stopped to look at the objects in the dust.

People stood or squatted to relieve themselves in full view along the road. No one paid attention.

Exhausted by heat and thirst, we talked of nothing but water and could think of nothing else.

"If we don't find water soon, we'll die here in the steppes," Tetya Valya groaned. "God, I'd give anything for a carafe of cold *kvass* [a fermented drink] with icy droplets sliding down the glass."

"I'd give anything for a downpour. Or even a drizzle. Remember when you and I and Svetik and his pal Sol piled into Papa's canoe? The water was lapping over the sides of the canoe, the sweet cold water. We laughed so hard we capsized and nearly lost the canoe."

"Where are the boys? Svetik, Papa?" she murmured.

Yes, where? Where is my papa? "It may be a while before we hear from them."

"How in hell will they get in touch with us? We don't know ourselves where we are . . . or will be. I should have stayed in Kiev." There was longing in her voice.

Mercilessly, the sun continued to beat down on us. Again our eyes skimmed the round unbroken horizon, searching for a lake or stream. We strained our ears for the sound of a train. Nothing. Not one motor vehicle was on the road, not a soul walked in the opposite direction. It seemed the whole of Russia was moving east.

By the end of the third day the crowd had thinned considerably. Carts and wheelbarrows and horse-drawn wagons had left us in their dust. Older people and women with small children had fallen behind. Ahead of us, the wide ribbon of road stretched to the horizon.

The endless steppes.

The following midday we were near a crossroads when a cavalcade of tractors and combines approached the highway. Tetya Valya and I surged forward. If they had water, there wouldn't be enough for everybody, and we wanted to be first. The front tractor, pulling a covered trailer, turned east, and its woman driver stopped. The entire cavalcade came to a sudden halt behind her.

The driver wore a crisp white head cloth. "How long have you been on the road?" Three days, we told her. She was sympathetic. "Get in." The motion of her head indicated the trailer. "We'll give you a lift to the railroad station at Orekhov." But at the moment, water was what we needed most. "Our supply of drinking water is limited," the driver said. "There are too many of you."

"What about the water in the radiators?" I pleaded. "Can't you part with some of it?"

"If you don't mind drinking that foul stuff, I'll let you have some." We gulped the oily, gasoline-smelling water and wished we could ask for more.

Several women in the trailer were relief drivers. Their shiny faces looked peaceful in repose. I took a window seat and tossed my worn-out sandals overboard.

The tractors and combine-harvesters in the caravan belonged to a machine tractor station, which supplied collective farms with implements. They were evacuating east, and Stalin's words came back to me: "The enemy must not be left a single engine nor a railway truck. The *kolkhozniki* must drive away their livestock. Grain reserves must be handed over to the state for evacuation to the rear." *Where is the rear? We've already covered some eighty kilometers on foot. How much farther do we have to go?*

It was stiflingly hot in the trailer. Tetya Valya closed her eyes. Her puffy eyelids quivered; her lips were cracked. She was covered with sweat and dust, and so was I. I looked at Tetya Valya's tight chestnut curls and heard Mama's voice: "The witch with shaggy hair, a clever husband stealer." And I thought, *But if not Tetya Valya, Papa would have found someone else. Someone else might not have made him happy and could not have been my friend. What would I do without her now?*

I made no effort to contemplate the might-have-been and returned to my vigil at the window.

★ ★ ★

The rolling motion of the trailer and the steady hum of the engines made me drowsy. Suddenly I saw a lake. I rubbed my eyes. No, I was not dreaming. It *was* a lake, shimmering invitingly ahead of us.

"A lake!" I shrieked.

On her feet at once, Tetya Valya called for the driver to stop. "How far are we from Orekhov?"

"One kilometer, two at the most."

Tetya Valya and I thanked the driver for the lift and grabbed our belongings, and the two of us rushed for the lake—in reality a water hole—and dived into the water in our underwear. We drank the sweet-tasting liquid to excess, bathed, and felt our sore muscles begin to relax and our spirits rise. We washed our hair, and then we drank more water, lily-of-the-valley-scented soap bubbles and all.

Ahhh, what joy to feel clean again!

We were frolicking in the water when the dull, laborious sound of a distant train reached us—the sound we had been longing to hear. We scrambled from the pond, slipped on our dresses over our wet underwear, and dashed for the railroad tracks.

Clusters of people lining the tracks waved madly for the train to stop. It did, and everyone around expelled a long breath.

Dripping wet but feeling almost human again, Tetya Valya and I climbed over the sideboard of an open flatcar and sank into its cargo of loose grain. Scores of people were on the car already. With everyone aboard, the train of boxcars and freight trucks belched steam and jerked into motion.

Refreshing breezes ruffled our hair, drying and blowing it in our faces. "Isn't it invigorating? I love it!" I cried. I also felt a sense of adventure riding an open train to an unknown destination. Tetya Valya, far more affected by the ordeal than I was, did not share my spirit of adventure.

"Where the devil is this taking us?" she grumbled, which made me feel guilty, my joy less intense. I had asked her to come to Zaporozhye, not to the devil and beyond.

I looked for a familiar face. All strangers, many swathed in tunics and scarves. "Does anyone know where this train is taking us?" Some shook their heads no. Most didn't bother to reply.

"Don't waste your breath," Tetya Valya snapped at me. "Can't you see they're *muzhiki* [peasants]?"

Many of our fellow travelers were indeed peasants, by nature phlegmatic and taciturn. In our "classless" society, there was a class distinction between city dwellers and town and country folk. The Kievans, moreover, considered anyone not from Kiev as inferior, just as the Muscovites looked down upon the Kievans. Tetya Valya said the *muzhiki* treated their responsibilities lackadaisically; she regarded them with disdain. As for myself, I had always thought the peasants were lazy. Now I felt they did not trust us city folk.

The train rolled on late into the night, slowed down, and finally stopped. We were ordered to disembark. Confused, we bleary-eyed and dazed passengers tried to gather our belongings and hurried to board a second train before it got away. The engine with a long train of boxcars and cattle cars was spewing steam across the tracks. Much shoving and elbowing accompanied the transfer.

A gravelly voice cried out, "Move your ass!"

"*U nego morda I sraka odinakovi*" ("His animal face looks like his ass"), a cheery female voice returned.

But peace prevailed. Tetya Valya and I climbed aboard a boxcar. Its sliding door closed from the outside, and the train took off.

I could barely see the shapes of those sprawled around us, but I smelled onions and heard them chomp and slurp—eating raw bacon and bread, probably. Saliva ran down my throat. Tetya Valya and I were famished.

Before long, heavy bolts were lifted, and the sliding doors were pushed open. More refugees crawled in over us in the dark. The train kept stopping at intervals, plucking refugees off the road. Soon our car was so packed and stuffy we gasped for air.

"I can't take this anymore." Tetya Valya was growing very irritable. "Leave them alone!" she snapped again when I tried to find out from the newcomers what town or village they came from. We had no idea where we were, ever. Stations were not identified, perhaps for security reasons.

"I've put up with this for as long as I can," said Tetya Valya. "Next time we stop, I'm getting off."

"Then what, more walking on the corroded washboard? My feet are full of scabs from broken blisters. They'll start bleeding again. You have sandals, I—"

"Don't argue. You've got to stop being so argumentative."

I resented being called argumentative. "I was not arguing. I merely told you how I felt. Besides," I added testily, "I have as much right to express my opinions as anybody else."

Tetya Valya's face flushed. After a moment she said, "I'd rather die in the steppes than suffocate on this damned train." Her voice now was softer. "You can hang a hatchet in the air, it stinks here so."

The air was thick with body odors and the smoke of coarse tobacco rolled in bits of *Pravda* or *Izvestia* newspapers.

My own anger dissipated in a flash. *If she prefers the steppes, so be it.* I felt increasingly guilty about having dragged her away from home and worried about what this prolonged ordeal would do to her disposition. Every time she snapped at me, I cringed.

The train stopped, the metal door slide was pushed, and the doors opened. Outside, there were no more anxious, dazed refugees. People piled out to stretch their limbs, to get a breath of fresh air. Tetya Valya and I detrained with our belongings. Through the early morning mist, we could see that we had reached a sizable railroad junction.

We cornered a railroad attendant. "What's the name of this town?" There were no signs. "Where are we?" The elderly man with the large purple nose was clearly reluctant to give an answer. I pressed ten rubles into his palm.

"Across the river from Rostov," he muttered into his beard, folding the money and slipping it into his boot.

Tetya Valya and I stared at one another as if in total disbelief. The news was astounding.

"Someone in heaven is looking after us," I said, smiling brightly at Tetya Valya, and she returned my smile.

Aunt Khilya, my father's sister, lived in Rostov-on-Don. I was a small child the one time I saw her in Kiev and remembered her only from a photograph. But Tetya Valya had been to Rostov with my father and knew Aunt Khilya and her family quite well.

We crawled under a coupling between two cars and started for the river. The old man came after us.

"You can't go to Rostov!"

"What's the matter, Grandpa?" Tetya Valya said. "You think we're escaped criminals? Ex-convicts?"

"It's *them* that make the rules, not me," he muttered. "Rostov is off limits for refugees." We ignored him. He called after us, "You'll miss your train!"

The train signaled its departure. Everybody climbed aboard. The sliding doors were shut and bolted. There were no windows. It was just another cattle train . . .

At the Don River we met a lone fisherman. "Can you take us to Rostov?"

He wouldn't think of it! "Not allowed, against the rules." We pressed twenty rubles into his palm, and at dawn he took us in his dinghy across the Don.

The rising sun glistened on the wide, calm waters of the river, which flows into the Sea of Azov just south of Rostov. The silent boatman rowed slowly, the line of his propped-up fishing rod trailing in the water. From time to time he pulled in his oars, listened, looked, then rowed on again.

★   ★   ★

Rostov was alive with people on their way to work, trolley buses gliding, streetcars clattering. Janitors were hosing down sidewalks. In a streetcar, two young women were discussing their dreams. A man was working on a crossword puzzle in the magazine *Ogonyok*. I looked longingly over his shoulder; it was "my" puzzle, "my" *Ogonyok*. Rostov was almost as beautiful as Kiev, I decided, and the people dressed and acted the same as Kievans.

Aunt Khilya hugged us when we arrived. "What a surprise! What a wonderful surprise! So happy to see you." She smiled and cried. Uncle Aaron removed his thick horn-rimmed glasses as we embraced. Cousin Gina, a student of medicine, and I were mutually excited about meeting at last. My sturdy aunt and the shapely Gina began to fuss over us, preparing breakfast, heating water for baths, sorting and soaking our dirty clothes, and raining questions on us.

Uncle Aaron later joined us in the front room. We didn't mean to cause panic and tried not to sound frantic as we related what was going on outside Rostov, what was happening on the road and inside the cattle cars. We talked about the destruction of the dam, the bridges, the sinking of the Dnieper River fleet, and the scorched Ukrainian earth. It was all news to them, and they were visibly shaken. No wonder the authorities tried to keep refugees from entering Rostov.

Revived after Aunt Khilya's lavish noontime meal, Cousin Gina and I took off for the harbor; large vessels, barges, motorboats, and sailboats cruised about. That night we tangoed and fox-trotted with other girls and boys on the open-air dance platform in the park. Who said there was a war going on?

Two days later I reported to DonURP (like DURP, a branch of the People's Commissariat of Inland Water Navigation) for instructions as to what I, a dutiful employee, should do next. I learned that several of our people were in Rostov now, and that a directive signed by Comrade Platonov had advised all stray employees of DURP to assemble in Kalach-on-Don, about seventy kilometers west of Stalingrad.

The signature hit me like a bolt of lightning. The pain I felt at having been teased with words of love and then rejected had diminished. Now the feeling returned, and I could feel the turmoil within me. Part of me insisted that it was my duty to go to Kalach, and I longed to see Aleksandr. But I would not allow him to hurt me again.

I hadn't told Tetya Valya how deeply his disappearance had affected me. She had told me that what I felt for him was girlish infatuation and that I would get over it. I had tried to convince myself that she was right and nearly succeeded. Still, I resented her belittling my emotions and didn't want to give her a chance to do so again. Nor did I feel the need to share my inner self with her or anyone else.

I had grown up in emotional isolation. No one had ever taken time to sit down and talk to me, to draw me out, to discover what thoughts, fears, and feelings occupied my mind and heart. I had become accustomed to fighting my own inner battles and now felt secure knowing that the conflicting emotions that beset me were tucked away within. I could at any moment change my mind about anything without being called childish or fickle.

I was, moreover, secretive. The political environment and the society's propensity to secrecy had taught me to keep my thoughts and feelings behind the closed doors of my mind. I had also learned to rely on myself, to trust my feelings and intuitions.

Tetya Valya was packed when I returned from DonURP. "I'm going back home," she said with determination in her voice.

Another lightning bolt.

"Oh no! I was so sure we'd continue together. An order came from Platonov for all DURP employers to assemble in Kalach-on-Don."

"Sorry, my girl. I don't know what's happening with Papa and Svetik. I need to be at home where I might hear from them. Surely you can appreciate how I feel."

"Yes, I do." Still, I was deeply disappointed.

Aunt Khilya said, "You're making a grave mistake, Valya. Kiev has been invaded before and might be invaded again. Stay here with us."

"Nothing could be worse than what we've already been through. But thank you for the offer. I would've gladly accepted if I knew how to get in touch with Misha and my son."

Remembering my history lessons, I thought that, yes, Kiev had been invaded many times in the past: by the Mongol hordes and the Turks, by Lithuanians, French, Germans, Austrians, and Poles. But I also remembered that Tetya Valya, half-German on her mother's side, had told me that she spoke German fluently and was not intimidated by a possible German invasion of Kiev.

All good and well, but would Tetya Valya be permitted to board a train? One had to have a good reason and an authorization for traveling west by train these days. Blithely, I issued a certificate written by hand:

Citizen Valentina Sergeyevna Orlovskaya, employed by the People's Commissariat of Inland Water Navigation, is authorized to proceed to Kiev to collect a typewriter registered in the name of DURP.

Yes, a typewriter. No Soviet citizen could own a typewriter in those days.

I saw Tetya Valya off at the station. She kissed me on both cheeks. She said, "Don't lose your head completely over Platonov. He's a grown man, and you're still only a girl." She pinched my cheek. "Remember, from now on you're entirely on your own and responsible for yourself."

Not thinking we might never see one another again, we said our fond farewells.

Tetya Valya boarded the train for the west. I sailed east the next day.

10

THE TURNING POINT

At the Great Don Bend, near the Volga, the tranquil river narrowed before Kalach. Its color changed from steely blue to sandy, as it wound and twisted through the steppes. Chance had brought me to Rostov, DURP had ordered me to report in Kalach. *What will Aleksandr's reaction be when he sees me? Will he be glad to see a loyal employee rejoin his team? Will he care at all?* I leaned forward against the railing and sighed again and again, to steel myself. I was frightened.

It was late at night when we arrived. The small boat inched its way slowly toward the pier. I looked toward the shore and caught my breath. I had expected to see Aleksandr soon, but not this soon. He stood at the landing with a serious expression on his handsome face, which was illuminated by a spotlight. I heard the ramp being dragged across the sand. Someone called, "Kalach!" There was a commotion as people began to disembark. Matveyev, a tall and rugged river captain from Kiev, came toward me, loaded with his luggage and mine. I gestured for him to proceed. *Let him carry it.*

Aleksandr exuded crisp authority, shaking hands with the men from DURP as they filed down the ramp. I took a deep breath, lifted my chin, and approached him with an air of confidence.

"Good evening, Comrade Platonov." I extended my hand. I hoped to put him at ease with my businesslike approach, not merely to protect myself from another rejection and still more hurt. *He'll feel more comfortable that way*, I reasoned, *and so will I.*

He took my hand and looked at me without speaking. More people came behind me, so I moved on, walking slowly as if in a trance. I heard the familiar baritone, "Zoya!" I paused but would not turn my head. Then I saw Matveyev just ahead, a cigarette hanging from the corner of his mouth. He beckoned me to follow him. I quickly turned and waited for Aleksandr to catch up.

"You're incorrigible." He shook his head without taking his eyes from mine. "I don't know what I'll do with you." His tone had a hopeless quality. I felt my tension melt away.

"Put me to work," I said cheerfully, unable to say more. Several men were approaching us to talk to Aleksandr.

He gave a deep sigh. "We'll talk tomorrow."

It was arranged for me to stay with a family whose neat house was near the Don. My room had a charming wicker rocking chair. A small round table covered with a colorful fringed shawl displayed faded photographs of medal-decorated, saber-wielding Cossacks on horseback. An icon perched on a corner shelf, and right beside it hung a picture of Stalin. The family didn't see a contradiction in that, and neither did I. The soft bed was made up with a pyramid of five white square pillows tapering in size, like the bed of my babushka, where my cousins and I had spent many a night falling asleep to the murmuring sound of her fairy tales.

The room was cleanly swept when I returned at noon the next day to get my swimsuit and drop off the milk, muskmelon, and soap I had bought at the local farmer's market. Aleksandr had left a note for me to meet him at the river after work. A fluffy old cat came up to me and pressed against my foot. I rubbed its gray belly, and it stretched and yawned.

The man of the house wore balloon pants tucked inside his boots. He was leaning against the willow-wattle fence, cracking sunflower seeds and spitting the hulls out of the corner of his mouth. His wife was digging in the garden. "You come eat with us," she called to me at the gate. I thanked her; I would. A dog growled in his box.

After lunch I strolled along the river's shore, tossing shells and colored pebbles into the water with my toes. I swam a bit, then sat with my back to the willow shrubbery, sifting sand through my fingers and daydreaming. I was thoroughly enjoying my solitude when the figure of Matveyev loomed over me.

"Phew, it's hot!" He plopped himself beside me.

"Why don't you go in the water? Better yet, swim across. It's cooler on the other side," I said to get rid of him.

"Excellent idea!" He leaped to his feet. "Come, I'll take you piggyback across." I didn't budge. He tried to pull me up by my hands and then began tugging menacingly at the straps of my swimsuit. "Don't resist," he warned laughingly as I clawed at him. "Anything can happen if you fight me."

I tore myself away and started for the river, then swerved and ran the other way.

"Be careful when you run! That swimsuit of yours won't support all that's bouncing in it!"

I had left my dress on the shore and had to go back, but I warned him, "If you so much as touch me—"

"Don't tell me you'll call for help." His nostrils quivered. *Like a rabbit's*, I thought.

"That won't be necessary," I replied acidly, gathering up my dress. "I can deal with men like you myself."

"Better not get angry with me. You can never tell, I might be of help to you someday."

"Go to hell!" I snapped, and I stomped away.

He laughed.

★　★　★

The sun hung low over the horizon when Aleksandr met me at the river. He was deeply tanned and looked good in a white shirt with open collar and sleeves rolled up.

He stroked my arm. "How brown you are. But you're so thin." He frowned. "What happened to you since I saw you last? Where's your aunt Valentina?"

"The trek across the steppes was rough on her. She turned back at Rostov. What about you? Where did you get that tan, vacationing?" I heard my father's sarcasm in my voice.

"In a way, I guess it was a vacation. I got sunburned recuperating in Rostov. In a hospital."

"A hospital!" I felt immediately contrite.

"Yes," he said, and he told me the story of his sudden exodus from Zaporozhye. He had been taken ill; he was rushed to a hospital on the eve of the flood and was nearly left behind in the pandemonium that followed. Comrade Gorsky had rescued him by commandeering an ambulance to drive them to Rostov.

He moved closer to the shore, his hands behind his back, head bowed as if in deep concentration. "So your aunt went back."

"I'm sure she's at home by now and all right."

"I'm sure she is. It's you I'm worried about. If anything happened to you, I'd never forgive myself for urging you to leave Kiev."

"You mustn't worry over me. What could possibly happen? Anyhow, I left because I wanted to."

I averted my eyes as I struggled to overcome my reticence to ask about his illness, afraid he might consider me too bold. Finally the desire to know overcame my shyness, and I said, "What was wrong with you? You were sick once before and I wondered. Was it serious?"

"Yet you never asked. You really don't care about me."

I swallowed.

"And the way you greeted me, so condescendingly. The pain you caused me here"—he placed his palm on his chest—"I don't know if that wasn't a greater agony than my kidney stones."

I didn't want to hurt Aleksandr, never dreamed a girl like me could hurt someone so powerful and worldly-wise. *Yet I did hurt him. He does love me*, I thought, and stammered, "Stones! How . . . how did you get rid of them?"

"Just pebbles." He smiled. "No, it isn't serious. Painful, yes, but I'm all right now."

The wind fluttered his dark hair. I stroked it smooth.

"You did worry about me, after all," he said.

"Oh yes I did, very much."

"But you don't love me," he said. Or asked. I couldn't decide which. I wanted to say "Yes I do," but the words stuck in my throat.

"Zoya, Zoyenka," he said, as he took me in his arms and kissed me. And in that dying summer light I returned his kiss to let him know that yes, I did love him too.

★   ★   ★

After about a week in Kalach our rapidly dwindling group moved on to Stalingrad. For me it was a welcome relief. Aleksandr had had another kidney stone attack and had been admitted to a Stalingrad hospital. Several men, though exempt from the draft, had gone to fight the enemy. Some business matters had been conducted in Kalach, but I was in no way involved and time began to drag. *What a waste of time*, I thought, *when I could be doing something useful somewhere else*.

I had been to Stalingrad twice since landing in Kalach. The city was quite narrow and seemed to stretch for many miles along the Volga. The population, friendly and energetic, appeared to live normal lives. I did some sightseeing; shopping was good. In the Univermag department store (where the Germans would make their last stand when they were surrounded in 1942), I bought a smart black leather purse and some French-blue silk crepe de chine for a "good" dress, which I hoped my mother's dressmaker would make me.

This time, the changes that had taken place since my first visit some five days before were staggering. Stalingrad was overrun with fugitives, and more were pouring in, humble and resigned. The prevailing mood among them was quiet confusion, but there was also hope.

The few refugees I talked to were from Odessa, which had been savagely bombed. "It was terrible, terrible." A frail, gray-haired *starushka* (little old lady) waggled her head. "I'd just left my bench in the park when bombs began to fall. Children were playing in the park. They were all killed, mercifully with their mothers." The old woman muttered a prayer. "God have mercy on their souls."

"The Fritzes will pay for it," a younger woman said. "Before long, they'll be running like rabbits."

A plump, cheerful blonde who sat beside me on the curb smiled. "I know I'll soon be back in Odessa, eating good Ukrainian borscht and drinking milk."

I visited Aleksandr at the hospital every day but was not permitted to stay longer than ten to fifteen minutes. He was in pain but tried to convince me the doctors were doing everything they could to make him comfortable.

In an attempt to lighten the mood—or perhaps he believed as I did—he said, "Our heroic troops are smashing Hitler's armies on all fronts. The war will probably be over soon after the winter sets in."

The situation, according to Aleksandr and news broadcasts, did not appear critical. The front lines were far to the west of Kiev; even Zaporozhye remained in our hands.

The center of Stalingrad was so crowded it was impossible to find a vacant spot to sit on a sidewalk, much less a place to sleep. I roamed the streets, lonely and bewildered, with no place to go and nothing to do. At night I slept on the barren floor in an office of VolgaURP with my coat for a blanket and my purse for a pillow.

On the fifth or sixth day, the strangeness of being in Stalingrad struck me suddenly and very strongly. *Why am I here? What am I doing among all these refugees?* Instead of serving some useful purpose, I was stagnating from inactivity. The sensation passed temporarily while I was with Aleksandr. When I left him, it returned, stronger and more intense. It was all right for the elderly, the very young, and the sick to be waiting on the Volga for the storm to subside in the west. Not for me, full of energy and going on eighteen.

I returned to the hospital and told Aleksandr that I wanted to go home. "DURP doesn't need me here. Kiev might. If the Nazis attack Kiev, I want to be there to defend it. I don't want to be left with a feeling of having deserted my town in its time of need. You do understand, don't you?"

He took a while to answer. As I waited, looking at him, I sensed his turmoil. His face reflected uncertainty.

My own mind at that moment was confused. I suddenly couldn't bear the thought of leaving him and wanted him to offer some opposition.

He did not.

"Yes, I understand," he said haltingly. "If only I were in a position to keep you occupied, I would. As it is . . ." He took a deep breath and exhaled slowly. "Comrade Frolov will issue an authorization for your return, and he'll accompany you." I felt it was unnecessary and tried to protest, but he was adamant. "I won't let you go alone. And I won't relax until Frolov returns and tells me you have reached Kiev safely."

"I wonder when we'll see each other again."

"It won't be long," he said. "We'll celebrate our victory at home on New Year's Eve, if not before."

He looked as though a great burden had been lifted from his soul. My heart sank. The relief I felt knowing that Aleksandr understood my reasons for wanting to go home was blended with a sharp pang of disappointment because he did not ask me to stay in Stalingrad.

"I'll miss you," he said, as I bent over and kissed him lightly on the forehead.

At the door, I glanced back and blew him a kiss, not knowing it was the final one.

★   ★   ★

I was headed for the railroad station, dodging pedestrians, bumping into them, tripping, with my suitcase in my right hand, briefcase and string bag in my left.

Midway, I turned and hurried to the river with a deliberation, a sudden urge to feel and taste the mighty Volga—the soul of Russia—once more. I took off my shoes, waded into the river above my knees, scooped my hands full of the water, doused my face, and let some of it trickle down my throat.

Beyond the calm and beautiful Volga stretched the vast unbroken landscape, an ocean of the perfectly flat steppe of Kazakhstan. *Asia.* I felt like I was standing at the edge of the world.

Ten months later, German troops reached Stalingrad. Soon the calm and melancholy Volga churned with blood. Fierce fighting raged in the streets of Stalingrad; shells exploded every minute of the day and night. Stalingrad became legendary as the turning point in the outcome of the war—the Great Patriotic War, as it is called in Russia.

The steps I now took irreversibly changed my destiny. Thus, Stalingrad was also the turning point in my life.

11

MY PURSE!

The long train that Comrade Frolov and I took on our way to Kiev was not crowded, but all the lower berths in our coach were occupied. For whatever reasons, other people were also going back to Kharkov, Kiev, or Poltava. *I am far from being the only one*, I thought, and felt vindicated and gratified, as though my action had to be justified.

As the train rumbled through the steppes, it struck me as remarkable that although I had covered some twenty-five hundred kilometers since leaving home, I hadn't had the pleasure of traveling on a passenger train before. And for the first time I was aware of just how far away from home I had gone.

At the railway terminal in Kharkov, a mob of people with heavy loads of bags and bundles on their backs began to board even before we had a chance to detrain. They pushed and shoved and complained vociferously: "Don't push!"

"For heaven's sake, let us get off first!"

"Boors!" I scoffed, as I pushed and elbowed through the mob.

An elderly man in a worn-out army tunic jostled Frolov as he passed. Frolov snarled at him, "Hey, *muzhik*, watch where you're going!"

More people were spilling out from the large gray building of the terminal onto the platform.

I looked around uncomprehendingly. "Why is everybody in such a hurry? What's the rush?"

My heavy-jawed escort in his leather jacket made a face. "They act as if they don't expect to see another train in their lifetime."

A smartly dressed woman, a fur coat over her arm, and a well-groomed man, each laden with two bulging suitcases, appeared to hesitate. "Let's take the train to Stalingrad. Just to get out of here," the man was saying to the woman. "With Poltava lost . . ."

Frolov stopped in his tracks. "Did you hear that?" He looked as if he had been hit by staggering news.

"Yes." I half-shrugged. Only the words *Stalingrad* and *Poltava* had registered, not the fact that with Poltava only 142 kilometers southwest from Kharkov and already in German hands, everyone around feared Kharkov might be next.

Frolov considered the situation for some moments. "Well then, Comrade Orlovskaya, that's it!" He flung his arms up into the air.

"What do you mean, 'That's it'?"

"There're no trains to Kiev. Let's find a seat before this one gets completely filled."

"How do you know? We have only just arrived. We can't give up. Not until we have exhausted every possibility."

"What other possibilities could there be? We cannot get to Kiev. It's as simple as that. Let's go." He tugged my arm.

"What about all the people who have just arrived with us? Some may also be Kievans and on their way home."

"No doubt they'll all be going back east."

"Not me." I remained convinced Aleksandr was relieved to see me go home. "I'll walk if necessary, but I'm not going to quit." *The pilgrims used to journey on foot from far and wide to pray in Kiev in the old days. So can I.*

"Well"—Frolov cleared his throat—"in that case I must leave you. I have no intention of bulldozing my way through the German lines."

"Neither do I. I'll bypass them, naturally."

"It'll be a long walk—some six hundred kilometers. Are you sure you're up to it?"

"I'll find a way to get home, don't worry."

"Well, then I must bid you farewell." He pumped my hand.

The train back to Stalingrad whistled brazenly. Moments later it was gone, with Frolov on board.

Once I had made certain that no trains were departing for Kiev or anywhere else to the west, I began to search the station for Kievans.

"Excuse me, please, are you from Kiev?" I asked a young curvaceous girl in a tight black skirt.

"Kharkov is my home," she replied.

Knots of people remaining on the platform were squatting on their bundles. Their weather-beaten, humble faces reflected the servitude of those long used to endure harsh life under the Gentle Father, *Batiushka* Czar, and now *Batiushka* Stalin.

I approached a rotund woman carrying a pair of felt boots and a fur hat in a string bag. "Excuse me, are you from Kiev, by any chance?"

The woman made a vague gesture, pointing to the north.

I threaded my way through the crowds in the departing hall and the waiting room. And here, as elsewhere, people waited for eastbound trains with resignation, with the incredible patience of those long accustomed to endless lines, inefficiency, and delays. But I found no Kievans, not a soul going my way.

With my luggage at my side, my feet tucked in, I slumped down on a bench in the waiting room. My confidence had deserted me. The night was dark. I was afraid to go on the highway by myself. Eelworms of fear wriggled in my stomach at the very thought of it. Again amid strangers traveling in family groups, I was alone.

I dozed off. In my stupor I heard Kiev mentioned, the magic word, and bolted upright. A man and a woman at the foot of the bench broke off their low-voiced conversation when I asked, holding my breath, "Are you Kievans?"

"I am," the man smiled, exposing a gold crown on his upper left tooth. The young woman in a crumpled dress was from Zhitomir.

"Oh, I'm glad. I'm so glad. I've looked all over for a Kievan."

"Why? I gather you're a Kievan yourself, but . . ."

I told them I had to get home, but I was afraid to walk alone and was looking for companions. They listened, regarding me with sympathetic curiosity.

"Sorry to disappoint you," the man said. "I'm on my way to Omsk. It so happens that we both are."

"Where are your parents?" the woman asked.

"My mama is at home, in Kiev. Papa is at the front."

"You have relatives in Kharkov, I presume."

"No, I don't."

"You might not be able to get through to Kiev. You might get killed if you tried."

We didn't know that following heavy battles and encirclement, Kiev had surrendered on September 17—two days before the Germans captured Poltava.

"Come with us to Omsk." The gold tooth sparkled again.

"No, thanks." Omsk, in Siberia, was not for me. "I've just arrived from Stalingrad."

"What possessed you to leave?"

I shrugged and said nothing.

The man invited both of us to spend the night with him in the apartment of his relatives, who had left.

Under the midnight sky, the streets of Kharkov were deserted. It was very dark and still. Not a single shaft of light penetrated the blacked-out windows. I couldn't keep from shivering, though I felt quite warm.

In the one-room apartment we undressed in the dark. The couple took the bed; I slept on a sofa. My presence did not deter them in the least from engaging in a frisky game of love. *People do get friendly in a hurry these days*, I reflected with indifference, trying to drown out the not-unfamiliar sounds by putting my head under the pillow.

"Your nipples taste like they've been dipped in vodka."

"Just be sure you don't gulp them down, Andrushenka," the woman purred. "Sip gently, sip . . ."

★　★　★

In the morning I woke up feeling good. Yesterday was past. This was a new day. With optimism intact, my confidence returned. I waved vigorously to my departing one-night friends.

The sky was a steely blue, the air cool, invigorating. I left the platform ready to take to the road. Quite apart from the strong emotional attachment I felt for the city of my birth, giving me wings to maintain my course, an inner voice kept urging me to go on. I made a promise to the Virgin Mary that if she helped me reach Kiev, I'd end my pilgrimage at the Saint Sophia Cathedral and say a prayer to her.

I was passing through the station when I stopped and stared at the vaguely familiar face of a man from DURP, now a Red Army officer. A Kievan! I dropped my luggage in the middle of the hall and ran to him as one runs to meet an old, long-lost friend. I really only knew the tall blond man by sight. Lieutenant Sharbin introduced himself with a firm handshake and told me he was en route to join his battalion at Zaporozhye.

"Zaporozhye! DURP has an office in Zaporozhye. I worked there. May I come with you?"

He lit a hollow-stemmed cigarette and gestured for me to follow him. Once outside, he said, "It's not that I don't want you to come along, but the firing zone is near Zaporozhye. The entire area in that vicinity is no-man's-land. Civilians, especially young girls, have no business passing through that zone. If they catch you—"

"I'm willing to take that chance."

"I expect some pretty heavy fighting to break out there at any moment. It's far too dangerous. Why risk it? I must go, but why you?"

"Because I'll be that much closer to Kiev. I was about to start my pilgrimage when I ran into you."

"You would never have gotten through alive. Don't you know what's going on out there?" He poked his thumb in a westerly direction. "Hell upon earth."

"Then you must agree it'll be less dangerous for me to go home through Zaporozhye than through Poltava. I know some people in Zaporozhye who could help me find a boat to cross the river. Or I'll swim across. It's far better than walking all the way from here and trying to bypass Poltava, no?"

"Why must you go back at all? You should be going east."

"I've just come from there. I want to go home. Then I'll enlist and fight like you."

At that he slapped my shoulder. "All right, Comrade. Let's go then. We haven't much time to waste."

We boarded a one-car train carrying a group of soldiers. They were singing en route, whistling, playing mouth harmonicas. It was heartwarming to see soldiers going into the battle with their spirits high. Sharbin and I joined the soldiers singing Dunayevsky's "Song of Homeland":

> Vast is my homeland
> There're many forests, fields, and rivers.
> I don't know of any other land
> Where man can breathe as freely.

The train took us southeast instead of due south to Zaporozhye. The Germans had already invaded the area between Kharkov and Zaporozhye and were about to crash into Donbass, the coal-rich Donetsk Basin. We skirted the front lines all along.

The grimness of the situation hit me hard when we were dumped at Donetsk. The train would go no further. To get some sleep, Lieutenant Sharbin and I followed the soldiers into a large auditorium near the railroad tracks. It was packed with unshaven men, their army tunics ringed with black sweat, their boots caked with mud. They lay sprawled on the floors and benches, rifles at their sides. We crept cautiously between and over them, looking for a vacant spot. Some stared at us without the energy to stir or swear; others tossed in their sleep. The air was thick with stale tobacco smoke and the pungent odors of boots and sweat. A heavy silence pervaded the auditorium, a sense of subdued despair. My heart cried out to these exhausted, listless men. They seemed so old. The strangeness of being in Stalingrad had been overwhelming—being here, the only female among some thousand dismal-looking men, didn't even approach reality.

A soldier wearing a formless army cap made half of his bench available to me. He took off his boots, unwound strips of cloth from his legs, and pulled his bare feet under him. I curled up at my end, slipping my purse under my head for a pillow. Lieutenant Sharbin sat on the floor beside me, his head resting on his elbow on the bench.

"Do you have children?" I whispered.

"Yes, a little girl. She's eight."

"Where are your wife and daughter now?"

"At home, I think. I don't know."

I closed my eyes, then opened them again. "Are these our combat troops?"

"Shhh. Go to sleep."

I lay awake wondering if these worn-out soldiers were about to be replaced by fresh troops, or if they really were our combat troops. *Where are all the young men who were called up when the war began?* I was mystified. *What happened to all our tanks and artillery, the airplanes and cavalry?* I had seen no sign of them anywhere.

At dawn, Lieutenant Sharbin roused me from a deep sleep by shaking my shoulder. "We had better hurry," he said in a muted voice. "I have to find a way to get you out of here, and it might not be easy."

I sat up, still drowsy and trying to remember where I was, and why. I reached for my purse. "It's gone," I cried. "My purse, it was under my head. It's gone!"

In my purse was my passport, used by Soviet authorities for tracking and identifying its citizens, the all-important document without which one could not make a move.

"Calm down, girl. Your purse must be here somewhere. It probably just fell off the bench when you moved in your sleep. We'll find it."

We searched under the benches and among half-awake, groggy soldiers, my panic mounting. We scoured the entire auditorium. The purse was gone, and with it all my documents and every copper kopeck I possessed.

People caught without a passport in peacetime were arrested and never heard of again. To be caught without one in wartime was unthinkable! I was, moreover, a stranger in these parts, and conspicuous. Every newcomer would surely be checked and double-checked to ensure that not a single spy had been overlooked. Of course I was not a spy, but could I prove it? Would the uncompromising police give me a chance to prove anything? I could be shot on the spot. Stalin had ordered spies to be annihilated. Posters demanded "Death to spies!"

Lieutenant Sharbin was upset by this turn of events. He had decided during the night to send me back to Kharkov. "Now I can't," he groaned. "I'll have to see to it that you get to Zaporozhye at all costs." We stepped outside. "If any of our DURP people are still there, they might be able to help you in some way. But how do we get you there?"

How, indeed? I wondered, standing beside Sharbin at the railway tracks. *Does he intend to walk through the no-man's-land?*

"Here's the situation," he said, rubbing the back of his neck. "I'll be taking a locomotive due here from the east shortly. Its mission was pulling freight cars with cargo of heavy equipment and bits and pieces of the Zaporozhye Steel Plant. The locomotive will be going back to Zaporozhye empty again for another load, and that's where you come in. Chances are the engineer would refuse to take you aboard. If he did, there'd be nothing I could do. So, we'll smuggle you aboard."

Two soldiers on the same mission as Lieutenant Sharbin joined us. Sharbin briefly explained my predicament, and they assured him full cooperation. When a steam engine with a tender full of coal pulled up, I instantly scrambled aboard the tender and hid in a burrow of coal—but not without my bottom being soundly pinched first by one of the friendly soldiers.

Grinning, Sharbin wished me a pleasant trip.

"Better than walking." I grinned back at him.

The redeeming features of the arduous journey inside my burrow were the incredible speed with which the locomotive moved and the fact that it moved unbending due west. Now and then I craned my neck to see what I could see: nothing but a trackless no-man's-land.

My traveling companions teased me on arrival at Old Zaporozhye: "You could pass for an African—your face is black, your teeth sparkling white."

The coal dust had filled my nostrils and settled in my throat. A water pump near the tracks yielded barely enough water to make my face a lighter shade of black. I brushed my hair and shook off coal dust from my coat.

We parted wishing each other a safe return home.

I called after them, "Onward to victory!"

The sound of their voices singing "Ekh Kalinka, Kalinka, Kalinka moya . . ." faded in the distance.

Silence and apprehension enveloped me.

12

STRANDED

Old Zaporozhye in the vicinity of the railway struck me as a ghost town, deserted but for a stray dog. The silence of the streets was interrupted when a shutter creaked and banged. House after house was damaged and apparently abandoned by the residents in haste; windows left unlocked rattled in the wind. Piles of broken glass were underfoot; two streetcars lay overturned. A crossroads was blocked by fallen telegraph poles; the wires rang a soulful note when I tripped over the tangle. Shell-pitted sidewalks, caved-in roofs, smashed windows. The wounds of war. The destruction wrought by the enemy warplanes wrenched my stomach. "The Fascists be damned!" I cried out into the void.

Some distance away, the damages were slight. But stores were empty, their doors and windows boarded up. Windowpanes were crisscrossed with paper strips to ward against blasts. I grew uneasy. *What if no one is in the office?* I didn't know where any of the DURP workers lived.

The center of town showed signs of life, and I relaxed a bit. People went about their business; womenfolk in padded jackets were clearing rubble off the sidewalk. A cluster of older women gossiped at their doorsteps, cracking sunflower seeds between their teeth and spitting out the hulls as they talked. They stopped their rapid chatter as I approached, and I felt—unreasonably perhaps—that they were curious about me. A "big-city" girl in high heels with coal dust in her hair must have been an odd sight. I felt self-conscious.

What amazed me most was the absence of uniforms. And, of course, there were no young men anywhere.

As I crossed a broad, water-damaged street, I saw two policemen strutting toward me. I came to such a sudden halt that a woman behind was unable to avoid bumping into me. Scared the police would stop to check my passport, I instinctively turned to run the other way.

"The devil take you!" the woman hissed in my face.

"Clumsy cow!" I spat the words and took off at a dead run, making myself more conspicuous than I could afford.

The sound of my running steps was loud in my ears; my heart pounded. I turned a corner into a narrow street and, without a backward glance, pressed myself into the recess of an old house with peeling paint. The recess reeked with urine. I waited. No one was following. I heaved a deep sigh of relief and proceeded at a brisk pace.

When I finally reached the DURP offices near the river, I was relieved to see they were not deserted after all. Nadya Dubenko and Ekaterina Petrovna were at the switchboard.

"Zoya!" Their faces registered great surprise. Never having expected to see me again, they bombarded me with questions the moment I stepped through the door.

"Have you been working in the Donbass coal mines? Where have you been? To Stalingrad! Why did you come back? How did you get through to Zaporozhye?" I tried to answer all their questions, but they just peppered me with more.

Nadya Dubenko wore a coil of thick hair around her head. She was a heavy-framed girl of twenty-two with soft brown eyes and a large bosom. "What are you going to do next?" she asked.

"First of all I'll need a place to sleep," I said, hoping one of them would invite me to stay with her. "Then I'll see about a job." I had DURP in mind.

"What, dismantling the steel plant? There're no other jobs. And nothing to do here either." Indeed, the telephones remained silent; the switchboard lights did not blink. "We're just marking time."

The stoop-shouldered Ekaterina Petrovna's chest looked hollow by comparison to Nadya's; she was about thirty and divorced. "You can stay with me," she said. "I live alone with my baby, Annushka. It'll be good to have company."

"Very kind of you, but I'll still need a job because I must eat too. I don't have a kopeck to my name. All my money was stolen. And my documents," I added uneasily.

"Your passport?"

"Yes. All of it."

Ekaterina Petrovna didn't seem perturbed. Nadya exclaimed, "Ay yai yai!" swinging her head like a metronome. After a few long moments, she called Dunya Kovalenko, an office clerk with an irritating shrill voice, and asked her to bring a blank employee identification card for me to fill out. "You'll at least have that," she said to me when Dunya obliged.

My fresh identification card, dated September 24, 1941, stated merely my name and the position I held with the Administration. It provided a tenuous sense of security at best. The blanks were pre-signed by Aleksandr Platonov.

"Don't fret over the money," said Ekaterina Petrovna. "If you stay with me, you'll eat with me. I've stashed enough potatoes and buckwheat to last the winter. I'll help you today, you'll help me tomorrow, no?"

"Sure. One hand washes the other, and both are clean," I responded with a grin. "I'll be glad to stay with you. You're most generous."

Ekaterina Petrovna, more than Nadya, who was a girl of few words, brought me up to date. They spoke of the looting that had gone on at the height of the panic after the flood, and of the foodstuffs people had hoarded. Most parts of town were without water, and there was no electricity since the power plant, the mighty Dneproges, had been destroyed.

"When I left Zaporozhye I thought for sure the Germans followed right on our heels. I was wrong, of course, and glad for it. Obviously our troops were too good for them."

"The Soviets are holding the other bank. Beyond that"—Ekaterina Petrovna dropped her strident voice—"nothing but Germans. We heard it from our soldiers on the run."

How else would we know what's going on? I thought and felt my resentment rising. *Why must we always depend on what people say? Why don't our leaders keep us informed?*

"The Germans have crossed the Dnieper," Nadya said. "They've established an outpost up north, not far from here."

Both women sounded indifferent.

"Dnepropetrovsk was lost some weeks ago."

"And Kiev?" I asked, afraid what the answer might be.

"Lost."

I swallowed hard and said abruptly, "I'm going to the river for a while."

The DURP was some thirty paces away from the Dnieper. I crossed the road and stood at the shore, looking at the skeleton of the once magnificent dam. I cursed the war responsible for this, and my own preposterous situation. The city that I loved had fallen to the enemy. I couldn't go home, couldn't join the army, or even go back to Stalingrad. I clenched my teeth from frustration. Without a passport, none of it was possible.

Nothing stirred across the Dnieper. It seemed to me only a matter of days before the Germans invaded Zaporozhye. Who could keep them out? There was no sign of our troops. No tanks. No airplanes. *Where could Lieutenant Sharbin have gone? Where is his battalion?* I saw nothing to indicate that the West Bank was the front line.

I turned to go back to the office. Raya Ginsburg, a slender girl with large, melancholy eyes and shiny black hair, ran up to me. Obviously she had followed me to the river. "Hello, Sonya. Remember me?"

"Of course I do." We shook hands.

"I was in the office when I heard you came back. I need to talk to you."

"Sure, Raya. What is it?"

"I'd rather talk to you at home, if you don't mind."

We walked toward her house in silence.

Raya and her mother shared a room in a basement flat. The mother looked frail, her thinning dark hair liberally streaked with gray. She welcomed me with a timid smile, pulled up a chair for me at the table, blew at it, and dusted the seat with her bare hand. There was something touching in that gesture. The yellowish oilcloth was warped from hot plates. The window was flush with the ground, and I could see the feet of the people passing by.

Raya closed the window. "Do you think it's all right for us to stay in Zaporozhye?"

"Why not? There're lots of people still here."

"We want to stay, but we're afraid. Our next-door neighbors tell us we should leave because we're Jewish. They heard it on the radio. But the warning was never repeated. I listened for it, our friends did. None of them heard it either. So at first I thought maybe the neighbors were just trying to scare us."

"Why would they want to do that?"

"So we'd leave. There're four of them living in one room."

"I see. They have an eye on your room. Some neighbors."

"Yes, but now others are saying that Germans take valuables away from Jews and chase them out of town. You've been all the way to Stalingrad, so I thought you might know if any of it is true."

"I don't know, Raya. I can't advise you what to do, but I wouldn't consider leaving for that reason. You can't believe everything people say. And if there was a warning on the radio, it was just propaganda, probably, so we'd all leave."

Raya's mother asked, "You're Jewish also?" Her gentle smile reminded me of Aunt Yulia's.

"I'm half Jewish, on my father's side."

"Ah, then you're not Jewish," she said, and tried to tell me that by Jewish religious law I could be considered Jewish only if my mother were Jewish.

Here we go again—religion, I thought resignedly to myself.

"Jewish laws don't apply in the Soviet Union," Raya said to her mother. "You ought to know better than that. We take our nationality from our father. I know Sonya did."

"After all, I'm half Jewish and only a quarter each of the other two."

"And you're not afraid to stay, Sonyechka?"

"No, not at all. The Germans were in Kiev for nearly two years during the Civil War of 1918–1922. I heard people say how civilized and gentlemanly they behaved. Many liked them better than they liked the Reds or the Whites."

"It's our own people we're afraid of, particularly the old-timers. They dislike the Jews. Mama has lived through some bloody pogroms. She remembers. Some still call us *parkhatiye Zhidi* [mangy, scabby Jews]."

"Oh, come on, Raya. The pogroms are a thing of the past. There hasn't been one since the czarist days. As for the Jew-haters, they're also relics of the past."

"True, and for that we're grateful to our wise leader Comrade Stalin. But"—Raya lowered her voice to a whisper, even though the windows remained closed and were steamed up now from the water boiling on the kerosene burner—"once the Soviets are gone, the anti-Semitic Ukrainians might start pogroms all over again. And if the Germans close their eyes to it, God help us."

It seemed inconceivable to me that our own people could be more dangerous than the enemy. And how absurd to even mention pogroms. I ignored the warning, such as it was, though it did settle inside my subconscious to be recalled later.

"Well, if you're afraid then you should leave. Now, Raya, before it is too late. Why stay if it worries you? If I could, I'd leave this minute."

"Why can't you?"

"My passport was stolen, so I must stay where at least a few people know me. I have no other choice."

"Good Lord, how awful! Then you won't be able to go home until after the Germans have taken Zaporozhye, I suppose."

"Yes, unfortunately."

Raya took her mother's hand into her own, looked at her and said, "Mama, Mama, what shall we do?"

"Listen to Sonya, darling. If she's not afraid, then maybe we shouldn't be afraid either. Let's wait another day and think about it." To me she said, "If we leave, there might be nothing left to come home to. We'd lose it all."

It saddened me, to think that this damp, rundown dwelling could mean so much to them: they were afraid to stay yet unwilling to give up what little they possessed. Not unlike my own mother—though on reflection, Mama's reluctance to abandon her quality stuff from the czarist days seemed more reasonable.

Raya was a bit relieved at having talked with me, and after a hot cup of tea I got up to leave, knowing Ekaterina Petrovna would be waiting.

"Thank you for coming." Raya's mother clasped my hand. "May Our Lord protect you, child." Raya and I hugged good-bye.

I never saw them again.

I often thought of the girl with the large, melancholy eyes and hoped she heeded her own instinct and did indeed leave.

13

WAITING FOR THE ENEMY

Old Zaporozhye was the sort of town where people seemed to know one another by sight, where newcomers were viewed with suspicion if they looked different or were better dressed than most by local standards. It was a community hungry for news and diversion, where people spread rumors with the speed of a virus. This in itself did not strike me as unusual. But why go so far as to wish anyone evil? Why start and perpetuate malicious rumors? "That honey blonde on high heels must be a German spy" ran the rumor about me. In those troubled times, such a reputation was virtually a death sentence.

In the Soviet society of collective responsibilities, communal dwellings, and common goals, we labored under the slogan "All for one and one for all." An individualist was sneered at: "Don't break away from the collective! Don't stand out in the crowd! Be like us! If you do stand out, it means you're not one of us. If you are not one of us, then perhaps you're an enemy." And Soviet logic maintained, "If *perhaps* you are, then you are."

As a Soviet-born citizen of the New Generation, I had always considered myself immune to such criticism. After all, I was one of them. So when Ekaterina Petrovna brought the rumor home, my immediate reaction was a blend of disbelief, anger, and dismay.

"Who are these people? Why are they saying this about me?"

"You know how it is," she said. "We've all heard so much about spies, we've seen posters depicting them. But how many have seen one in the flesh? I'm sure I never have. To detect a spy is to be honored," she added with sarcasm. "And with the Germans at our doorsteps, people are losing their heads a bit anyhow. You do look German, you know."

"That's very funny. So my looks make me automatically a spy."

"My dear girl, it isn't funny, the more I think about it. Your German appearance—plus you don't have a permit to reside in Zaporozhye, do you?"

"Of course not. How can I register with the police without a passport?"

"That's just it. Once the rumor reaches the ears of the police, they'll start looking for you."

"This is absolutely idiotic. I'm not a spy. You know me."

"No I don't, not really. And personally, I don't care what you are, believe me," she said. I wondered dimly if I *should* believe her. "But you asked me who and why. Well, I'm telling you, some spiteful women, probably. Now listen, don't leave the house. Stay in until the air clears. If anybody knocks at the door while I'm gone, don't answer it. Keep quiet as a fish."

Before going to work the following morning, Ekaterina Petrovna took her Annushka to her mother's house in the country, where the baby would stay "until the air clears."

Left alone, I was quieter than a fish. My fears mounted. Every time the stairs creaked, I froze. When I heard footsteps on the landing, I was afraid to breathe. I was exhausted by the time Ekaterina Petrovna came home that night.

"The rumor is still only a rumor. The police are not on your trail," she said. "Don't fret." But then she suggested I sleep in her baby's bed, and she added a sinister note by slipping her baby's bonnet over my head. "Just in case someone comes unexpectedly in the night."

In my dream, the grinning Mephistopheles that had guarded the entrance to my hideaway at home in Kiev came to haunt me. I was tortured slowly while the Mephistopheles in NKVD uniform interrogated me: "Tell us the truth! You're a Fascist spy. You are a spy. You are!" I struggled, tried to scream, but couldn't. From afar, I saw myself in a casket mounted on a cart pulled by a horse. "Don't bury me! I'm alive!" I screamed, and I woke up in a cold sweat.

Ekaterina Petrovna tried to soothe me. "It won't be long now. Don't despair."

On the fourth day of my agonizing confinement, she came home earlier than usual. She was distraught and spoke in a sequence of short, rapid-fire sentences.

"You can't stay with me any longer. You must leave. The police are looking for you. If they find you here it will be my head, too. I'm sorry, but that's the way it is."

Good God, I thought in pure panic. *Where can I go? Is there any place in this godforsaken town where I can hide?* I remembered Uncle Vanya. *Now I know what it's like to live in fear. Now I understand why Uncle Vanya felt relief when he was told his name was on the list and he knew he would be arrested by the secret police . . . to get it over with.*

"I'll go to the police and report myself," I said, not really meaning it. I was not brave enough to commit suicide.

"No, no, don't do that. Let me think . . . Yes, yes. Nadya's would be a good place for you to hide. I'm sure she'll let you stay with her until the Germans have taken over."

"A crazier thing has never happened to me. It's absurd that I should be waiting for the enemy to rescue me."

"What options do you have? I'll get in touch with Nadya. She'll come for you."

★   ★   ★

Nadya and I waited for twilight. By crossing the city, going through alleys, and lurking in doorways, we reached the outskirts of New Zaporozhye late at night.

The area where she lived was a hybrid of a village and a shantytown of dreary, identical shacks. She had two brothers, fourteen and seventeen, and a fifteen-year-old sister. Her father had a job in town and also helped his wife tend their stock and a private garden plot.

The mother was illiterate and quite religious. Like most Russians of the older generation, she was superstitious: she prayed to God but was careful not to offend the devil. Her children, like me, had been conditioned against religion. Yet we did not hesitate to ask God to grant us a favor and to thank him for this or that. We were not superstitious, but we religiously knocked on wood, tossed a pinch of spilled salt over our left shoulder, and avoided crossing the path of a black cat. Just in case . . . As a child, I believed in angels; they were sweet and kind, and they looked after you. My angel, according to my mother, had kissed me when I was born, leaving his mark on my cheek, the dimple. Now I wanted to believe an angel was hovering over me.

The family's seedy cottage had three rooms: one was a kitchen, the second was for sleeping and eating. In the third room, the family was hiding a cow (it was against the law to own one) and two pigs. Everyone slept, ate, and washed in one room. The parents slept in one bed and the two boys in another; Nadya and her sister shared their bed with me. In the center of the room stood a long table with benches on either side. A bench against a wall served as a washstand, and near the door were hooks and pegs for coats, hats, aprons, and towels. A lightbulb hung from the ceiling in the middle of the room. The windows were tiny and the doors so narrow that I thought the cow must have been born and raised inside—until I saw her squeeze through the door to be watered and fed at the back of the garden plot.

Extremely grateful to these people, I tried to be useful whenever I could. I was scared of the cow and wouldn't go near her, but I cared for the chickens and rabbits, and I helped Nadya carry water for the family and their livestock. Twice a day we went to the river, a good kilometer away, filled two pails each with water, and carried them on a yoke swung across our shoulders.

My fear of the police or of the rumor reaching this sleepy shantytown was so great that I was careful whenever I went outside, even to the outhouse at night. To be as inconspicuous as possible, I wore one of the mother's long skirts fastened with pins, for she was more than twice my size, and a kerchief pulled far down over my forehead, my light hair tucked in. I walked barefoot.

So as not to offend the kind folk who sheltered me, I tried to imitate them in everything they did. I brushed my teeth with my index finger, wiped my greasy palms on my skirt, licked my fingers or wiped my mouth with the back of my hand, and slept in my underwear. But I couldn't slurp or smack my lips quite as well as they did when we ate. To wash my face as they did, I filled my mouth with water from a community tin mug, spat the water into my cupped hands, and then doused my face with it. I hated it.

The tasks of feeding the animals and fetching water from the river just barely managed to fill the days. The evenings were dreary. There were no books to read, no games to play, no puzzles to solve. The family communicated in monosyllables, went to bed early, and got up at dawn.

Nadya came home at noon on the last day of September and told us Zaporozhye was utterly deserted. She would not be going back to work.

"New fighting broke out all around us," she said. "The Germans have been moving so fast, the Soviets can't stop them."

"Sure they will be stopped," I said. "The Red Army is the mightiest army in the world."

"You think."

"They're letting the Hitler troops swallow enough territory to choke on, that's what I think. Just as happened to Napoleon's troops in 1812."

"Maybe. Let's fetch water. It may be our last chance for some time."

"You think the Germans will be here soon?" I hoped so. I couldn't stand this kind of living any longer, and I had become afraid of my own shadow.

"It looks that way."

"Are you afraid of them?" I asked.

"No. Why should I be? They're just people. Peasants and workers like us. The soldiers, I mean. As for the rest . . ." She shrugged her shoulders.

I couldn't tell which side she was rooting for. Her sentiments seemed to reflect my mother's: "Fascists, Communists, they're all the same to me."

"I'm not afraid of the Germans either," I said without conviction. "Some people say Hitler's soldiers are vicious. Anyway, the sooner they come, the better. We can get rid of them faster that way."

"Sure," Nadya said, also without conviction.

We made several trips to the river until all the barrels, a trough, and every pot and pail were filled with water. The cow was squeezed back into her room. The doors and windows were locked, shuttered, and barred.

What I had been waiting for finally arrived as darkness fell.

Huddled inside by the feeble light of a naked bulb dangling from the ceiling, we listened to the sporadic outbursts of cannons and the rapid fire of machine guns. The shooting sounded near and frightening, then faint and far away. There was some air activity. We could see a red glare across the northern skies.

The next day the firing grew fainter, then stopped. By nightfall, the quiet was absolute, and more frightening than the ear-splitting bursts of cannon fire. We were overcome with an eerie feeling, expecting the storm to break over us at any moment.

But the storm passed us by.

Part III

GERMAN OCCUPATION

14

FACING THE INVADERS

On the morning of October 2, 1941, the German troops were there. We saw a motorcycle zoom by and heard the rumble of heavy trucks and tanks.

Nadya's younger brother burst into the cottage. "The Germans are marching up the Lenin Prospect. Let's go!"

I shed my peasant disguise and decided to dress up a little—a white pullover, dark-blue skirt, gold locket with the picture of my father—and with Nadya followed her pigeon-toed sister to New Zaporozhye to see what the Germans looked like.

"Hurry up," I goaded Nadya. "The Germans might be gone by the time we get there."

"What's the rush?" she said, quickening her pace. "The Soviets have given up too easily. They might never come back."

Yes, I thought, *too easily, without any resistance at all*. To Nadya I said, "Maybe. We'll see."

What a spectacle! Crowds lined both sides of the Lenin Prospect, as for a May Day parade, while German soldiers in immensely flattering gray-green uniforms marched in relaxed parade formation in the middle of the sun-flooded street. They appeared proud and self-assured.

Some people stood passively with the indifference of those who felt neither hatred nor joy. But the majority openly welcomed the invaders. Among them were *Volksdeutsche,* ethnic Germans who had lived in Russia since czarist times; they embraced the soldiers whose language and heritage they shared. The Ukrainians with strong nationalistic feelings, whose dream was to break away from the Soviet Union to form a free and independent Ukrainian state, also welcomed the Germans, who they hoped would help them fulfill their dream. Artisans and small shopkeepers of the old generation looked forward to free enterprise, which they expected to be restored under German rule. Still others in the crowd were Ukrainian peasants who had bitterly resisted the ruthless collectivization and had never forgiven Stalin for the brutality with which their resistance had been crushed.

Soldiers with crash helmets raced by on motorcycles with sidecars, machine guns on the handlebars. A countless flow of huge trucks teemed with men in gray-green. Then more cheerful, fresh-looking troops on foot. Car horns were honking; the soldiers sang marching songs. The crowds smiled and waved, exuding enthusiasm. White kerchiefs were flying like sails on a stormy sea.

The soldiers don't look sinister at all, I reflected. They beamed with satisfaction and waved back at the spectators, who were clearly overextending their Russian hospitality, though without the symbolic bread and salt.

What an impressive army! I felt admiration, but resentment also, and dismay. *How will we defeat them? The Soviets lied to us about how well prepared we were. We weren't prepared at all! How else could we have lost so much territory? And in such a short time—three months!* The adulating crowds sharpened the sting. *Why are these people cheering so? Such enthusiasm! What happened to the pride we had in our country?* Even my contemporaries were cheering. Suddenly I realized how many unhappy people there must have been among us all along. My mother and her family were not the only ones who loved Russia but hated the Soviet regime and wished for its downfall.

I too was glad to see the Germans, glad and greatly relieved to be rid of the Soviet police. Now that the threat of being shot as a spy had passed I felt a sense of liberation, and I laughed inwardly at the irony. *Imagine being liberated by the enemy!* But I could neither wave nor cheer. The Germans were enemies, and as I watched the spectacle, I prayed to a God I didn't believe in to please let our troops beat them. I no longer cared for the Soviets, not since Uncle Yosif's arrest and then Uncle Vanya's, and because they lied to us. But I did care about Russia.

A high-ranking officer drove by in an open car, his right hand outstretched, and I assumed he was gesturing for the troops to disperse. Soon after, the procession came to a halt. Knots of spectators began to mingle with the soldiers. Guttural German and melodic Ukrainian and Russian voices floated on the surface of the becalmed sea.

Nadya and I were crossing the broad avenue on our way home when I suddenly found myself surrounded by rosy-cheeked soldiers. Their questions, fired at me in rapid German, were left unanswered. I could not understand German. But I did understand their curiosity, for I was equally curious about them.

"Skad pochodzisz?" ("Where are you from?") A Polish-speaking soldier came to the rescue.

"Z Kijowa," I answered in Polish.

"Are there many such pretty girls in Kiev?" I was slightly embarrassed by the oblique compliment. When the soldier added, "My comrades like your dimples very much," I thought, *How amazing that the enemy could be human enough to know what to say to make a girl feel good!* While patriotism said I should hate our enemies, I felt no hate for these boys. I smiled instead.

And then I laughed. "I'm free, Nadya! Free at last to go home."

"I figured that," she said. "Now that the Germans are here, you won't need us anymore."

Did I hurt her feelings? I felt thwarted and a little annoyed. "You invited me to stay with you until the air cleared. Well, the air is clear."

I had picked up scabies by sleeping in their house, and the tiny blisters between my fingers itched constantly. I had also picked up ticks, which I pulled off with my fingernails. I needed a steaming hot bath and was anxious to get going. But I stayed two more days so that Nadya would not think me ungrateful.

★ ★ ★

Old Zaporozhye appeared uniformly gray: the buildings, the pavement, the sky, the clothing people wore. The center of town was lively as it had been in July, before the destruction of the dam. Crowds milled about, among them rugged Russian men, men under the age of thirty. *Where did they all come from?* I wondered. Of course, they had been in hiding, as I was, waiting for the German front lines to pass by. But why weren't the young men in the army? They must have escaped from the battlefields. *A rotten bunch of deserters,* I thought with contempt, and wondered how much more territory we would have to surrender before the Red Army could successfully counterattack.

I dismissed the troubling thoughts from my mind, didn't dwell on them, and concentrated instead on finding a way to get home to Kiev. *Today, if possible.* Mentally I was already on my way.

It galled me to see the Germans so well organized. Within two days of occupation, they had set up their *Ortskommandantur* (local headquarters). Russians seeking jobs, permission to leave town, or residence permits, formed a queue in front of the *Ortskommandantur.*

On my way to the end of the line, I ignored a group of the "rotten deserters" and joined a cluster of chattering females. The Germans, they were grumbling, had closed the gates to the city, and no civilians could enter or leave Zaporozhye.

I winced and scurried across the street. At the side entrance to the building occupied by the *Ortskommandantur,* I approached the sentry. He stood at attention with no emotion on his face. He didn't blink. *Intimidating!* I forced a smile, and pointing at myself, I asked, *"Kiev, ja?"*

He shook his finger in my face and snapped, *"Nix Kiev, nix! Kiev— cholera!"*

I stared at him. *Cholera!* Tears welled up in my eyes. I turned and inched away, my eyes blurry, without seeing where I was going. I had lived through epidemics and knew what cholera meant. I had visions of my mother, friends, and relatives in convulsions, people trying to burn their dead and everything the deceased had touched. *Kiev in quarantine . . . and I'm stuck,* I sobbed unabashedly, *stuck in this God-awful Zaporozhye.*

An animated group of local women encircled two German officers who towered over them. The officers noticed me sobbing in the middle of the street. They detached themselves from the group and approached me. Both spoke excellent Russian.

"Why are you crying?" one of them asked. I was helpless to stop the tears and couldn't answer. "Come along," he said, and guided me into a small, empty house across the street. I followed automatically, my mind on Kiev and the cholera.

The younger of the two officers gave me his handkerchief. "Tell us why you are crying. We might be able to help."

I sniffed, rubbed my tears roughly away with his handkerchief, and told them what the sentry had said.

His face turned red with anger. "I assure you there is no cholera in Kiev." He explained that the sentry had used the word *cholera* as a sort of curse, directed against the people of Kiev who were aiding partisans in acts of sabotage. The man's Russian-speaking voice made me less apprehensive. I sighed a deep sigh of relief and then I smiled, all at once proud of my townspeople for making it difficult for the occupational forces and hopeful that the officers, who looked like generals to me, would help me get home. Both men were very tall, with an air of supreme self-assurance.

Sonderführer (special-rank officer) Karl Mannheim had a wholesome complexion, was proud but pleasant-looking with expressive brown eyes, and in his midthirties. He asked my name.

"Sophia Orlovskaya."

"What brought you to Zaporozhye?"

I told them how I happened to be there and all alone. There was something arrogant about his posture as he sat straight up on a desk, his long legs crossed, one knee over the other.

I felt rather than saw both men watching me closely as I talked, and I was suddenly ashamed of my once beautiful, now stained black coat. I was uneasily conscious, too, that I hadn't had a hot bath since Kalach-on-Don.

Sonderführer Paul Osterberg, close to fifty and from my point of view far too old to be in the army, was a distinguished-looking man with sunken cheeks and sparse blond hair. His skin was sallow, but his nose was pink. "I knew a fine Russian family in Heidelberg by the name of Orlovsky," he said. "It's an aristocratic surname, isn't it?"

My father's Jewish family name was Gorlovsky. During the revolutionary upheavals, many Russian Jews changed or shortened their names to sound Christian, while retaining their Jewish identity. And so did my father. He assumed the Christian name Orlovsky by dropping the letter G. *Is it an aristocratic surname? Sounds good to me!* I looked into Paul Osterberg's light-blue eyes and said yes.

"Indeed it is forbidden for civilians to leave town," Osterberg confirmed. "It might take months before you will be allowed to go home."

"Months!" I gasped.

"At your age, it can seem an eternity. Time flies to us," he said with a rueful little smile.

"Come to our quarters on Gogol Street tomorrow," *Sonderführer* Mannheim said to me. "Would eleven suit you, Paul? We should be settled by then. Yes, come at eleven, Sophia, and we'll see what we can do to help you." He offered me his hand and smiled encouragingly.

"*Auf Wiedersehen, Fräulein Sophie.*" Osterberg stressed the last syllable of my name, which reminded me of our French teacher, nicknamed Mademoiselle Trolley Bus, for she was huge. He bowed slightly from the waist and also shook my hand.

I left them with a bright, trustful smile. An adage often uttered by my mother sprang to mind: "The world is not devoid of good people." *Yes, even among the enemy*, I thought, as I walked to Nadya's with my usual jaunty stride. The day was still gray but not as gloomy as it had appeared earlier.

15

TO REGISTER—OR NOT?

The two officers had established their residence in a one-story brick house on Gogol Street. A tall wooden fence with a small squeaky gate faced the street. The entrance to the house was behind the fence and through the yard, which was gray and dismal; not even weeds grew there.

Herr Mannheim's room was pleasant enough in its simplicity. On a desk between two narrow windows lay a dagger commonly worn by German officers, a neat pile of mail, and a framed photograph of a young boy and a little girl. A mess tin of ersatz coffee and some cookies his wife had sent him were on the table. An officer's cap with silver insignia, a greatcoat, and a gun in a holster hung on a coatrack by the door. The room smelled of soap and boot polish.

Herr Osterberg wasn't there when I showed up; I was painfully punctual, as usual. While waiting for him, Herr Mannheim told me they were attached to the *Wirtschaftskommando* (Economic Task Force), Wi-Kdo for short. He explained that Wi-Kdo was a nonfighting military unit for industrial and agricultural rehabilitation in the Ukraine. Their task was to rebuild the plants and factories that had been reduced to skeletons and to make them produce again as quickly as possible.

With no money to rent a bed, and no family to feed me occasionally, I had to have a job. Yet I could not cook or sew or mend, and I had never done any real housework in my life. The only other positions open to Russian women under German military rule were kitchen helper, office charwoman, and street sweeper. The thought of sweeping the streets made me cringe.

"Could you find a spot for me in the kitchen?" I asked Herr Mannheim. "I can peel and slice potatoes, I can wash dishes and scrub frying pans." With the food situation looking grim, kitchen work would be ideal, I reasoned. But these choice positions had already been assigned.

Herr Mannheim placed another cookie on my plate. "We'll need someone to clean our rooms and could hire you," he said. "How would that be?"

"That's fine, Herr Mannheim." *Far better than sweeping the streets*, I thought to myself.

"I'll suggest it to Herr *Sonderführer* Osterberg. Apart from cleaning, you'd have to start fires in the morning and keep them going when it gets colder. Can you do that?"

"Goodness, yes." I knew how to start logs burning in a fireplace. But only the devil knew how to feed that monster of a furnace with coal and keep it going.

"Very well," Herr Mannheim was saying. "I was afraid you might consider the position degrading."

"No job is degrading," I said. "More degrading is not to have a job at all."

Mannheim nodded. The older man arrived. He agreed to have me as a cleaning woman, but he was not pleased. "It's utterly unsuitable for you, my child," he said. And I thought, *Such a sweet old man.* He had even touched my "aristocratic" hand lightly with his lips when he greeted me. Wouldn't Mama love to hear about *that!*

★   ★   ★

I returned to Nadya's that afternoon and thanked them warmly for the care they had given me. I had found a job and an apartment, I told them. "You will visit me, Nadya, won't you?" She said she would but she didn't, and in fact, I never saw her again. It was not possible for me to visit them.

With my suitcase, briefcase, and the string bag stuffed with shoes, some boiled potatoes, apples, and dried fish, I walked back to Old Za-porozhye around seven o'clock that night. I hadn't had time to read the announcements posted by the occupational authorities and didn't know about the curfew.

En route, I was stopped by a German patrol. Pointing at their watches and at the evening sky, they made me understand that I was not to be outside after dark. They asked to see my passport. I gulped, then shrugged and tried to smile.

One of the two patrolmen asked, "*Jude?* Communist?"

I had no idea what *Jude* meant, but I said, "*Nix, Nix*," dropped my luggage and with an imaginary broom in my hands swept an imaginary floor, repeating, "Wi-Kdo, Wi-Kdo."

The men exchanged a few words in German, turned on their hobnailed boots, and strutted away.

I was rightly alarmed for the wrong reason. I feared my lack of documents would continue to haunt me. *Will I ever breathe freely again?* I thought angrily, not realizing that lacking a passport had saved my life. Soviet passports, which among other statistics specified ethnic origin, were used by the Germans to identify Jews. Caught off guard, I would have shown my passport to them, and that would have been the end of me.

The janitor, whom I asked for the keys, came upstairs with me. He was an inquisitive, swarthy old man with a bulbous nose.

"What are you doing coming here so late?" he said, entering my apartment. "Don't you know it's forbidden to roam the streets between sundown and dawn?"

"Yes, yes, I know now. Thanks for telling me."

"They shoot violators. You ought to read the notices: 'This is verboten, that's against the law.' " He spat on the floor. "But it'll pass. The Germans are smart, they know we're on their side."

Speak for yourself, Grandpa, I said in my head.

"They're hard-working, too. With them around, we'll have plenty of bread and butter. We'll soon have a good life, like before the Revolution. The young ones will—my son and you," he corrected himself, scratching his head. "My woman and I, we're too old to gain from the new order."

The old man was making me nervous. I wished he'd leave. I wanted to unpack and get acquainted with my new surroundings.

As soon as the nosy janitor left, I explored my new home. To be the sole occupant of a two-room apartment and a bathroom with a tub pleased me at first. There was running water (cold only, of course) but no electricity. In one room stood a sofa with horsehair and springs sticking out through the upholstery, a dining table with chairs, a mirrored wardrobe, and a brass bed frame. The kitchen was bare but for a wood-burning stove and a narrow leather cot. I pushed the cot out from the kitchen to sleep on. But the uneasy feeling that the previous owners had never left was too strong in that room; I dragged the cot back into the kitchen again and tried to make my nest near the stove. The spot looked warmer and made me feel more comfortable, anyhow.

The comfort evaporated when my candle burned out and I had no other. There was no oil for the lamp. I had no blankets, no sheets, and no pillows, only stacks of old newspapers that the greedy stove consumed rapidly. I lay down on the bare leather cot, covered myself with my once-beautiful summer coat, tailored by Uncle Lazar's father-in-law, and still awake, dreamed about my own nest back home, suddenly so dear to me.

★   ★   ★

Mannheim stayed at home one day to nurse a cold and watched in silence as I flooded his linoleum floor with buckets of water and scrubbed it on my hands and knees, as I had seen women scrub their wood floors. My mother's highly polished parquet was cleaned with wax rather than water.

Unlike the floor in Osterberg's room, Mannheim's was spotless. Clearly he took care of it himself. I wondered why he did it. Maybe I didn't scrub hard enough. And so I asked.

"There's no need to scrub linoleum," he said with a hint of a grin. "It's enough to mop it with a damp cloth."

I was glad I asked. Cleaning turned into an effortless task. But the benighted furnace was a constant source of irritation. The hard coal was dumped in the middle of the yard. Wielding an enormous ax, I had to break the huge chunks into smaller pieces and chop kindling wood. I didn't mind as much when the sun was out, or even when it rained, but when the blizzards dropped the temperature below zero, I hated it. I had nothing warm to wear.

When my daily chores were out of the way, I often lingered in Mannheim's warm room, reading German proverbs in his wall calendar and learning many by heart. Every now and then Herr Mannheim dropped by at noon, translated the proverbs, and corrected my pronunciation. He stayed no more than fifteen minutes or so, but it broke the lonely day and I looked forward to his visits.

My blisters had spread to most of my body, and the itch was intense. *What to do about this filthy disease?* I was ashamed and bit my lips rather than scratch in Mannheim's presence.

One day he noticed the tiny blisters on my hands, and he asked, "Do they itch?" I looked at the floor and nodded. "You have scabies. Don't be ashamed. It's something anyone can pick up. I'll help you cure it," he said. And he did.

Lacking medicine in Zaporozhye, he wrote his wife, who sent the necessary salve from Germany. Eventually the itch stopped, and I stopped scratching.

* * *

The *Ortskommandantur* was busy printing announcements in Ukrainian, Russian, and German and posting them in prominent locations throughout the city. Following the janitor's advice, I took time to read the depressing messages and found that civilians were forbidden to leave their places of residence without special permits, forbidden to shelter nonresidents, forbidden to approach railroad installations . . . curfew . . . careful blackout of windows. Furthermore, looters, partisans, and saboteurs would be shot; anyone harboring a fugitive would also be shot.

I also learned that all Jews and Communists must register with the German authorities and that to appropriate property belonging to Jews was a punishable offense. The fact that Jews were singled out did not sound so good. I recalled my conversation with Raya Ginsburg and decided not to register. *To hell with them!*

Some days later, a notice pasted on a wall near my house ordered Jews who had failed to report to do so immediately. Anyone caught disobeying the order would be shot. I got so scared I trembled. *Jesus Maria, perhaps I had better obey.*

I let another day crawl by.

The janitor's pimply son of twenty-one, a rotten deserter, came to fix the lock on my door.

"The Germans hate the Jews so much they're rounding them up and marching them off far beyond the woods somewhere. They say *Zhidi*"— that derogatory name for Jews again—"are the greatest enemies of the people." And he added with a sneer, *"parkhatiye Zhidi,"* a clear indication of how he himself despised the Jews.

A cold chill ran up my spine. I felt an odd pulsating sensation, as if all the blood in my body had suddenly rushed to my head. Shocked and terrified, I made a monumental effort to sound casual. "How do the Germans know who's a Jew and who isn't? I mean, if they don't report themselves."

"We have our passports, don't we? Are your blackout shades all right? Well, good night then."

Of course, the passports . . . I felt weak. Now I knew what *Jude* meant and why the patrol had asked me about it. *Dear God, what luck my passport had been stolen! And what if Mannheim or Osterberg had questioned my ethnic background the day we met? I would have told them the truth.*

To Hitler, a Jew was anyone with even one Jewish grandparent.

I couldn't sleep, pondering in the dark of night what to do about reporting, wondering how many of my former coworkers at DURP were still in town. Some had seen my passport and knew me as a Soviet Jew. One of them might report me and I would be shot . . . unless I obeyed the order to report.

In the morning I was still troubled but calmer. I resolved not to report, and I told myself: *Sophia, you must keep quiet. Don't implicate yourself by raising questions. Act the way you have always acted. Above all, keep on pretending you're ethnic Russian and don't let Mannheim and Osterberg know you're scared.*

I hoped the occupation would not last much longer and that I could bluff my way through. My instincts were all I could depend on, to deceive by pretending my only hope.

I came to work in a sullen, melancholy mood, knowing now that I could not go back to Kiev while it was occupied. I had no idea how many of the innumerable forms I had filled out with my ethnic identity were floating around. Nor could I risk being identified by those who knew my father was a Jew.

My face must have revealed my gloom. "What's wrong?" Mannheim asked the moment he stepped into the room. "Tell me, what is it?" I uttered a sigh. "My concern for you is the same as for my own daughter. You can trust me."

"It's the war," I said, not looking at him. "When will it end?"

"Ach, so that's what's troubling you." His face lit up. "It won't be long, Sophia. Soon you'll be able to go home. The Wehrmacht is on the threshold of Moscow. There might be a cease-fire when the city falls."

"Never!" I could not believe I said it.

"This sort of remark is extremely ill advised."

I flinched at the tone of his voice. Suddenly he was a Nazi officer. *How stupid of me, how dangerous to antagonize Mannheim*, I berated myself, then heard my own sulky voice, "I don't care."

"I care," he said. The awesome mask of the Nazi officer had dropped from his face as quickly as it had appeared, but the voice was still stern. "Remember, certain things are better left unsaid. Think them, if you can't help yourself, but have the good sense not to say them out loud. That wasn't wise."

A faint smile softened his expression, and I smiled back, thinking that no matter what he said, there was a lot of Russia beyond Moscow.

★   ★   ★

The first snow began drifting to the ground and stayed there, first snowdrifts and frost, then icy winds. A thin layer of ice appeared on the Dnieper, growing thicker, stronger every day. As a child I had eagerly looked forward to the coming of winter, the time of skating and sleigh rides and snowball fights.

Now, thinking of my thin-soled shoes, my summer dresses, I knew how different, how dismal this winter would be for me. My lightweight coat, which also served as a blanket, was useless against the fierce winds and driven snow. The janitor had promised and then forgot to find me a blanket in one of the abandoned apartments, and I was not about to remind him. I was jittery around him and his family, the only people, apart from the two German officers, with whom I had any contact at all.

In my solitude, I talked to my mother. "Mama, Mamochka, how I argued with you when you complained about our communal apartment existence. 'This living in one room and waiting in line to use the toilet, it's abominable!' you said. It didn't bother me, I told you, and it's true. Everybody lived like us. What bothered me was your attitude, forever complaining about something so trivial. You made the best of our circumstances; you created a home for us within one room—a lovely home surrounded by friendly neighbors. You should have been content. Look at me, a sole occupant of an apartment with my own bathroom, and I hate it. It's cold. I have nobody to talk to. I'm lonely, Mama. If only you knew how miserable it feels to be utterly alone."

The apartment was cold. Now and then I collected enough fuel to start a fire. Like a squirrel, I dragged home anything and everything that was burnable, picking up small pieces of coal, kindling, and old papers on my way home from work. But even old paper was hard to find. I was by no means the only squirrel in search of fuel.

One morning I found the green wood already snapping and popping in the furnace in Mannheim's room. He had started the fire—a small gesture, but it filled me with gratitude. Chilled through, I basked in the cozy glow of the fire before tending to the chore I dreaded most: separating and breaking the hard coal outdoors. The ice-cold ax seemed to weigh a ton; its metal shaft adhered to my bare hands like glue when I gripped it.

The winter of 1941–42 was particularly severe; the temperature, already below freezing, was dropping. Grocery stores sold canned spinach for a time, nothing else. People with foresight had hoarded enough staples to last the winter. The others faced starvation. It was forbidden for civilians to leave town, yet desperate souls sneaked out to nearby farms to trade clothes and whatever else they possessed for food. My predicament was twofold: I had nothing to trade, and without papers I could not afford to be caught sneaking out of town. The fear of dire consequences overwhelmed even my great hunger pains. I would have starved to death had it not been for Mannheim, who now and then left food for me in his room, sharing the rare parcels he received from home. It was enough to dull the pain.

I accepted Mannheim's help without hesitation. As a child, I had run errands for neighbors, held their spots in the queues, and taken an old man for walks, holding on to him; he shuffled his feet and couldn't talk following a stroke. I had helped others without ever expecting anything in return, and I assumed Mannheim's motivation was the same. *It makes him happy helping me because*, I thought, *if you do things unselfishly for others, it makes you feel good about yourself.*

Osterberg never left anything for me to eat. One afternoon he said, "It's time for supper, my child. What are you having tonight?"

"Spinach, I guess. If some is still available."

"Is spinach the only thing you know how to prepare?"

I was flabbergasted. *Doesn't he know how grave the situation is for the local population in the city? Herr Mannheim knows.*

"The stores are empty, Herr Osterberg. Canned spinach is the only thing they have. And it isn't even green. It's brownish, rotten probably. It tastes horrible without salt."

He grimaced in disgust. "I'm sure it does. It sounds dreadful."

"Money is of no use. You can't even get salt nowadays—at *any* price. Or did you know that?"

"So I hear." He stood up. "Come with me. We'll see about getting you a decent meal."

I put away my cleaning paraphernalia and trotted happily beside Osterberg to the kitchen of the Wi-Kdo across the street.

He introduced me to Maria Ivanovna, an interesting-looking woman about forty years old. Her smooth olive skin, high cheekbones, and slightly slanted dark eyes appeared to be of Tartar origin. She wore her black hair in a knot at the nape of her neck. She filled a mess tin with turnip soup for me to take home and whispered into my ear, "Come visit me. Sometimes I get to take leftovers home with me."

I dashed home holding on to my mess tin with a blush of warmth left in it. The piercing cold seemed to penetrate my entire body. I feared my blood might congeal unless I moved vigorously.

Day-to-day life had grown increasingly miserable, compounded, moreover, by fear. At home at night, I felt like a castaway, utterly alone and isolated from the world. I tried to give myself a lift by recalling the happy, carefree prewar days. But it didn't work. The thought of my lost youth and shattered dreams intervened. I chased the reflection away and tried instead to concentrate on the hungry but cheerful little girl I had been, free to do as she pleased. I had felt sad at times to think how little I had meant to my mother, how I missed having her take care of me, read to me, keep me fed and warm. Now I appreciated what Mama had unwittingly done for me, and I felt grateful. Had it not been for my unorthodox upbringing, which encouraged independence and self-reliance, I couldn't have endured. Mama's words spoken a decade ago came to mind: "Don't you worry about my Zosik. She's a bright girl and full of spunk. She'll be all right." I felt good about it then, and I felt better now. Mama's attitude and belief in me had given me the strength to persevere and cope another day.

I tried to look at my survival as a challenge, an exciting game—the only drawback being that I didn't always know who was on my side and who was against me.

16

A PROMOTION

It was snowing heavily that morning, and the yard wrapped in bridal white appeared less bleak. I was standing at the coal mound with the ax in my hands when an officer in a leather greatcoat passed by. I noticed him glance at me.

Soon after, as I was stoking the fire in the furnace, Mannheim entered the room. "Sophia, I have good news. From now on," he announced, "you're my office help."

I sat down in a daze. "Are you serious?"

"Herr *Oberst* [colonel] saw you struggling with the coal and asked me about you. I told him you're a fine girl stranded here away from home, no family, and he recommended we give you an office job."

"Thank you, Herr Mannheim. Thank you very much."

"Don't thank me." He smiled modestly. "Be grateful to my commanding officer. I'm merely obeying his orders."

"Well, then I'm grateful to both of you."

"It would help if you could speak German," he said. "We'll concentrate on it." How like a father he sounded.

"I'm ready any time you are."

The *Wirtschaftskommando* occupied a gray building with inset balconies flanked by tall columns. In front of the main entrance was a fountain, surmounted by a crude statue glorifying Soviet women-workers. The fountain, now used for water storage, was boarded up.

Mannheim sat at his office desk, his back to the windows, beyond which the trees on Gogol Street bent beneath the weight of ice on their branches. My desk faced the wall.

One day I asked, "How much longer before the trains start running again? When can I go home?"

"You must learn to be patient," he said, not for the first time.

Patience was not my virtue, and Mannheim knew it. But he had no way of knowing that it was a game I played. Afraid as I was to return to Kiev, I had to go on pretending it was my ardent wish. Otherwise, Mannheim might grow suspicious.

None of this game playing would be necessary if Mama had come with me, I thought, also not for the first time.

"The railroad presents some difficulties, but we're slowly overcoming them. Even so, it will be some time before civilians are allowed to travel. Your countrymen took all the locomotives and cars with them when they left. The problem is that we can't use our rolling stock here because the Russian gauge is wider than it is elsewhere in Europe. This is why we have to bring in military supplies and personnel by trucks."

"That must slow down your operation," I said innocently.

"Not in the least," he snapped. "The Wehrmacht is proceeding briskly and unopposed."

"Really, Herr Mannheim, it is mind-boggling how well organized you are, militarily and otherwise."

That pleased him.

The officers among the military men attached to the Wi-Kdo were, for the most part, arrogant, class- and rank-conscious, and stiffly correct. I was so happy to have a job in a centrally heated office that I nearly didn't mind these "typical Nazis" regarding me as a nonentity. Others, like Mannheim and Osterberg, couldn't possibly be Nazis, I decided. They were too kind for that. I thought of them instead as victims of the draft, benevolent enemies.

How fortunate, I thought, that my surname, Orlovskaya, had led my benefactors to assume that I was ethnic Russian and that I did not deny it. I was keenly aware that even Mannheim, the kinder of the two, wouldn't hesitate to turn me in if he knew I was a Christian and a Jew.

As the days went by, I learned that Mannheim was born in Latvia. Like many Baltic Germans, his entire family had escaped to Germany before the Russian-German nonaggression pact went into effect in 1939, permitting Soviet troops on Latvian soil. Now I knew why Mannheim spoke perfect Russian. Most Latvians did; the Russian Empire had dominated Latvia for a hundred years (1817–1917). I assumed this was the reason why he felt compassion for the Russians. He spoke to people on the street, trying to ease their pain with a kind word, helping them as he did me.

Among the civilians were several Russian women employed in the kitchen and as charwomen. Nine local girls and several men of German origin worked as interpreters in the office.

My duties were filing, adding up long columns of figures, and pretending I was busy when I was not. Mannheim could not generate enough work to keep me fully occupied. Clearly the position had been created solely to get me off the pile of coal. The salary for my services was generous and worthless. Money could not buy food. Now as before, I depended on handouts from Mannheim and the officers' canteen.

But most of all I depended on Mannheim, the man who had saved me from danger, perhaps from death, whom I regarded with respectful affection and deep gratitude.

Mannheim's concern for me was the same, he had said, as for his own daughter, and I believed him—and took advantage of him, sometimes aggravating and irritating him. I was thoughtless and impulsive. When he flared up, and this happened periodically, I knew I had gone too far and sometimes apologized. I was stubborn too, and young—not yet eighteen. In some ways I was mature, streetwise, and able to manage my own affairs. In other ways, I was quite naive—and also unaware of how deeply Mannheim cared for me.

Mannheim asked me on a Monday, "What did you do yesterday?" The expression on his face was genial; it was streaked with almost boyish innocence. I loved to watch his face, a constantly changing panorama of expressions: one moment warm and compassionate, the next stern, forbidding, and arrogant.

"I visited with Maria Ivanovna. She's jolly. I like her." In some ways she reminded me of my mother, and like my mother, she loved to entertain. That Sunday she had had two visitors, an officer friend of hers and *Sonderführer* Klinger, who was very handsome and younger than most officers at the Wi-Kdo. Klinger was a marvelous pianist, and I enjoyed listening to his impromptu concert of rhapsodies by Liszt. Maria Ivanovna had served wine, but all I told Herr Mannheim was that she and I had had tea.

"I'm glad you were with Maria Ivanovna and not alone. As I said before, you ought to meet the *Volksdeutsche* girls. They're Mennonites, good girls, younger and more like you."

Soon after, *Sonderführer* Klinger walked in. Klinger and Mannheim greeted one another with the Hitler salute and shook hands. Klinger turned to face me. I guessed that Mannheim was about to introduce us when Klinger smiled charmingly and said, " . . . Karl. Fräulein Sophie and I have met . . . yesterday." Klinger did not speak Russian, so this was all I understood. Mannheim glanced at me, his nostrils flaring. My face burned.

They turned to business matters. I remained at my desk, watching Mannheim's expressions and waiting for the sign of a changing mood. I counted on his anger to dissipate.

When the door closed behind Klinger, Mannheim loomed at my desk. "Why did you lie to me?" he demanded furiously. "Why didn't you tell me you had met *Sonderführer* Klinger? You invented an evening with Maria Ivanovna, didn't you?" He was asking one question after another without giving me time to answer. "Stop chewing your lip and tell me why you lied to me!"

"I didn't lie."

"Of course you did."

"I did not lie. I was with Maria Ivanovna. I merely didn't tell you Herr Klinger was there too."

"I'm sure you didn't." And he proceeded to remind me how he had found me, lost and homeless, how he had been helping me and overlooking my hostility and impudence. "I believed in you. And what do you do? You repay me with deceit and subterfuge."

I kept quiet, squirming in my chair and waiting for him to calm down. Finally he returned to his desk. "You had better go to my room and wait until I get there."

I left with my chin on my chest. *What have I done that's so terrible? So I omitted a small detail, so what! Or does he expect me to tell him everything? He already knows more about me than either of my parents ever did or cared to know. I should disobey and go straight home*, I thought defiantly. But then . . . *I'm expendable. He'd fire me.*

As I waited for Mannheim, nervous about what his verdict might be, I noticed an open box at the door. It was the package he had received from his wife a few days before. It was almost empty. He had given most of it to me.

Only the last Saturday, when I came to work, Mannheim had urged me to open my desk drawer. I looked inside to find a note: "A surprise is waiting for you in my room." I rushed across the street and was very pleased to see a warm breakfast on the table. While devouring pumpernickel bread and scrambled eggs made from egg powder, my eyes fell on a parcel with my name on it. The parcel was neatly wrapped in coarse brown paper and tied with a fuzzy string. I ripped it open and found it filled with nuts, bonbons, *Lebkuchen*, and sugar cookies shaped like stars and half moons. I danced back to the office and thanked Mannheim for the wonderful surprise, but I had no words to express the gratitude I felt. The expression on his face was that of a man totally gratified at having pleased someone. I couldn't decide who was more pleased.

Only last Saturday.

I couldn't wait for him to come so I could magnanimously apologize for whatever it was that had upset him so.

"Here you are at last!" I said the moment he stepped in.

"Sorry it took so long. I thought you'd gone home by now."

"I did think of it."

"What stopped you?"

"I didn't want to wait until tomorrow to find out what you have decided to do with me," I sputtered. "Are you going to fire me?"

"Yes," he said, "I could do that. But I won't." He looked at me, then out the window. "The minute I saw you crying your heart out in the middle of the street, I made a promise to myself to protect you and help you in any way I could. I'm determined to keep that promise, even though you're making it difficult for me at times. You seem to forget there's a war going on. Soldiers surround you. If you're not careful—" He broke off and wheeled around to face me. "Take Klinger, for instance. I know him and his reputation with women. Anything could happen if you associate with him. You're too trusting, I'm afraid. If your reputation means anything to you," he continued in softer tones, "don't see him again. That's all."

"Sure." I shrugged. Klinger wasn't worth arguing about. "But what am I supposed to do, hibernate? I can't help it if I run into him." Moments later, I asked, "How is a girl to gather the experience you talk about if she is not to experience anything? Not by being overly protected, surely."

Mannheim sat down and crossed his legs.

"I knew a girl at home, a pretty girl," I went on. "I may have told you about Nora, the girl I used to envy because she had felt boots. Anyway, her mother didn't allow Nora to play with us and wouldn't let her out of her sight until she was fourteen. By that time we already knew enough to stay out of trouble. Nora didn't. She gave birth to a fatherless child when she was sixteen. Sixteen! She was the only girl I knew who had anything to do with boys while still in high school. And I knew lots of girls, Herr Mannheim. So you see, her mother did Nora more harm than good. Nora wasn't only overprotected, she was pampered as well."

"Hmm. So you think I'm overprotecting you?"

"Somewhat. At least I'm not being pampered."

"And you resent it?"

"What, that I'm not being pampered?" I laughed, feeling secure about my job once again. "Or your protective attitude? No, no, I don't resent it. I appreciate your concern. I truly do. Only you shouldn't worry about me quite so much."

"I'll try," he said, and his frowning face melted into a friendly smile.

★   ★   ★

The streets were covered with a thick blanket of snow, the crisp, crunchy kind that used to be fun to walk through. Today, shivering my way home, I did not enjoy it.

The civilians I met on the way were all bundled up from head to toe: boots, leather caps with furry earflaps, fur collars, wool scarves. I imagined them rushing to their warm homes and loving families. I envied them.

A group of Italian soldiers were singing a joyful song and flapping their arms like penguins to keep warm. Germans strutted by, always in twos or threes. I wondered if any of the Italians could speak German or vice versa. It seemed peculiar that the so-called friends-in-arms never mingled or talked to one another.

I had a sudden image in my mind of Tamara Fortoloni, my childhood friend. She had had to leave Kiev for Italy because her father, an Italian by birth, refused Soviet citizenship. How awful she must feel about the Italians, her people now, at war with her native Russia. And her father—was he fighting against his brother in the Red Army?

At a crossroads, all pedestrians had to stop. An endless column of Russian prisoners of war was being escorted—to a prison camp? Poor wretched souls. I shivered from the cold and from the pity I felt for the prisoners. They looked wasted in strength and vitality, their uniforms in woeful condition. So many had no boots; their feet were wrapped in tattered rags. Their faces reflected utter hopelessness, and it seemed I was not looking at just these few thousand forlorn souls but at the hopelessness of our whole situation.

I searched for a familiar face among the prisoners but didn't see one, and I was glad. My papa could have been one of them. *How could I possibly have helped him escape? Where is he now? O God, what if he is wounded, seriously wounded, or . . .* I left the unanswerable suspended in the cold air, afraid to even think that something might have happened to him.

Several women remained standing beside me at the curb long after the last of the prisoners shuffled by. Their heads were bent, their hands clasped under the chin, as though in prayer.

All that night I kept thinking about the prisoners, feeling sad for them and angry at the sense of hopelessness I shared with them. My mind kept swinging between them and my father and mother. I didn't know how I was going to endure the worst of winter yet to come. *If only Mama were here.*

17

"YOU HAVEN'T LOST EVERYTHING."

I looked at the French-blue crepe de chine I had bought in Stalingrad for a dress and debated whether to sacrifice it for a headscarf or find a dress-maker first. *Is there enough for both?* I put the fabric in my briefcase to take to the office the next day.

My stomach throbbed with hunger. I ate a crust of black bread, sucking on it like a piece of candy. Still hungry, I put on my damp coat, stepped outside, and cringed. A fierce Siberian wind blew ice particles in my face. I ran up two rickety flights of stairs to Maria Ivanovna's apartment. Her door was padlocked. *She must still be at work*, I thought, and dashed for the Wi-Kdo, hoping I was not too late for some leftovers.

When I entered the office building, I could hear encouraging sounds of activity way down the corridor: voices from the officers' dining room and noises from the kitchen, where pots and pans were being scrubbed. I stepped in through the kitchen door.

"What in the name of God brings you here on a night like this?" It was Paul Osterberg. He and several other officers were still in the dining room. He came toward me.

"I'm hungry," I said in a small voice. Maria Ivanovna was nowhere in sight.

"My dear child, you're blue with cold. Here, sit down." He pulled a stool forward and slipped off my shoes, which he gave to someone to be dried at the kitchen range. He then crouched on one knee and proceeded to rub my feet, oblivious to the fact that he was in full view of the other officers. "They feel like icicles."

Tears filled my eyes and rolled off my cheeks as I looked down on the balding head of this kind old man.

He looked up, and his light-blue eyes smiled. "There now, do they feel better?"

"Much, much better. Thank you."

Someone brought me a bowl of soup and a patty made of boiled beef. It was so good I barely restrained myself from licking the plate.

A few days later, driven by the sharp, ringing December frost, I hurried home firmly clutching my mess tin filled with hot soup. Tonight, I thought cheerily, I would burn all the trash I had collected over the last few days. It would keep me warm while I ate leisurely in the comfort of my own home at the stove. I rounded a corner, ran up the stairs, unlocked the door to my apartment—and my happy mood crashed.

My apartment had been ransacked. Everything I owned was gone: dresses and shoes, every single bar of soap, swimsuit, stockings and underwear, pretty little handkerchiefs, and a funny-looking plastic purse, all gone. The golden locket Babushka Rosa had given me before she died was gone, and with it the only photograph I had of my father. I hadn't had very much; now I had only the clothes I wore. *It's like a nightmare*, I thought. *Or maybe it's a joke? Maybe the janitor's son . . .* I had forgotten to look in the bathroom. A spark of hope sent me flying into the bathroom. Cotton stockings that needed to be mended, the few pieces of underwear left to dry, were all gone.

With the back of my hand I wiped the tears that were streaming down my face, drank the now cold soup, picked up my toothbrush and back scrubber—*of no use to the thief*, I thought grimly—and left. I didn't much care where I would sleep tonight as long as it was not in that apartment. I couldn't stand the sight of it. Beyond that I did not think. All I wanted was to be with someone, someone I could pour out my heart to. *Karl Mannheim.*

I ran most of the way. My damp eyes stung, my face and ears were hot from the cold, my fingers felt numb. I knocked at Mannheim's door.

"Herein!"

I walked in.

"Sophia!" He dropped a book, came to the door, and looked anxiously into my face. "What happened?"

"I—I've been robbed. The thief took everything." I burst into tears.

He put his arm around me, just as I'd always longed for my father to do, and I nestled my head on his chest. With his other hand he stroked my hair, until my sobs subsided.

"Now tell me exactly what happened. Do you have any idea who could have done it?"

I did, but I shook my head. "I don't." *The Germans would kill that son of a bitch. And what's the use? The janitor's son has probably left town already to trade my things for food.*

"Did you say your door was locked when you came in?" I nodded. "Then it must have been someone in the house, someone who had access to your apartment, a passkey. We'll find that thief, and God help him."

"I don't want to go to that . . . that miserable place ever again." I was near tears once more.

"Hush, don't cry. You don't have to go back there if you don't want to. We'll help you find another place."

"Tonight . . . maybe Maria Ivanovna will put me up."

"Lie down and rest a while. I have an idea." He put on his greatcoat.

It felt good to put my head on a pillow. It was so soft. Somehow I was very tired. He covered me with a blanket. It felt so warm.

"Don't worry about a thing." His voice was soothing. "You haven't lost everything. You still have me."

★   ★   ★

Bright light from the overhead lamp woke me.

"You were sound asleep, curled up like a kitten. I hated to disturb you, but I have some news."

I sat up quickly. Reading Mannheim's face, I knew the news would be good.

"I talked with Maria Ivanovna. She's expecting you. And tomorrow you will move into your new home."

"Where? How did you find something so quickly?"

"It's a surprise. Get ready and I'll take you there."

My face was smudged, my hair a mess. I splashed my face with cold water and ran a comb hurriedly through my hair.

We crossed the street, turned the corner and there, facing a four-story office building across the yard from the Wi-Kdo, Mannheim stopped. He pointed at one of the large, totally blacked-out windows on the first floor and said, "That is your room." The modern L-shaped building was now used as a residence for the *Wirtschaftskommando*'s servicemen and noncommissioned officers. The nine *Volksdeutsche* girls who worked at the Wi-Kdo occupied six rooms on the first floor, dubbed *Damenstift* (ladies' establishment).

"Helga Weiss is making the room ready for you to move in tomorrow. She'll be sharing a room with one of the other girls across the hall."

"I'm so grateful to you, Herr Mannheim. Just imagine, no more wading through the snow, no more stiff limbs, wet feet, blue hands. It'll take seconds to run across the yard to get to work." What I was most happy about was that I would no longer be alone and isolated from the world. I was used to hunger, I was used to cold, but I could not get used to solitude. The girls, moreover, were all about my age. "Mennonites, good people," Mannheim had said.

Barely hiding his boyish smile, Mannheim claimed to have forgotten to tell me that the building was centrally heated.

"You didn't forget. You were saving it for another surprise. I know you."

"Well, since we're on the subject of surprises, I have still another one." He paused, to heighten the suspense, no doubt. "You'll be fed two meals a day from the mess, like all the girls at the *Damenstift*."

I was too moved to speak. What a day this has been, I marveled: one godsend after another, and all because of the robbery.

"My patron saint Sophia is looking after me," I said on our way to Maria Ivanovna's.

Maria Ivanovna, dressed in black, bustled us in from the cold. A black shawl with vivid red, green, and yellow flowers was draped across her shoulders, gypsy-like. Her black hair, usually in a tight knot, cascaded freely down her back.

She touched my arm. "I'm so sorry about the robbery. It's dreadful! Dreadful!"

I startled her by saying how glad I was I had been robbed.

"Please come in. Come in, Herr Mannheim."

We followed Maria Ivanovna into her room, warm and inviting with water boiling in the samovar. The dining table, covered with a white lace cloth, was set for tea.

"I've put aside a few things for you. Not much, but . . . Now eat, Sophia. Herr Mannheim?"

"A glass of tea would be fine. Thank you."

"A glass!" I cried. "How could you hold on to a glass filled with boiling hot tea? You'd need pot holders."

"Don't men in Russia drink tea from glasses? In silver holders, if I recall. Only women drink from cups, no?"

Maria Ivanovna's eyes crinkled with amusement. "You're absolutely correct, that's the way it used to be. Who in Russia has silver holders anymore? I'm sure I don't."

Without further ado, I helped myself to a thick slice of dark bread and smeared it liberally with black currant jam. I ate slowly, savoring every bite. I poured the steaming hot tea from the cup into a saucer and saw myself as a child again, lifting the saucer with both hands, sipping tea and hearing the adults talk but paying no attention to what they were saying.

When Mannheim had sauntered from the apartment, Maria Ivanovna presented me with some underwear, a black wool skirt, and a dark blue flannel dress with a white detachable collar. Nothing fit me, but I didn't care.

"You're drowning in it!" Maria Ivanovna laughed a quick, throaty laugh. "Never mind, my dressmaker will alter it."

"Dressmaker! I just remembered. My briefcase is in the office! I keep my photographs in it. The fabric for a dress I bought in Stalingrad is also there. Oh, Maria Ivanovna, I'm so thankful, most of all because my cherished photographs were spared."

"Well, then let us have some wine to celebrate." She got a bottle and struggled with the cork. "Horst Klinger has been asking me about you. He wants to see you again but—" The cork popped. She filled our glasses, and smiled as she lifted hers in a toast. "What is the relationship between you and Mannheim? I don't mean to pry. Just curious."

"He's my father-protector—from the soldiers that surround us." I laughed.

"Nothing more?"

"Certainly not. If you want to know the truth, Herr Mannheim is the best friend I've ever had. Ironic, isn't it?"

A faint smile crossed her lips. "Well," she drawled, "if you can keep him as a friend, good for you. I'll be curious to see how you manage it without . . . hmm . . . getting involved. Perhaps I can learn a few things from you myself."

My eyes felt heavy. *It's been a long, long day*, I thought. Seeing me stifle another yawn, Maria Ivanovna made a bed for me on the sofa and sat beside me talking while I fought the waves of sleep.

"Next time you come, I'll tell your fortune. Klinger likes for me to read cards for him. But all I see are spades, foreboding misfortune, death . . ."

★ ★ ★

The girls' wing at the end of the long corridor was secluded. The six rooms were bright, with daylight shimmering through the frost-covered windows. The large bathroom had a deep tub and hot running water. Talk of luxury!

I filled the tub and purred as I lowered myself in to take my first hot bath in months. I wallowed in the tub, and it wasn't even Sunday.

Feeling like a newborn babe, squeaky clean, I went to the dressmaker. Like all dressmakers, she did the sewing at home. I asked her to make me a dress as well as a blouse from the silk fabric I brought her. Who needed a head scarf?

"If you insist on both, the dress will barely cover your knees," she protested.

"That's fine," I said. In Kiev, short was in style.

"A flared skirt takes a lot of fabric."

"I want it straight, not flared. A formfitting dress, but not tight, please. You could add short slits on both sides of the skirt. Make them rounded."

She measured me for size. "You have a lovely bustline and such a small waist."

"Such flattery! But thanks anyway."

"I meant it sincerely. As for the blouse, the sleeves will be short. Would you like me to dye it black? I'll embroider it around the neck and the front opening."

I nodded. "That's what I want."

As I was leaving, she said, "You'll catch your death of pneumonia wearing a summer coat in this freezing weather. You don't have a winter coat? Buy one, or get a blanket and I'll make you one."

"Buy one? You can't be serious."

"Go to the flea market. You'll probably find one there."

I asked Herr Mannheim for a few hours off on Saturday so I could go to the flea market. "I forbid you to go there," he said.

"Why? All I want is to see about a winter coat."

"I only make the rules to help you. But you must obey them. It's unsafe for you to venture into that part of town."

I was soon to find out that Mannheim was right. The open-air markets were raided periodically. To be caught in a raid might mean rape. To satisfy the sexual appetites of their soldiers, the German occupational authorities had established army brothels. Initially they intended to fill these brothels with volunteers and made announcements to this effect. But there were no volunteers. And so the ruthless hunt for healthy young women began, and with it mass rape.

★   ★   ★

The Saturday before Christmas I left the office earlier than usual. At home the furniture had to be dusted inside and out, floors and windows had to be washed. The Germans were sticklers for cleanliness, and an officer on duty checked to see that our rooms were spotless.

As I was scrubbing the floor on my hand and knees, I heard "Ooh la-la!" behind me. I turned to face two young men in Luftwaffe uniforms standing in my doorway. They were trying to tell me something, but I couldn't grasp a single word. The one with large dark eyes was staring at me.

Soon I heard their footsteps diminishing down the corridor. Moments later Helga Weiss and Karina walked in.

I had a warm spot in my heart for Helga, the girl who had moved to make room for me. She said, "The two sergeants are from TK-1, a Luftwaffe transport column. They're celebrating Christmas tonight and asked us to invite you." Helga had a square face and a firm jaw, and dark hair cut short.

"If they all speak like these two, I'd sit there all night like an idiot."

"No party is complete without an idiot. We promised Guido Schneble you'd come with us. You really made an impression on him, I must say. He's the one with unusually shaped dark eyes, a Bavarian from Munich. Seppi Irschik, the nice-looking blond, is a Viennese."

"We had a terrible time understanding them ourselves at first. It's their d-d-dialects." Karina was a shy girl, and she stuttered. Her blond braids were wrapped around her head. "Don't feel bad, Sophia. Come with us. They'll probably have a Christmas tree."

Because religion in the Soviet Union was derided as the opiate of the masses, people celebrated Christian and Jewish holidays in secret. Only my dying Uncle Kazimir, shortly before joining his patron saint, dared to publicize his celebration of Christmas with an evergreen tree. He decorated it with oranges and tangerines, hung dozens of tiny bottles of vodka known as *merzavchiki* (little villains), and strung a long line of miniature hot dogs all around the tree to symbolize, he told us, a nation in chains. His visitors were invited to eat and drink from the tree.

A few years before the war, it had been decreed by the Supreme Soviet authorities that the *yolka*, a pine tree, had no religious significance and was therefore acceptable for New Year's Eve. I had a tree every year thereafter. I loved its smell and the magic it radiated when all lit up. What fun I had shopping for ornaments, trimming my *yolka*, and lighting it with candles—on New Year's Eve.

An invitation to see how Germans celebrated Christmas was too tantalizing to pass by. "I'd love to come."

Mannheim was expecting me that night. As I was dressing, my conscience began to stir. *I must run over and tell him. "I can't see you tonight. I have far more exciting things to do than study German with you."* That sounded awful. The truth would only hurt his feelings. *I'll think of something tomorrow,* I said to myself with an abstracted look at my image in the mirror. *But tomorrow is Sunday. Hurrah! I won't see him until Monday. And Monday? Anything could happen by then.*

The two sergeants from TK-1 came for the ten of us in a gray truck with a canvas cover. We giggled like schoolgirls as they heaved us into the back of the enormous truck.

Joyful greetings and accordion melodies accompanied our entrance into a plain hall, as large as the garage below where trucks were parked. Some thirty gregarious young men were clearly delighted to have girls among them, especially since all but one spoke their tongue fluently. All around me was laughter and hilarity. I sat quietly between Guido Schneble and Seppi Irschik at one of the long tables placed around the room and felt uncomfortable. I could not join in the conversation fired around the table and over my head. I didn't know the lyrics to the songs they sang and could not participate. *What in the world am I doing here?* I wondered, squirming in my seat and glancing around uneasily and in disappointment. There was no food but plenty of beer, which we girls did not drink, and plenty of cigarettes, which we did not smoke.

And no Christmas tree.

The next day, looking forward to a Sunday afternoon with Maria Ivanovna, I was disappointed when she told me that her friend and Klinger were joining us. "Pleased?"

"I guess so," I temporized, searching for a plausible excuse not to stay. I knew she wanted to fix me up with Klinger. I was not interested, nor was I in the mood to break my promise to Mannheim after having stood him up last night. I decided on a compromise. "I really can't stay very long."

The sun was sinking when after a detour to the river I returned home. I had just pulled down the blackout shades and turned on the lights when Helga Weiss came darting across the hall. "Where have you been all afternoon? Herr Mannheim was worried about you. He came twice to look for you."

This spelled trouble. *I should have told him I couldn't see him last night,* I chastised myself, and crawled under my blanket with a nagging feeling of guilt.

A tapping at the door made me jump. It was Mannheim.

I slipped into a dress and let him in. "Won't you sit down?" I pulled up a chair for him. He did not move. I waited for him to speak, but he stood perfectly still, as if stricken suddenly mute in my presence.

The silence was unnerving. To break it, I asked, "What time is it?" I couldn't think of anything else to say.

"So sorry I woke you up," he said irritably, with a sardonic overtone. "I didn't expect Miss Recalcitrant to be in bed already. It was nearly eleven when you returned last night. And where were you today?" He looked narrowly at me. "You *did* go to the flea market, didn't you?"

"Oh no, no!" So that's what worried him. I breathed normally again. "I was with Maria Ivanovna for awhile. Then I took a brisk walk to the river. Couldn't resist taking a peek at the snow-white beauty under the winter sun." I rattled on until he sat down. A smile unfurled his compressed lips.

"The girls must have told you how I worried. I was afraid you had gone to the flea market, after all. And last night, I waited and waited."

"I'm truly sorry, Herr Mannheim."

He waved my apology aside. "It doesn't matter. I'm glad to see you unharmed. You had forgotten our German session, hadn't you?"

I bobbed my head, pleased he had made it so easy for me to extricate myself.

"It's my fault, I guess. I should have reminded you. I knew you couldn't be so thoughtless and inconsiderate."

A few days later he came by carrying a sizable bundle under his arm. "I was here last night to give you this, but you had already disappeared. You were with the soldiers from TK-1 again."

He sounded scornfully aloof, the way he uttered the word *soldiers*. I didn't like that, nor the stringent rules he made for me to obey, the curfew he imposed on me, his strict discipline. The attention and fatherly concern he lavished on me were just what I had craved all my life. But he carried the role of a protector too far to suit me. *So what if there's a war? What am I to do, see no one, go nowhere, and wallow in self-pity until the world is sane again? Why must he always make me feel guilty? I'm not doing anything wrong.*

"Yes, I was with the soldiers. But how did you know?"

"Never mind. Just remember, nothing ever escapes me."

The girls all disappeared together. So how would he know? Unless . . . he waited outside and saw us return. He spied on me! I tightened my lips and was trying to conjure up some kind of retaliation for his supervision when I heard him say, "Aren't you going to look at what I brought you?"

The steam in my samovar instantly evaporated. My mouth fell open. *A winter coat!* I waltzed around the room with the brand-new coat flung across my shoulders. It was made from a mouse-gray blanket and trimmed around the neck and down the front with white rabbit fur. I stroked the fur, so soft, so cuddly. I buried my face in it.

"It's beautiful, Herr Mannheim. Thank you from the bottom of my heart."

In addition to his gift, inside the bundle was a parcel from Frau Mannheim. My spirits escalated as one by one I drew out stockings and underwear, a colorful silk scarf, mittens, and of all things, knee-long pantaloons.

"How thoughtful of Frau Mannheim," I said, holding up the pantaloons with what I hoped looked like sincere appreciation. When Mannheim had departed, I put on the pantaloons and burst out laughing.

★   ★   ★

Christmas Eve. Most girls whose families lived in the vicinity had gone home for the one-day holiday. The shy Karina and I were darning our stockings in my room when a heavy truck rolled into the yard. Guido Schneble arrived with another Bavarian.

Guido was a friendly young man with sparkling white teeth and a sturdy build. Karina translated for him: "It's hell to be alone on a holy night. Put your darning away and come with us."

Karina and I gladly accepted their invitation and enjoyed the evening with them. Guido had a small Christmas tree in his room behind the garage; the tree was decorated with ginger cookies and candies in variegated wrappings. He opened a box of chocolates. "They're for you to enjoy." Then he treated us to thick, delicious eggnog. And I thought to myself, *How generous he is, so thoughtful and kind. Imagine feeling sorry for two girls left alone. But what does he think?* Guido and I found that we could communicate somewhat.

I had no idea that two weeks earlier the Japanese bombers had struck the American fleet at Pearl Harbor, or that the United States had entered the war. Such momentous events! All I knew was what Guido managed to convey—the Wehrmacht could not cross the threshold to Moscow. And because he said that so only I could hear him, I imagined Guido to be on my side.

On the last day of 1941, two days after I turned eighteen, Aleksandr's words came back to me: "We'll celebrate our victory at home on New Year's Eve." He couldn't possibly have been such a fool as to believe that. But I had believed it.

At the beginning of the war I was convinced Russia would win. When I saw for myself the superior-looking German troops, my conviction began to waver. Compared to the German war machinery, our equipment seemed puny. The Germans continued to push eastward and were making tremendous progress on two sectors of the front; nearly all of the Ukraine was in German hands. Karl Mannheim had said that.

Guido Schneble tipped the scale. He was the only German who would tell me that the Wehrmacht had suffered some setbacks and could not break through to Moscow. Their soldiers were severely handicapped by a shortage of winter clothing. Fighting, he told me, was practically impossible because of the severe weather that congealed the oil in their mechanized units and made it difficult for the infantry to advance.

"Your winters are brutal," he said as we sat in my room. "I've never seen so much snow in all my life as here in the Ukraine." Driving to Zaporozhye in a convoy of heavy trucks loaded with supplies and spare parts for the Luftwaffe, they had gotten stuck in deep snow, shoulder-high, and nearly froze to death before another convoy could rescue them.

Guido's candid revelations restored my confidence. Again I thought of Napoleon and his defeat in the winter of 1812. Unlike the Germans, Russian soldiers were conditioned to harsh winters. The blizzards, snowdrifts, and subzero temperatures, in addition to the vastness of Russia and our superiority in numbers of men, must triumph over the enemy, if not this winter, then the next—or so I hoped.

18

GERMAN STUDIES

As the winter of 1941–42 drew to a close, the town stirred. Private businesses opened: barber and shoe repair shops, two beauty parlors, a photography studio, and a movie house, with two or three shows a week for the Russians; the Germans used the theater the rest of the time. The curfew was lifted for "good behavior," as there had been no sabotage or partisan activity in the area. Old Zaporozhye was less depressing now that it was waking up.

Lydia, a ballet dancer turned kitchen helper, and I rushed about inspecting everything. *Die Symphonie des Lebens* was playing at the movie house. The beauty parlor smelled of fresh paint and looked impressive with all the hair dryers and electrical equipment for permanent waves.

Nor did we overlook the *banya*, a public bathhouse loved by all Russians. We carried bundles under our arms with fresh underwear, lye soap, and towels. Inside the steam room, we beat each other's bare backs and bottoms with birch twigs to cleanse the pores.

Our limbs still aglow, faces scrubbed and shiny, we trotted to the photography studio. Lydia posed in a floor-length Russian costume, complete with *kokoshnik*, a headdress worn in old Russia. She looked stunning. I wore my new blouse and assumed a thoughtful pose. Both pictures turned out well, but it was mine that the photographer chose to enlarge; he colored it in pastels and (to my detriment) displayed it in his window.

Lydia and I visited Maria Ivanovna, the fortune-teller. She told me I would soon meet a man, and a romance would develop. She predicted a long journey and even saw marriage in the cards. Would I marry the man I was about to meet? "No, you have already met the man you will marry," she said. I could think of no one but Aleksandr and wondered if he was still in Stalingrad.

My mother also read cards, but her predictions were predictable: a gentleman visitor on the doorsill or a merrymaking company. We always had one or the other. How could she go wrong? Or she prophesied tears of sadness or happiness, and there were always some of each. I had sneered at it. Why, even I could have predicted that, without looking at the cards.

★   ★   ★

On a Sunday in February, a noncommissioned officer approached me in the corridor outside the girls' wing, his forage cap under his arm. "Fräulein Sophie?"

I was surprised he knew my name and looked at him with mild curiosity. "Sophia," I corrected him.

"Forgive me." He inclined his head in a slight bow and introduced himself. "Otto Schubert, your neighbor two floors removed."

As we shook hands, my coat slid off my shoulders and fell to the ground. I bent to pick it up, and so did he. Our heads collided. We rubbed our heads and laughed. He helped me put my coat on and dropped his forage cap. Again we laughed, and I couldn't stop. I was just happy, so happy to still be alive.

I had never seen him before and wondered how I could have missed an attractive young man like him. He had a dimple on his chin, his mouth was sensuous; his eyes looked like hazelnuts with humor in them.

"Going for a walk, I see. May I join you?"

"I'm on my way to see Herr Osterberg," I said regretfully. "Do you know him?"

"Yes, of course. Well, perhaps you'd join me later on? It's such a fine day."

"I'd love that." We agreed to meet in an hour. I walked off sedately, and then darted across the yard.

Paul Osterberg was going to Germany on leave and his face revealed his happiness. His itinerary was a busy one: Heidelberg, his ailing mother, sisters . . . Düsseldorf . . . Cologne . . . I listened but absorbed only half of what he was saying. I wished I knew what time it was. Otto might not wait for me.

"You're not very attentive today. What's on your mind? A young man, no doubt." Osterberg nodded knowingly. "You look radiant."

I felt my cheeks turn crimson. "*Unteroffizier* [noncommissioned officer] Otto Schubert and I are going for a walk," I confessed.

"Ah, yes. A splendid young man." I wished him bon voyage. "Have a good time. But keep your head," he added at the door. "You know the situation."

Yes, I knew. For a Russian girl to fall in love with a German could lead to nothing but heartbreak. A German would never marry a Russian. It was verboten. Anyway, I had no intentions of marrying anyone, least of all a German. After the war was over and I had graduated from the university, there would be plenty of time to think about that.

Otto stood at the same spot where our heads had collided earlier. Our eyes met from a long way off, and we walked toward each other, smiling all the while. We strolled toward the river.

"You're from Kiev, I'm told. It's an ancient Russian city."

"A thousand years old, and beautiful. It sits on three hills, high above the Dnieper. Some streets are so tall—"

"Steep, you mean."

"Steep," I repeated, and carried on in my broken German. "Instead of sidewalks some streets have sidestairs. Parks and flowers everywhere, linden and chestnut trees."

"Berlin is famous for its linden trees."

"Are you from Berlin?"

"No, Vienna is my home."

"I read about Vienna in books. Is it as beautiful as they say?"

"Yes, it is. Vienna is a city of striking Baroque architecture, of good cheer and music and song. Some of the most beautiful music ever composed was by the Viennese: Joseph Haydn, Johann Strauss, Franz Schubert—no predecessor of mine, sorry to say. And we claim Mozart as a Viennese."

Otto spoke High German, clearly and distinctly for my benefit. I understood him well. But not when in his enthusiasm he got carried away and reverted to his native Viennese. It was softly spoken, not guttural, and very pleasing to my ears.

"What did you do before the war?"

"I studied law at the university. After Austria's Anschluss [joining] with the German Reich, I was called to serve in the Wehrmacht."

The town was alive with young people: Russian couples drifted by, the men carrying their girlfriends' purses, their arms interlocked; German soldiers hand-in-hand with local girls. Fraternization was frowned upon officially but largely ignored.

Light traffic rolled across the Dnieper. We stood at the shore and observed German soldiers and the *Hilfswillige* (Russian prisoners of war who had volunteered to work for the Wehrmacht) laying planks on the ice.

Spring will be here soon, my heart rejoiced. Any day now, the mighty roar of the ice breaking up would resound in the air.

I kept glancing at Otto from the corner of my eye. He was fairly tall, his hair dark and wavy, like my father's. He radiated confidence and vitality. I liked the way he smiled, the way he walked with a light springy stride.

"The Dnieper reminds me of the Danube," Otto remarked. "I wonder what it looks like in summertime."

The wind off the river was cold, but I did not feel the chill. I removed the silk scarf from my neck and held it away from me in this direction and that until it puffed out like a sail. The wind whistled around us.

"You'll catch cold." Otto took the scarf away from me and wrapped it around my neck. "We had better start back if we want to be fed," he said. I didn't care if I missed a meal.

At the door to my room, Otto hesitated, and I realized neither of us wanted to part quite yet. "Well," he said, "I really must run."

But soon he was back, and we spent the rest of the day together. I showed him my photographs, including several of the Dnieper in summertime. All that was left of my previous life was in those photographs, and as we looked at them I recalled all the pleasant things that had happened to me in the past. I thought of Aleksandr, my first love, of how our time was over like a brief gust of wind, and wondered when, if ever, I would see him again.

Some days later Otto brought a pocketsize book wrapped in brown paper and insisted I read to him. I examined it and read the title, "*Deutsches Wörterbuch*. That's a dictionary!"

"Read to me."

"*You* read." I propped my elbows on the table and put my chin on the palms of my hands. "I refuse to be ridiculed."

"It's a matter of grave importance. I'm serious." His eyes with their long lashes smiled.

Using the dictionary as a guide, Otto began to teach me German, adding zest to my anemic vocabulary. He made a game of it, selecting words at random and explaining each one in great detail. He was clever and resourceful. We had no German-Russian dictionary, so he drew pictures to illustrate an animal or an object, or created a situation to explain words that could not be drawn. His demonstrations, such as acting out various moods and emotions, were so comical they made me laugh.

More often than not, he laughed at me. Once I showed him my hands and said, "My leather is so dry." (In Russian, the same word is used for *leather* and *skin*.) Otto roared with laughter. Then he painstakingly explained the difference between leather and skin. Another time I wailed: "You stepped on my finger!" when in fact it was my toe.

To learn German from Otto was pure delight.

As he stood behind me at the table one evening, he pointed at the verb *stehlen* (to steal). "Do you know what this means?"

I was about to say, "Yes, I do," when he bent down and stole a kiss.

Another time he brought a gramophone, an ancient model with a crank, and one record for us to dance by. I looked at the label and started laughing. It was an old Ukrainian folk song, "Bandurist," melodious but slow. "As the bandurist strums his lute-like instrument, he praises the beautiful eyes of his beloved," went the song.

Otto feigned indignation at my laughter. "I searched the world for it!"

"It's just that . . . it's not exactly a dance tune."

"We," he declared, "can dance to anything." He made a formal bow. "May I have this dance, *gnädiges* [gracious] *Fräulein?*"

I lowered my eyes demurely, the way I had seen ladies do on stage, and rose slowly. He held me close as we waltzed, and all at once the scratchy record made the most romantic music ever composed.

"How old are you?" I asked him once, even though it was indiscreet, according to my mother, who claimed to be at least ten years younger than she was.

"Twenty-six. Twenty-seven, actually, in March."

"Twenty-seven!"

"Shocking, isn't it?"

"Oh, no. I thought you were older."

"That's better still. You're very comforting."

"It's the way you look . . . I don't mean that exactly. What I wanted to say—how do you say it? You . . . you look so experienced. That's it!" I cried exultantly. He started to laugh. "Well, you are! You've studied at the university, you've traveled a lot, and you've seen so much."

"Yes, I have seen most of Europe. War-torn Europe, I must add, so none of it for pleasure."

"And before the war?"

"I toured Germany and Italy on a bicycle. Other than that, I stayed pretty much close to home."

"I visited all the large cities, crossed every river, and climbed the highest mountains in the world," I told him.

"In your dreams?"

"No. With my fingertips on the map."

Otto drew me close. "By the time you've reached my old age, you'll probably have seen the world."

I put my head on his shoulder, content just to be near him. I never thought of the war when I was with Otto. And neither, I intuitively believed, did he.

My room was my refuge. Within its walls was peace.

19

A LAMB IN SPRING

Mannheim rarely got angry or upset with Miss Recalcitrant anymore. I was, of course, a "sensible girl" who stayed close to home. I never told him about Otto. If Mannheim knew about him—and he probably did, since nothing ever escaped him—he no longer lectured me on being careful around soldiers. He still kept a close eye on my activities, but this did not bother me. My father had started to do the same thing. Besides, I had nothing to hide.

It did cross my mind that Mannheim's love for me was more than fatherly. But I ignored that scarcely comforting thought out of an instinct for self-preservation. Not to ignore it would have destroyed the friendship I valued and depended on. His behavior had always been above reproach and made it possible for me to continue looking up to him as a father figure.

At the end of a busy day in March, Mannheim said, "I have received a parcel from home. Come over tonight—I'll share it with you."

Otto and I never made plans in advance, as though we had agreed never to speak of tomorrow. It was always today or yesterday. Tomorrow, after all, might never come. I could spend an evening with Mannheim. And I should.

"I'll be glad to," I said, even though I would rather have been with Otto.

The evening was pleasant indeed. We ate smoked ham and boiled potatoes with salt, and we talked. He had promised to write to my mother, but months had passed and he never mentioned it. "You haven't written to my mama yet, have you?"

His answer seemed evasive. "The best way to get in touch with her would be for me to go to Kiev myself."

"Does that mean you might?" I pretended it would make me very happy if he did.

"I will, as soon as an important matter here is resolved," he said mysteriously.

I trusted Mother to say nothing about my father to Mannheim. But could I trust our neighbors? Could I be sure Mannheim wouldn't check up on me with the authorities? There were ample ways to discover that I was a Jew. That worried me.

I had heard at the beauty parlor that all Jews had been driven out of town. "The poor souls are starving in ghettos," my hairdresser said, and I believed it. But if anyone had told me that most Jews had been killed, I would not have believed it. The innocent people—old men, women, and children—had obeyed the order to report for resettlement into ghettos be-cause they did not believe the rumors that the Nazis were murdering Jews. Who could have believed that the civilized, cultured Germans were capable of such unspeakable brutality?

As time went by, I had begun to feel secure. I hoped there were many Jews who had refused to obey the order to report for resettlement, not knowing that other people did the reporting for them. The Germans were not satisfied that all Jews and Communists had registered and constantly encouraged the population to inform on them. Many eagerly obliged, de-nouncing their neighbors, former coworkers, and one-time friends.

Neither Karl Mannheim nor Paul Osterberg had ever asked to see my passport. The subject had come up one day, and I told Mannheim I had none. It did not matter to him, he assured me. But, he said, it was just as dangerous to be without papers now as it had been under Soviet rule. He urged me to apply to the Ukrainian civil authorities for identification papers, which he believed I would get with ease.

He had never been more wrong. The identity card I received stated: "The bearer of this certificate says she is Sophia Mikhailovna Orlovskaya, born in Kiev, Ukraine." What did this piece of paper prove? Nothing. Nothing but that I was indeed a female. *Callous bastards!* I fumed. *They could have closed an eye and issued a valid document. Certainly the Germans would not have known the difference.*

To make matters worse, some obsequious bureaucrat from the civil authorities notified the *Wirtschaftskommando* that I had no valid documents, and an officer demanded that I be dismissed. I learned only later of the in-ternal struggle both Karl Mannheim and Paul Osterberg had had within the Wi-Kdo on my behalf. Obviously this was the important matter to which Mannheim had alluded. At considerable risk to themselves, Mannheim and

Osterberg forestalled an investigation, defended me, and at the same time shielded me from any knowledge of the threat.

★ ★ ★

The days rolled on toward May. I could smell the unmistakable scent of spring in the air, and it had an exhilarating effect on me. Mama used to say I was like a bouncing lamb in the spring. *She should see me now*, I thought as I hurried across the yard on my way home from work. I was humming a Johann Strauss waltz and wished Otto and I would go for a stroll, the Russians' and Germans' favorite recreation.

I glanced at his window and saw him standing there. He waved to me and within minutes he was downstairs, saying, "Would you like to—"

"*Spazierengehen?* [Go for a walk?]"

"You would, would you?"

"*Wunderbar!* I'm glad you asked."

"I did?" He arched his brow in mock surprise. "Tell you what, *Schatz* [dear], we'll go out first. And then we'll go up to my room for a change. How would that be?"

"That's fine." I had no qualms about it. I was, as Mannheim had astutely observed, a trusting soul. I had been fantasizing for weeks about his room and wanted to see the chair in which he sat, the desk where he wrote letters, the bed in which he slept.

We crossed town toward the railroad tracks. Acting silly, we skipped and jumped over mud puddles, walked on top of the rails to see who could stay on longer, and had a race. I was declared the rail-balancing champion, but Otto won the race and demanded a kiss as the prize.

"Later!" I laughed, dodging him.

When we got back to our residence, I found Otto's room furnished with the same Spartan simplicity as the girls' rooms downstairs.

I had barely had a chance to look around when Otto folded me in his arms and started kissing me. His passionate kisses took my breath away. Abruptly, he rose from the edge of the bed where we were sitting and crossed the room.

I heard him lock the door. The sound of the clicking key brought me back to reality with a jolt. All the sensuous excitement evaporated, turned off as if by a switch.

"Unlock the door," I started protesting when he sealed my lips with his and leaned over me on the bed. I jerked out from under him, jumped up, and ran to the door, steaming with resentment at having been duped. "Let me out!" I snapped.

He followed me to the door but made no move to unlock it.

Frustrated because there was not one German word in my vocabulary strong enough to express my indignation, I blurted out *"Idiot!"* in Russian (with an accent on the last syllable).

Idiot is "idiot" in most languages, though I didn't know it then. Otto unlocked the door, and I stormed out.

A few nights later I heard his official voice outside my door, alerting me: *"Verdunklung!* [Blackout!]" Otto was an officer on duty that night.

"What's wrong with my blackout shades?"

Otto's voice again: "I can see a beam of light."

The room was dark.

"Check the shades yourself, if you insist." My voice was stern, belying the gladness I felt. The idea of not seeing me while we were still under the same roof must have bothered him, as it did me.

Otto walked in and closed the door. "Switch on the lamp," I said, "so you won't stumble in the dark."

"I guess I made a mistake." He grinned sheepishly.

"Did you?"

He sat down beside me and slowly ran his fingers through my hair. Then he kissed me, just once, as if to ask forgiveness.

On a drizzly day in May we were sipping lukewarm ersatz coffee when Otto asked, "Still no news from home?"

"None."

"I'll try to get in touch with your mother. Write her a note, and I'll pass it on to her. I might even be able to stop over in Kiev for a day. I'd like to meet your mother."

"Oh, I wish you could." I planted kisses on his cheeks. *He must really care for me. Why else would he want to meet my mama?*

"Just wait till I see her. I'll tell her what an unruly, headstrong, naughty girl you are."

"She knows that already. If you want to shock her, tell her how docile, sweet, and agreeable I am. If you want to please her, tell her how beautiful she is. . . . There's so much I want to tell my mother, a note will never do."

"Then you had better start writing now." Only then did I realize what he was trying to tell me. "I'm leaving tomorrow."

Instantly I forgot my mother. *This then is the end.* I heard him say, "I'll be back," but he didn't sound convincing, and a feeling of irretrievable loss swept over me.

Otto put his arms around me and held me tight, close to him. We sat without speaking for some time.

At last I asked, "How long will you be gone?"

"Hard to say. Two, three weeks, maybe longer."

I wrote a short letter to Mama. I addressed the envelope in both Russian and German and told Otto, "If the train doesn't stop in Kiev—just in case it doesn't—toss the letter out the window. Somebody will pick it up and maybe pass it on to my mother."

"All right"—he smiled—"if the train doesn't stop." Otto wrote his home address in Vienna on a piece of paper and handed it to me. "Hold on to it, in case the train doesn't stop in Zaporozhye when I'm ready to come back," he said, his smile broadening.

Suddenly he was on his feet. A quick good-bye, another kiss, and he was gone.

20

RESCUED

Will I ever see Otto again? I wondered if perhaps he had only said he would come back to make the parting easier. But I had no inkling that I would no longer be there when he did return.

To make the time go faster, I jumped at Mannheim's invitation to go on an outing the following Sunday. "Where?" I wanted to know. "It's a surprise" was all he said.

But the day before our scheduled outing, I found a note under my door from Guido Schneble: *"Liebe Sophia! We're going on a boating trip tomorrow and want you to come with us. Everything is arranged to make the day guaranteed enjoyable. We'll pick you up at ten. Bring your swimsuit."*

Great! If only my swimsuit hadn't been stolen. Unthinkable that I should be sitting in the boat while others swam. The shy Karina offered a dark blue jersey tank top. I gratefully accepted, hand-stitched the jersey under the crotch, and *voilá*—a swimsuit!

My date with Mannheim escaped my mind, totally.

Six men from TK-1 and three of us girls from the *Damenstift* were on the truck by ten, speeding toward the Dnieper. With the dam destroyed, the melted ice–swollen river spilled over its banks, flooding the woods I had roamed while staying on the houseboat—where only last August I had heard the distant salvo of machine guns and shouted: "The Germans are coming!" and was accused by Comrade Zhuk of panic mongering. . . . Now we sailed in a rubber dinghy between the trees. Once it was tied up, the men and I dived into the murky depths below. The water was cold and the swim bracing. We had a picnic lunch and afterward let the current propel us through an eerily beautiful clearing, like a haunted forest lake.

It was dead calm, and no one in sight.

Quite suddenly, a boat appeared; it headed in our direction at full speed. Mannheim stood at the bow, straight as a ramrod in his impeccable uniform, his right hand ominously clutching his dagger. A feeling of wild panic came over me. I tumbled off the boat and swam to the thickly wooded shore, undoubtedly reaching it in record time. But my attempt to escape Mannheim proved futile. He had seen me, and by leaving the group I only made matters worse.

From my hideout in the bushes I saw our boat approach the shore, Mannheim in hot pursuit. I could not see what happened after that, but I could hear Mannheim's voice rise and fall like an angry wave. Fear flooded my innards. *I've done it again,* I moaned, crouching in the undergrowth. *I've really done it this time. He'll never let me get away with this.*

Some twenty minutes later, Mannheim chugged away. I emerged from my hideout and rejoined the group. I was trembling.

Guido said, "Your boss is really something."

"What happened?" My teeth were chattering like castanets.

"The *Sonderführer* came storming up to us and demanded you cross over to his boat at once—'or else,' he threatened. He refused to leave without you."

"We told him," Seppi Irschik said, " 'Sophia came with us, and she'll leave with us.' He got furious! At first he tried to pull rank on us. In our swimming trunks, he couldn't tell any of our ranks and called us *soldiers* as if it were a dirty word."

The men roared with laughter. The two girls crouching in the boat were scared into utter silence and immobility.

"So then what happened?"

Still laughing, Lieutenant Zitzmann said, "He kept taunting us, as if looking for a fight. So Fritz told him, 'If you don't shut up, we'll dunk you!' "

"And you know what Fritz did?" someone else said.

"Don't tell me . . . what?"

"Your boss stood in his boat, tall and omnipotent," Guido snickered. "He didn't believe that anybody could do such a thing to his exalted personage—even when Fritz jumped into his boat and began to rock it. The boat quickly filled with water and the *Sonderführer* was forced to wade ashore—in his full uniform! What a sight he was. Wet from the waist down and madder than hell.

"And he still wouldn't give up . . ."

★ ★ ★

I suspected Mannheim would be more than angry with me this time, but I decided not to make excuses for myself. His involuntary swim must have been a tremendous blow to his pride and dignity, so the less I said the better. *I'll apologize for forgetting our date, that's all,* I thought with bravado, *and I'll take what's coming to me.*

"Good morning, Herr Mannheim." I greeted him respectfully the moment he came into the office on Monday.

"Good morning." He looked straight ahead, his voice gruff and low. He sat down at his desk and frowned at the stack of papers in front of him. For a time he appeared very busy, making endless notes. Then he tossed the pencil aside with an angry gesture. I tensed. *Here it comes!* My nerves began to vibrate like mandolin strings. I braced myself.

But nothing happened. I watched him lean back in his chair. For a minute or two he drummed his fingers on top of the desk. Then he went back to work.

He neither looked at me nor spoke to me that day. Even when I mumbled my apologies, he said not a word.

The next morning he acted as if nothing had ever happened.

"Go on," he said, his eyes flashing kindness and generosity. "I left breakfast for you in my room. The food is getting cold." This was his way of telling me I was forgiven.

I smiled at him and scurried out the door.

★ ★ ★

A few days later, Mannheim said, "I must speak to you after quitting time." His voice sounded urgent, and fear that my secret had been discovered gripped my chest.

Only that week, my ballerina friend Lydia had asked me if I were Jewish. "What makes you ask that? No, I'm not," I had answered. *Did my voice tremble? I hope not.*

"Oh, I was sure of that," said Lydia generously. "And that's what I told Dunya Kovalenko, my school chum. She's pretty sure you're a *Zhidovka*. She knows you from before the Germans took over. You worked for DURP. And so did she."

I thought about Dunya. A girl with broad hips and a shrill voice who had seemed pleasant enough the few times we talked.

"Anyway," Lydia continued, "that's what *she* said when I showed her your photograph displayed in the photographer's window. She's crazy . . ."

I had the sick, familiar feeling in my stomach that comes from fear. *Crazy or not*, I thought, *Dunya's vicious. And Lydia, can I trust her?* One word from either one of them to the German authorities and . . . *Has Mannheim heard about it?* My heart was beating like a drum summoning troops into battle as I entered the yard through the squeaky gate on my way to see him.

"Here I am," I said with forced lightheartedness. I gave him a twig of new soft green leaves.

He gave my shoulder a squeeze. "Beautiful spring day, isn't it?" He pulled up a chair for me at the table. He himself remained on his feet and was taking entirely too long to come to the point of my summons.

"What did you want to talk to me about?"

"Your future," he answered evenly, his half-closed eyes inscrutable. "You're leaving Zaporozhye."

My heart skipped a beat. It was not safe for me to stay in Zaporozhye any longer, but to go back to Kiev was infinitely more dangerous.

"Why, Herr Mannheim? I thought you had forgiven me."

"Whether I forgave you or not has nothing to do with it. But why do you look so alarmed?"

"I don't want to go to Kiev just now. I like it here."

"Kiev isn't what I have in mind."

"Then why did you say I was leaving?"

"Because you are. You are going home, my home."

I stared at him, nonplussed.

"How would you like to be adopted?"

"What?" I truly didn't understand what he was talking about. "At my age? What about my mother?"

He laughed. "I'll adopt her too."

"Now I know you're joking."

"No, I am not. I've been thinking about it ever since I first saw you. That's when I adopted you."

I felt as if I were just coming out of a trance. My ears had received everything, but my mind was slow in registering. I dug my fingernails into the palm of my hand. *Yes, I am awake.*

Most of my childhood dreams had flashed through my mind, tickled my fancy for a spell, and then dissolved as quickly as they came. But the dream of seeing the forbidden world outside Russia had lingered, lodged in my heart, and Mannheim was now making that dream come true. He was sending me to Poland! Never mind that Poland was now part of Germany.

"You really mean it, Herr Mannheim, don't you?"

"I always mean what I say."

"But—" I wanted to ask about his wife and what she thought of it. What about my mother? Would he let her know and could she join me, later maybe? How did he intend to ship me off if there were no trains for civilians?

"No buts. First hear me out," he said. "Gut Birkenhof is the best place for you to be right now. You'll be safe there and well protected, and there's plenty of good food. You'll like your new home. My wife is expecting you, and my children are looking forward to having you. You'll love them, I know, and they will love you too." He was walking about the room with his arms behind his back. "And later, as soon as it is possible, I'll send you to university. I promise you. In the meantime you will keep on studying German with my wife. You couldn't find a better tutor, I can assure you."

His walking up and down was making me dizzy; I was glad when he stopped. I couldn't take my eyes off him lest I miss a word, a nuance, anything. And through the shock of it all I wondered, over and over: *Has the rumor reached his ears? Does he know my secret or doesn't he?* And yet, how strange that his decision to send me off to the safety of his estate should coincide with the new wave of malevolence against me.

Mannheim sat on the top of the table, his legs crossed, his hands on his knee. He looked at me for long moments. And then he said, "It's with your welfare in mind that I'm doing this. I will get in touch with your mother; you can depend on that. I've made arrangements for you to travel on a military train. *Sonderführer* Boltze will look after you en route."

"What if I refuse to go?" I asked, hoping his answer would provide some clue to his reasons for sending me away.

His hands tightened in his lap. "That would be very foolish. If you don't go now, you might have to go sooner or later anyway. But that," he said slowly, emphasizing every word, "that would be in altogether different circumstances. The destination might be far less desirable . . . Sophia, *mein Kind* [my child], I've told you before, and I'm telling you again—trust me. There are certain things I'm not at liberty to discuss, and therefore you must take my word for it. Go to Gut Birkenhof, and go now."

At the back of my mind, an uneasy thought formed: *Mannheim could find out the truth about me after I'm gone.* I hesitated while considering the "after," then firmly said, "I'm willing to go, Herr Mannheim." Because now, no doubt about it, my life was in jeopardy if I stayed. "When do I leave?"

"Tomorrow. Tomorrow at noon."

I thought I'd faint. My palms were moist. I couldn't breathe. I couldn't think of anything but that soon I would be far away from the danger that lurked around me. I was leaving Zaporozhye behind me, and with it the bitterness I felt toward my countrymen who most definitely did not wish me well.

My mother, 1930.

My mother, an ambulance attendant.

Red Army comrades' reunion, Kiev Arsenal, 1933. My father, top row, second from left; me on the right.

Me, fifth grader, age twelve.

Me, age fifteen.

The Dnieper River Dam at Zaporozhye,
destroyed on August 28, 1941
(photo from 1942).

Kreshchatik, the main thoroughfare, Kiev, 1941–44.

Refugees trying to return home across the Dnieper.

The front of the pre-signed ID card reads "USSR/Peoples Commissariat of the River Fleet." Inside it states that Sophia Mikhailovna Orlovskaya is employed by DURP in the position of secretary. Self-issued and dated September 24, 1941.

Soviet youth at the newspaper stand, Zaporozhye, 1942.

Guido Schneble and Seppi Irschik of TK-1. They had never seen that much snow, not even in the Alps.

Otto Schubert, 1942.

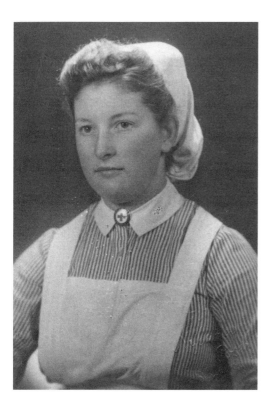

My one day as a German Red Cross nurse, Posen, 1942.

Gottlieb Brune, mayor of Wannefeld.

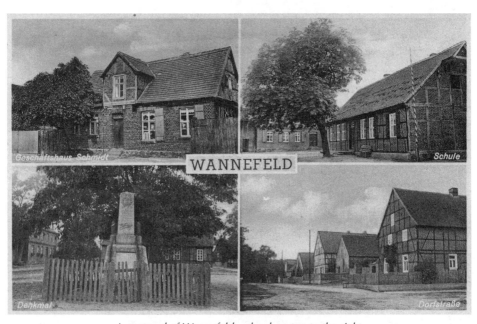

A postcard of Wannefeld; school on top to the right.

Girls from Poland and my two Hungarian roommates, Heli and Resi Kozin, at work in Gottlieb Brune's cannery.

Girls from the cannery at harvest time.

Guido, from Paris with love and a marriage proposal.

Gathering cornflowers, June 1944.

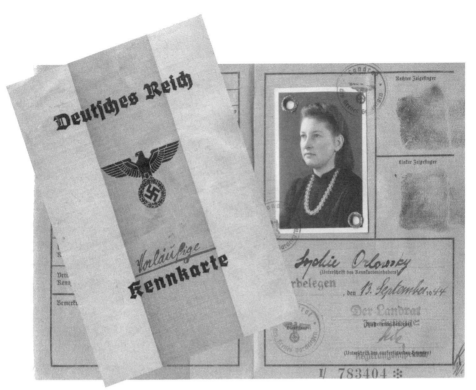

My Provisional Identification Card, issued in Gardelegen, September 13, 1944.

My refuge in Ruhpolding, 1944–45 (photo from 1997).

Me, Munich, 1949.

Our business card.

Guido, Munich, 1949.

Opa Schneble and O'ma Anni on their wedding day, July 26, 1950. He dedicated this picture to his grandchildren (from left): Isolde, Bernhard, Karola, Guido, Sylvia, and Richard.

Guidoli and his teddy bear.

My little marvels frolicking in the Alps: Sylvia (age six) and Guidoli (four and a half). Törwang, 1951.

Summer in alpine meadows, 1951.

Guido and his mistress, Bavarian Alps, 1951.

Guido's lady love is taken for a ride in our Ford Taunus.

*With my children,
Edmonton, Canada, 1968.*

*Jim and I attend a ball at
the Savoy, London, 1972.*

I was the only female draftsman employed by EBASCO at the time. New York City, 1953.

My favorite pastime: playing duplicate bridge at EBASCO after work.

The engineering team faces a model of a petrochemical plant under construction. San Francisco, April 2, 1965.

Part IV

EYE OF THE HURRICANE

21

ON A NAZI TRAIN

K arl Mannheim's resonant voice rang out as the wheels began to roll: *"Glückliche Reise!* [Happy journey!]" Leaning out of the open window of the train carrying the men of the Wehrmacht home to Germany, I waved and waved until the tall and proud silhouette in full dress uniform was a mere dot.

Sonderführer Boltze, to whom Karl Mannheim had entrusted me for the duration of the trip, sat beside me in a coach filled with Nazi officers. Behind us were boxcars crammed with soldiers. I was the only female on the train, and a civilian, yet my presence prompted no questions.

My blue-eyed, middle-aged escort was a disturbingly quiet man with a scar on his face and plastered-down blond hair.

"Will the train stop in Kiev?" I asked him politely, hoping to catch sight of my hometown and to drop the letter I had written to my mother for delivery by a passerby.

His clear blue eyes flashed, then narrowed. "I think not," he replied, as if worried I might run away and try to get to Kiev before he had a chance to deliver me into the hands of Frau Mannheim. After that he spoke to me only to say that under no circumstances was I to leave the coach without him.

But the train passed Kiev in the dark of the night or bypassed it altogether.

Deeply disappointed, I consoled myself that Otto's train had taken a different route and he was able to let my mother know I was alive and well. I couldn't wait to write Otto. How surprised he'd be to hear I had left Russia. His recent words came back to me: "By the time you've reached my old age, you'll probably have seen the world." And I had laughed. Now, glued to the window of a train rolling to the west, I believed anything was possible. One moment I had feared my life was coming to an end, the next I was running to a place where old fears might never find me.

Would the Soviets exile me to Siberia when I returned after the war? *Probably*, I thought, remembering Shura Prudnik's brother-in-law, who had been exiled there upon his return from a short time abroad. I heaved a dejected sigh, but then I shrugged. *To hell with the consequences! With the war going on and its outcome uncertain, the future is a question mark. Why worry about it?* Far more worrisome was the possibility that the Nazis might win the war, or that I might not live to see a Russian victory.

I asked Herr Boltze, "How much longer before we cross the border?"

"*What* border?"

"The old one, between Poland and Russia."

"I have no idea."

The train clattered on through the night. By the time the new day dawned, the Russian Cyrillic lettering had disappeared. Stations were identified in the Roman-English alphabet. We were in Poland. People darted by like butterflies. I could not see them very clearly, but the atmosphere was brighter and lighter.

I, too, felt lighter and brighter. I had fully expected to be searched and thoroughly probed upon leaving Russia. Nothing of the sort happened, and I marveled at the simplicity with which I crossed what used to be the heavily guarded Russian-Polish frontier. It seemed a forbidden adventure. It was an altogether intoxicating feeling, not unlike what an escaped convict must feel who believes himself safe and free.

I laughed out loud, and Scarface arched his eyebrows. Then he crawled back into his shell.

The train came to a screeching halt in the middle of nowhere, and the soldiers of the Wehrmacht rushed toward barracks to be processed through a delousing station. Scarface took me to the women's section, where a brusque German matron took her time examining her lone customer. I was instructed to strip naked and to shower using strong lye soap. Afterward the matron handed me a towel and sprayed powder under my armpits and between my legs. Washed and disinfected and smelling of insecticide, I was at last declared lice-free and clean enough to proceed toward the Third Reich.

We boarded the train, changed to another train in Lublin, and the morning after arrived in Posen—Poznan to the Poles. Warthegau, previously the province of Poznan, had become part of Germany after the Nazis and the Soviets partitioned Poland in 1939. To me, all of Poland was still Poland.

I had been waiting anxiously to step on foreign soil for the first time. The moment came; I clutched my briefcase and followed Herr Boltze off the train in a daze. Scarface telephoned Gut Birkenhof, the Mannheims' estate near Pudewitz, to announce my arrival. He came back and said, "My train leaves shortly before yours does." He escorted me to my platform, then left to continue his journey to Berlin.

As I stood waiting for a local to Pudewitz, I noticed that my hands were shaking. I tried to steady them by folding and unfolding the letter Herr Mannheim had written to whoever might challenge me before I reached his estate. The trembling disappeared. My ears perked up, and as I listened and understood the languages spoken around me, the foreign country didn't seem quite so foreign, after all.

The platform teemed with civilians, Germans and Poles. Soldiers of the Wehrmacht were leaving or returning from the Russian front; they were quite handsome, in high spirits, singing and laughing. The wounded, escorted by nurses in Red Cross uniforms, were also laughing. *Glad to be alive*, I thought.

A group of young Polish women with bulky bundles on their backs trudged by. They were not laughing.

★   ★   ★

I stepped off the local train at Pudewitz in exhilarated anticipation of being greeted by Frau Mannheim. *No doubt she is kind, like Herr Mannheim.* I scanned the small crowd on the platform. No Frau Mannheim. *She might have been delayed, of course. Maybe she won't come at all?* I sighed, growing more and more tense. Apart from one other woman, the platform was empty now.

The woman came up to me. "I see you're also waiting for someone." She looked well fed and had deep-set, piercing eyes.

"Yes, Frau Mannheim from Gut Birkenhof. Do you by any chance know her?"

"Are you Sophie Orlovsky? Herr Boltze telephoned to say we were to meet you at the station. I nearly left without you."

"I'm glad you didn't."

"I thought you had gotten on the wrong train or got off at the wrong station. Can you read German?"

"Of course I can. I was waiting for Frau Mannheim, thinking she might meet me."

"Frau Mannheim is visiting her sister in Potsdam. I came in her stead. . . . You're not at all what we expected."

What did they expect? I wondered, following the woman behind the station where a carriage was waiting. A proud-looking Polish man jumped off his high seat as we approached. He had short legs and a long torso. I greeted him in his mother tongue, and he smiled.

"Ah, you speak Polish."

"My mother and her sister speak Polish at home when they're sharing a secret," I explained. The coachman smiled again and helped us into the carriage, drawn by a dappled gray mare.

"You certainly don't look Russian," the woman remarked as the coachman prodded his horse along the broad country road. "I've always pictured them robust, rather coarse, you know. And the way they dress." She screwed up her nose. "I suppose you have to wear boots and over-stuffed jackets and whatnot. Your country is so dreadfully cold."

Good Lord, what an ignorant woman! I wondered who she was. She didn't bother to introduce herself, and I did not have the temerity to ask.

"It is dreadfully cold only if nobody loves you," I said, with more sarcasm than I had intended. "The Soviet Union is very large and climates vary from tropical to bitterly cold. Not unlike the North American continent, incidentally. I only know this, of course, because we learned at school about all the climates of the world."

"What school did you attend?"

"A high school in Kiev."

"Aren't you from around Zaporozhye somewhere?"

"I was born and raised in Kiev."

"Well, well," she drawled, "a city girl." She was gazing into space and seemed puzzled. "Why would Herr Mannheim pick you to work on his farm?" *What is she talking about?* Now I was puzzled. "Unless farming was part of your education." She looked at me. "Did you spend summers working in the fields?"

I ignored this, my eyes skimming the fields and orchards flanking the road. *Why should I tell her that while I've been on a farm and loved it, I've never worked on one? And never wanted to.* Horse buggies and oxcarts clattered by. People rode bicycles; the fluorescent white stripes painted on their rear fenders, so as to be seen at night, brought me back for a moment to the war and blackouts.

I could feel the woman's raisin-like eyes fixed on me. Then I heard her say, "What a pretty dress you're wearing." I acknowledged her compliment with a smile. "Did someone send it to you from Germany?" My smile faded, and suddenly I despised her with all my heart. Instead of answering her arrogant question, I asked if she lived in Birkenhof. No, she said, she lived in Posen. I rolled my eyes to heaven and thanked God.

The coach turned off the main road, crossed a deep ravine, and lurched along a bumpy country lane. We reached the Mannheims' estate, Gut Birkenhof. A murmuring creek ran through the woods on our right. On the left were freshly plowed fields of wheat and potatoes. A lake shimmered in a far-off field where cattle were grazing.

We stepped down from the coach in front of the main entrance to the manor, an impressive gray structure with a red mansard roof and stone stairs leading up to the first floor.

Before I could look around or meet anyone, the woman ushered me upstairs into a small attic room.

"This is your room," she said. "Come downstairs for supper when you have rested a bit. After four days en route," she added, not unkindly, "you must be tired."

I lay down on the bed fully clothed. "God forbid Frau Mannheim is like this woman," I said to the blank wall. *Or even remotely like her . . .* I pressed my face into the pillow and fell instantly asleep.

22

"GOOD LITTLE FARMER"

A dog was barking, horses neighed, chickens were clucking. *Where am I? Ah, yes . . .* Daylight was peeking through the dormer window. *What time is it?* I wished I had a watch. I looked for a mirror to straighten up, but there was none. I dashed downstairs for supper and was embarrassed to discover breakfast being prepared. I had slept for eighteen hours.

Gretchen, the eleven-year-old daughter, was in the kitchen with the cook. "Good morning," I said brightly and conveyed her father's greetings. She smiled faintly and scrutinized me with her bright blue eyes, uncertain what to make of me.

The cook, a Polish girl, asked me in German, "Hungry?"

"Famished," I said. She filled a soup plate with a delicious-smelling hot cereal and placed it on the table.

Gretchen shook her finger at the cook. "You haven't served us yet, Jadwiga. You're always late when my mother is away. And I am hungry."

"Why don't you eat, then?" I asked. "Join me."

"We"—she stressed the word—"don't eat in the kitchen." And she flipped her flaxen pigtails and ran off.

"Overbearing little creature," I muttered in her wake.

Willi, a handsome boy of thirteen, flaxen-haired like his sister but with his father's brown eyes, peeked through the door and vanished before I could speak to him. A thin-lipped Polish girl came in, nodded her head in my direction and busied herself piling plates and pitchers on a tray. Both servants wore starched pinafores, their fair tresses held back with silvery combs.

I was hungry but could not swallow. The lumpy cereal lodged in my throat. I felt uncomfortable, unwanted, and lonely in a household full of people too busy or disinterested to welcome me to Birkenhof. *How can people be so cold, so insensitive? Not one pleasant word from anyone!* I left the kitchen, tears prickling behind my eyes, and mounted the creaking stairs to the attic. *They must not see me cry.* I clenched my teeth and leaned against the door inside my room. An *ugly* room: a narrow, sagging bed, washstand, one chair, and a tiny window. A cowshed would make me happier, if the cows liked me. I closed my eyes and tried to make myself believe it would be different when Frau Mannheim returned. *She will make me welcome. If not, I can't possibly stay.*

"May I come in?" Gretchen stuck her flaxen head in the door and looked around the room as if seeing it for the first time. "That's my father's suitcase," she proclaimed. Yes, he had given it to me. "Why haven't you unpacked?" I hadn't felt like it. I told her that I wanted to see Birkenhof first. "I'll show it to you. Come with me to the stables. I want you to see my favorite horse."

The barn and the stables faced the house across a wide-open yard. It smelled wonderfully of the country: freshly mowed grass and horses and straw and cow dung. At the back of the house were a strawberry patch and a garden ablaze with color: blue, pink, and purple of the fragrant hyacinth, and orange nasturtium. In the orchard, the cherry trees were heavy with pale pink blossoms.

Gretchen's sorrel stallion was beautiful. After I had suitably admired him, we wandered through the barn, climbed to the hayloft, and sat talking in the hay. Gretchen was bright and inquisitive, but with a superior air that verged on arrogance.

"Let's go back to your room and I'll help you unpack. Do you have many pretty dresses?"

"Just one. But you are very pretty," I said. And she was.

A vivid rose stained her perfectly round freckled face. "When you get your clothes coupons, I'll go shopping with you for a dress."

"Sure. But there are more important things in life than dresses, Gretchen."

"Like what?"

"Learning and reading, for instance, and being with friends. I miss my friends. Tell me about yours."

"Renate is cute and a good student. Inge is stupid, and I don't want to be friends with her anymore."

"Do you ride horses with Renate? What do you do together?"

"She doesn't have a horse. She lives in Pudewitz. I don't see her except at school."

"Ah, then it must be lonely for you here when the school is out. Do you play games with Willi? Can you swim?"

"Not yet. But Willi can. He paddles in the water like Rex. That's his dog," she said earnestly. I leaned back in the hay and laughed, and after a moment she responded to my laugh.

"Would you like me to teach you to swim? I'll also teach you to play checkers and dominoes, or chess if you like. My friends and I also played volleyball. We attended the Theater for Young Spectators, and we danced and skated in our courtyard. One summer we took bricks from a construction site and built a puppet theater, made our own puppets, and staged a show for other children and adults."

She blinked at me. "You've done all that?"

"Once upon a time. But then, you're not interested in a fairy tale. You haven't asked me about me, how I feel about being so far away from home."

"Well, tell me then. I want to hear the fairy tale. How *do* you feel?"

"Much better now that you asked." And I began, "Once upon a time, there was a happy, carefree girl . . ."

★ ★ ★

Soon after dinner, served at noon, the coach rolled up and Gretchen, wearing a dirndl and knee-high white socks, climbed in; they were going to meet Frau Mannheim at the station. The woman from Posen, with a valise in hand, went along. I had finished my solitary meal and was outside when the coach returned. The cook and the maid were at the door to greet their mistress. Willi showed up with Rex at his heel. I stood slightly to the side, watching.

Frau Mannheim descended from the coach, a sturdy woman with fine facial features and clear blue eyes. Her round face was flushed, her brownish hair windblown. Although she was my height, she appeared taller, somehow. She wore brown wedge shoes and a gray belted suit with the swastika emblem pinned on the lapel.

She greeted everyone, then came toward me prim and composed, like a strict schoolmistress, and shook my hand with a firm grip. "Welcome to Birkenhof, Sophie."

"Thank you, Frau Mannheim."

"I had no idea when to expect you." She said this in German, and then switched to Russian. "Did you have any difficulties getting here?"

"None, really."

"That's good. Tell me more later." Speaking German again, she gave curt instructions to the coachman, who led the horse away, and she dismissed the maidservants. She put one arm on Willi's shoulder, the other around Gretchen, and motioned me to follow them. The mongrel dog, thinking he was also invited, wagged his tail and ran up the steps to the front door. "Willi, don't let the dog in!" Frau Mannheim's voice was stern. It gave me the shivers. Willi, not in the least perturbed, grinned at his mother, hopped on his bicycle, and took off with the dog.

What struck me most about Frau Mannheim was her purposefulness: every move she made, every word she uttered was deliberate.

In the downstairs sitting room, she took off her jacket and smoothed her permed hair with her hand. I noticed her hair was graying; I remembered plucking my mama's gray hairs for a kopeck each and smiled to myself.

"Run along, child," Frau Mannheim said to Gretchen, and the girl's short pigtails flipped behind her. "Now tell me about your trip, Sophie." My tale was short. "You were lucky. Most Russians are shipped to Germany by freight cars. They're on the road for weeks, I hear."

"What Russians? Do you mean prisoners?"

"Prisoners too, I suppose. I'm talking about the young women who are being sent to Germany to work. Didn't my husband speak to you about it? Well, then, forget I ever mentioned it. *Wie geht's meinem Soldat?* [How is my soldier?]"

"Herr Mannheim looks well. He works hard and seems to thrive on it. He often talks about you and the children," I thought I should add that. "Birkenhof is just as beautiful as he described it. And your garden, Frau Mannheim, it's lovely. Gretchen tells me you take care of it yourself. I'd love to help you if I may." My words were spilling over each other. I was nervous. And I kept smiling; I wanted to let her know how grateful I was to be there. I wanted her to like me.

"You certainly can help. There will be more than enough work for all of us. Birkenhof is a busy place in summertime." She tilted her head. "How long have you known my husband?"

"About eight months, since the Wehrmacht occupied Zaporozhye early this past October. It's been ten months since I left home," I volunteered.

"How did you meet?"

I described the scene at the *Ortskommandantur* and how I was crying and why, when Herr Mannheim and Herr Osterberg happened by. I also thanked Frau Mannheim for the medicine and her Christmas present. I expected her to say "You're welcome" or "Think nothing of it," like most people would. But she didn't.

"I had an altogether different picture of the person who was receiving my donations," she said bemusedly instead. "I never thought she would be like you."

"I hope you didn't expect a booted peasant girl with a scarf over her head." I smiled feebly, the woman from Posen still on my mind.

"Not necessarily booted, Sophie. But I did rather expect a country girl. How old are you?"

"Eighteen," I answered, and suddenly I realized something was terribly amiss. *Frau Mannheim knows nothing about me. How could she have taken me into her fold without knowing how old I was, and nothing of my social and educational background? Yet Herr Mannheim told me I would be part of the family. And what did that woman from Posen say? She couldn't understand why Karl Mannheim picked me, a city girl, to work on his farm. Clearly, Frau Mannheim is also wondering.*

"Didn't your husband write to you about me?"

"Well, yes, some time ago. He said he would be sending a girl from the Ukraine to help me at Birkenhof. The help I need is mostly for the fields. So naturally—"

She assumed I would be a peasant girl, someone to give her a hand. A farmhand. A wave of resentment rolled over me. How could Herr Mannheim have promised me so much—a friendly home, a chance to continue my education—and not say a word about what his true intentions were? "Don't ask any questions," he had said. "Just trust me." Well, I trusted him. I still do. Implicitly. There must be some misunderstanding. Maybe his detailed letter hasn't yet arrived? That must be it. No wonder Frau Mannheim was caught by surprise and doesn't know, like all the others, what to make of me. Clearly, Herr Mannheim did intend to send a peasant girl, initially. His decision to send me instead was made in such a rush that there was no time to inform his wife. Yes, that must be it, I concluded, and found comfort in that, and tried to decide how to win Frau Mannheim's goodwill in the meantime.

"I'm here to help you in any way I can," I said, adding with yet another smile, "only please don't make me milk the cows. I'm afraid of them."

"That won't be necessary. But I will need you in the fields. You're not afraid of work, are you?"

"Afraid?" I laughed. *What nonsense!* "The busier I am, the better I like it. I'd rather work than be idle any time," I said, and meant the words. *But work in the fields? Ugh!*

She rose to her feet, and as if reading my mind, patted me on the back and said, "Don't worry, farming isn't all that difficult. You're young and strong; you'll get used to it. You might even get to like it and become a good little farmer after all." With this I was dismissed.

I bristled at the sarcasm I thought I had heard in her voice: "good little farmer" . . . "get used to it." "I'll *never* get used to it," I muttered on the way to my dismal room, the prison cell. But then, I was strong. Farm work wouldn't kill me. The Nazis could.

I resigned myself to my fate and decided to do my best, much as I hated it. But I could not decide just then whether to like or dislike Frau Mannheim. She might be kind, but was her kindness as genuine as that of Herr Mannheim?

I put my head on my pillow and closed my eyes.

★ ★ ★

Gretchen nudged me. "Wake up! Supper is on the table." We rushed downstairs. "You won't have to eat in the kitchen anymore," she said in a breathless whisper.

Jadwiga, the cook, smiled obsequiously and stepped aside to let us through a passageway to the main room. Frau Mannheim and Willi were already seated at the damask-covered dining table. The chairs and a sturdy sideboard were of mahogany. It was a friendly room overlooking the garden. A grandfather clock ticked rhythmically between two tall windows. Freshly cut flowers were on the mantel of a stone fireplace.

"Feel better, Sophie?"

"Yes, I do. Thank you."

"She was asleep!" squealed Gretchen.

I glared at her. *Little idiot*, I thought while smiling at Frau Mannheim. "The journey was more strenuous than I thought," I said, and stopped myself from adding "emotionally more than physically."

"Don't apologize. I understand. Sit down," she said, pointing to the chair on her left. I took this as a good sign.

The breadbasket was passed around, and my spirits rose. Frau Mannheim urged me to eat—"to cover my bones with some flesh," as she put it. That wasn't difficult, since an everyday supper in Birkenhof was a feast: freshly baked bread, a variety of sliced sausages, cold pork, farmers' cheese, and butter. Milk was poured from a pitcher as large as the one my mother used for draft beer at home. I was in heaven!

Stacia, the maid, entered the room bearing coffee and apple strudel on a silver tray. She, too, was suddenly respectful toward me. And I thought to myself, *I'm not a better person today than I was yesterday. They probably think I am, because I have been invited to eat with the family.* Yet I found this promotion most agreeable; the maids' subservient attitude amused me.

Frau Mannheim poured ersatz coffee and while passing out the strudel on little china plates decorated with rose petals, she told her children, "Instead of Luise, Sophie will keep you company the next time I go to Potsdam." I wished she would stop calling me Sophie but did not dare correct her.

Gretchen burst out with excitement about the swimming lessons I had promised to give her. "She'll help you too," she said to Willi.

"And Rex," I added. "Don't forget the dog, Gretchen. Then Willi and Rex will have a race to see who wins." The children and I started laughing. Frau Mannheim smiled.

Willi seemed eager to reciprocate. "You can ride my bike any time I'm not using it. Do you know how?"

"I never had a tricycle, let alone a bicycle."

"It's easy," he said. "I'll show you."

After supper, Frau Mannheim and I sat up and talked long after the children had gone to bed. She wanted to know about my life and asked questions about Zaporozhye. It was peaceful in the house, with the sounds of crickets and the ticking of the grandfather clock emphasizing the quietude. We conversed in Russian. In my eagerness to befriend Frau Mannheim, I told her about my budding romance with Otto, something I had not wanted to share with anyone before. Throughout the evening, our conversation quite naturally kept returning to Herr Mannheim.

"I'm amazed that my husband couldn't arrange it so you could have gone home to see your mother first."

"We were not allowed to leave Zaporozhye. Besides, there were no trains for civilians. When suddenly I could leave, there was no time to even think of a stopover in Kiev."

"Suddenly? Why suddenly?"

"I don't know." Her question caught me off guard. *Yes, why?* I wondered anew. *Did the rumor reach his ears? He may know the truth. Why else the urgency? But his wife doesn't know. My life will be in danger if she discovers I am half Jewish.* I looked at Frau Mannheim and saw her watching me. "Probably because Herr Mannheim was able to find a seat for me on the military train. He said he would let my mother know where I am."

"Then he will. My husband never breaks his word."

"I believe that. He is a very kind man. Otto Schubert told me that because Wi-Kdo is not a fighting unit their provisions are quite small. Yet Herr Mannheim often gave me something to eat. If it hadn't been for him,

I would have frozen from the cold or starved to death—whichever came first," I added with a grim little smile.

"It is my husband's humanitarian nature. He knows how to give of himself."

"Yes, he helps people in whatever way he can. I'm very grateful to him—and to you, Frau Mannheim. I cannot thank you enough for taking me into your home."

"No need to thank me. It's enough to say you appreciate what my husband did for you." Abruptly she got up. "No doubt you'll want to write to your benefactor. And of course to your . . . what's the name of the young man again?"

"Otto Schubert," I answered. *How could she forget? I just mentioned his name.* Her skepticism did not escape me, though I could not imagine what she was skeptical about. *Didn't she believe my story about Otto?* I thought she was peculiar and decided then that I didn't like her after all.

Please, Otto, write to me, I said in my head, folding the letter I had painstakingly composed. I had asked about him, and whether he had enjoyed his sojourn in Vienna. I also described Gut Birkenhof. "When you left Zaporozhye I wondered if you'd ever come back," I wrote. "But I never dreamed I wouldn't be there when you returned."

I also wrote to Herr Mannheim.

23

A RED SILK CAMISOLE

Frau Mannheim, with Gretchen in tow, took me shopping in Pudewitz, a pleasant town centered on the market square. The two- and three-story houses around the cobbled square were narrow and clung to one another as if for support. A church, brooding over alder trees, looked more like a medieval fortress. I remembered with nostalgia Kiev's light blue, pale yellow, and white churches with golden onion domes.

We collected my ration cards and clothes coupons, and then I agonized trying to decide what to buy. Bolts of fabric and dresses filled the shop. And this in wartime! I bought some underwear, a pair of shoes, and a dress of synthetic silk, light blue with yellow petals—and my precious coupons were all gone.

The misguided German clerk had given me German as opposed to Polish rations when I told him I was from the Ukraine. Germans received more coupons than Poles. No doubt he assumed I was Ukrainian, and he considered Ukrainians superior to Poles. He knew that Ukrainian nationalists were collaborating with the Germans and fighting alongside the Wehrmacht—to "liberate" the Ukraine from the Soviets.

What he didn't know was that outside his narrow sphere of activity, the race-conscious Germans treated the Ukrainians with the same contempt with which they treated the Russians, Belorussians, and Poles.

"Now, Fräulein Sophie," said Frau Mannheim jovially, "we'll take you for coffee at the *Konditorei* [pastry shop]." She was in a good mood, very likable, and I was thrilled to be able to treat them to pastry with my own food coupons. We spent a leisurely hour drinking coffee and leafing through the magazines at the café.

Frau Mannheim managed the estate with skill and tenacity. She was firm but fair to the Poles in her employ. She often rushed out with a pitchfork and joined the crews at their work in the fields. When potatoes had to be dug, she would go out with the women and work side by side with them. They, in turn, respected her for it.

In spite of his wife's capabilities, Herr Mannheim was regarded as the lord of the manor. Any major decisions had to be approved by him.

I, too, respected Frau Mannheim, but I was in awe of her. She was brusque and so unreasonable at times. Or so I thought. *What exactly is expected of me?* I did not know how to respond to her demands, or rather her lack of demands.

When I asked her if there was anything she wanted me to do, she always replied, "Nothing at the moment." I thought that her kindness was genuine, one that expected nothing in return, like that of Herr Mannheim. It seemed odd, though, in view of what she had told me, that I should be idle when there was work to be done. Very odd . . . until a thought came to my befuddled mind. I had a hunch Frau Mannheim was playing a waiting game: waiting for a letter from her husband, the lord of the manor, with instructions as to what my role in the household was to be. And now so was I—waiting, and enjoying my unexpected, albeit unearned, vacation.

There was much to see, and everything was a novelty. Apart from Pudewitz, I explored Gut Birkenhof, an estate of some two hundred acres, and swam with the children in the lake, a lovely lake covered with water lilies near the shore. I rode Willi's bicycle to nearby villages where the estate workers lived with their families. Everyone in the Mannheims' employ was Polish. I felt close to the Poles and enjoyed visiting with them. Though German was the official language and German masters wanted only German spoken in their households, the Poles continued to speak their own tongue.

Most of all I enjoyed driving a horse-drawn buggy on errands to Ebersfelde, where Herr Mannheim's mother lived with her older son and his family. I loved the gentle old lady and her cloud of snow-white hair. She spoke to me only in Russian and always greeted me with a kiss on both cheeks.

Finally, in June, we received a stack of letters from Herr Mannheim. One was addressed to me, and the rest to Frau Mannheim. She stayed in her room that afternoon—poring over the letters, I guessed. She was rather quiet at suppertime.

"I've made a room available for you downstairs," she said to me later.

Ah ha, the letter we were waiting for has arrived! I was so glad, and felt happy as I dashed upstairs to retrieve my things and closed the door to the attic behind me. My new room was light and airy; the bed was firm. A desk at the window and a map of Europe on the wall pleased me most of all. A framed mirror hung over a chest of drawers.

Frau Mannheim emptied one drawer. "It should be enough for your things," she said. "I need the rest."

"More than enough. It'll take two years' supply of clothes coupons to fill this one alone." I thanked her profusely and on impulse kissed her on the cheek.

Her reaction surprised me. My exuberance seemed to embarrass her. She turned away and then, in a hostile tone of voice that startled me, she said, "I trust this room will make you happier." And without looking at me she said, "Good night."

I was crushed to see my gratitude rejected. There were so few ways to show my appreciation except by being demonstrative. Up until this time Frau Mannheim had accepted my thanks with grace and on several occasions had even put her arm around me.

The following day offered no explanation. If anything, I was more confused. *What could Herr Mannheim have written to upset her so?* If only I could ask. But I was in no position to probe. *What did his letter say?* I lay on my back in the meadows and studied the wind-scattered clouds as if trying to extract some answers from their formations that would make sense. I had expected Herr Mannheim's letter to bring good tidings, to clarify my status in the household. Instead, it had created confusion. *Is she angry with me, perhaps thinking I had complained to her husband about sleeping in the attic? To move me downstairs was his idea, surely. I had nothing to do with it.* I must show her the letter I had written to him to set that straight.

The letter I had received from Karl Mannheim was the one I had written him, in German, its many spelling errors heavily marked and underlined in red. "I am disappointed," he wrote in the margin. "If you have not resumed studying German grammar, I suggest you do so without delay. Be good."

Frau Mannheim skimmed through the letter when I showed it to her. She smiled a little, saying, "What a colorful reply."

"Next time I write to Herr Mannheim—and it may be a long time before I do after what he did to my masterpiece—he won't find a single mistake."

"Indeed," she said. "Starting tomorrow, you will be devoting one full hour to studying German."

"You're not going to make me study now," I said in jest. "It's summertime!"

"That's too bad," she said tartly. "And another thing: I have work for you to do in the garden, so don't run off."

Glad to be of help at last, I worked with a vengeance, weeding the strawberry patch. Popping berries into my mouth, I speculated about what could have upset Frau Mannheim. He must have told her I was to be a contributing member of the family and treated as such, not as a farmhand. She had already accepted me for what I was, a mere city girl—and I liked her for that—but to be told she must, that may have given her a jolt and angered her.

During the next few days, when Frau Mannheim spoke to me it was as if she had to, rather than because she wanted to. "German only!" was a new rule. I grew uneasy. Her attitude had changed. And though she was polite, she lacked warmth and spontaneity.

Some days later, when Frau Mannheim had gone to Ebersfelde for the evening, I snooped through the chest of drawers we shared. Among her neatly folded panties and nightgowns I came across an intriguing garment— a red silk camisole. I decided to try it on. In the midst of my prancing, standing on my bed in front of the mirror, who should walk in but Frau Mannheim. I jumped at the sight of her.

"How *dare* you snoop through my drawers?" She was clearly furious. "Take that off!"

To lose her composure was uncharacteristic of her. I stripped and stood naked before her, stunned and unable to equate the magnitude of her anger with my crime.

"I'm sorry," I said in a small voice. "I was only trying it on. Childish impulse. Please, forgive me."

Frau Mannheim would not listen and stormed out of the room.

I still was uncertain what had happened to change her attitude toward me. Gretchen, like a weather vane, reflected her mother's mood and also behaved with unaccountable coolness.

After several unbearable, cold-shoulder days, I told Frau Mannheim I was leaving. I had no idea where I'd go and didn't care what I'd do. Anything would be better, I thought, than to stay in Birkenhof.

She was aghast. "But that's absurd! I won't let you go."

"Why not?"

She took a while before answering. "I will write my husband. He must be informed."

"I don't want to be disrespectful, Frau Mannheim, but I feel it would make you happier if I left. I'm sorry to have upset you. I didn't want to part this way."

"I'm glad to hear you're sorry. You should be." The tone of her voice was softer now. "Since you cannot leave without my husband's consent, you will have to stay until we hear from him. You owe it to him. You are his responsibility. He is the only one who can decide what should be done. Not you, nor I."

★   ★   ★

Waiting for Karl Mannheim's reply was not unbearable. Frau Mannheim did not ignore me, as I feared she might. I sensed her resentment but also her willingness to help. She kept me occupied in the garden, sent me on errands to Pudewitz and Ebersfelde. She now studied with me, and I read German novels of chivalry and romance. Now and then we listened to the radio together.

Listening to the German broadcasts blaring out news of conquests annoyed me. Germans believed in Hitler as though he were a god, infallible. They were sure his leadership would bring them victory. The soldiers sang: *"Heute England und Morgen die ganze Welt!"* ("Today England, tomorrow the whole world.") German arrogance was irritating, but the war news sounded convincing.

The news of heavy fighting inside the Don Bend, with the Wehrmacht poised to advance toward the Volga and Stalingrad, depressed me. *That's it*, I thought. *If the Germans ever cross the Volga, nothing will stop their tanks from rolling over the perfectly flat Eurasian steppes.*

24

LORD OF THE MANOR

Two weeks passed. On my way home by bike from the post office and shopping for groceries in Pudewitz—one month following my arrival at the end of May 1942—I noticed fresh tracks made by a coach on the dirt road to Birkenhof. *Frau Mannheim must have gone somewhere*, I thought. *Or maybe a rare visitor has come to call?* But the yard was deserted—no sign of visitors, no coach. I was wheeling the bike to the rear of the house when I saw a familiar figure standing at the door. I caught my breath.

"Herr Mannheim!" I dropped the bike and flew across the yard. He came down the steps and opened his arms, and I ran into them. Tears filled my eyes. I had not realized how happy I would be to see him. It was as if my own father had come home at last.

"When did you arrive? I'm so happy to see you." I laughed and cried. He wiped the tears from my face with his handkerchief, like old times, and all at once that gesture erased three weeks of despair and uncertainty. It made me hopeful that his presence would exert a calming influence and defuse the emotional atmosphere. "I didn't know you were coming."

"No one knew. I wanted it to be a surprise."

"You and your surprises." I laughed. "You haven't changed."

He smiled. "I must say, for once I have not been disappointed." Then his face clouded. "I hear you want to leave. What happened? Tell me, why—"

"There you are." Frau Mannheim came floating through the door. I had never seen her look so radiant.

Gretchen poked me from behind. "Mutti nearly dropped the receiver when she heard Vati's voice. He was already in Pudewitz when he called!" She was beaming.

An ultimate surprise, I thought. *Only Mannheim is capable of pulling it off.* "It's wonderful to see your *Vati*, Gretchen. But where is Willi?" I turned to Frau Mannheim. "Does he know? He's probably at the lake with Rex. I'll go find him."

"We were about to look for him ourselves," Frau Mannheim said. "We can't deprive him of his surprise. It wouldn't be fair."

"I would've loved to see his face," I murmured.

"Aren't you coming with us?" Herr Mannheim asked.

"No, I can't." He hadn't seen his family in more than a year. To tag along, now *that* would really be unfair. "I just remembered the groceries—they're still strapped to the bike."

In the days that followed, Frau Mannheim was all smiles. Willi and Gretchen could hardly contain themselves, leaping with joy around their proud father. It made me happy just to watch them at mealtimes. I tried to make myself as unobtrusive as I could. This did not escape Frau Mannheim's notice, and she rewarded me with a nod of approval or a kind word.

★　★　★

I was perched on a sprawling branch of a cherry tree, gathering the fruit into a basket.

"Do you need a helping hand?" Karl Mannheim startled me. I looked down and grinned at him. "Surprised I found you?"

"No."

"Glad?"

"It depends."

He tugged on my skirt playfully and then pulled me off the tree and into his arms. The cherries spilled on the ground.

"Now look at what you have done. You should be ashamed." I smiled uneasily and freed myself from his embrace.

"I need to talk to you," he said, and stood in silence gazing at me, as if he had forgotten what he wanted to say.

Something about the way he had embraced me, the way he now gazed at me, made me retreat. I leaned against the tree.

"Well?" I squinted in the sun.

"Birkenhof agrees with you," he said, stepping back a few paces. "I know you don't like to be complimented. It embarrasses you. Just accept it gracefully when I tell you how lovely you look."

"Is that what you came to talk to me about?"

"Among other things." He pulled a booklet from the inside pocket of his gray-green jacket and handed it to me. "I'm sure you'll find better use for this than I would."

I flipped through the clothes coupons he had received as an officer on leave and cried out, "Many, many thanks, Herr Mannheim. Now I can really do some shopping. I'd love to buy a suit, and I need a bigger suitcase."

His facial muscles tensed. "You're not going anywhere."

"Even if I want to?"

"I won't let you go. Not now. Is that clear?"

"At least tell me why, if you don't mind."

"You have no idea what life is like in Germany for people like you. Foreign workers are confined to labor camps. They toil in heavy industries under nightly bomb attacks. Nor do they get enough to eat, I'm afraid."

I listened impatiently, unimpressed. *Surely he is exaggerating.*

"There is danger of another kind," his voice more urgent. "Remember, you would be all alone again. Who would protect you from evil tongues? Who would care what happened to you if, suppose, someone accused you of being a Communist?"

"Now you really exaggerate."

"What would you do?"

"I'd laugh in his face."

"It is not a laughing matter."

"I couldn't possibly be a member of the Communist Party because I only recently turned eighteen," I declared, feeling triumphant.

"You have no proof of your age nor of your nationality. What would you do if someone questioned it?"

I panicked momentarily and said nothing.

"Don't leave Birkenhof. You're free here, shielded and secure. Wait till the war is over." His eyes reflected kindness and goodwill.

My anxiety dissolved, and I relaxed.

"It's not that I'm anxious to leave. I seriously doubt that Frau Mannheim would want me to stay, because I am a snoop."

He was laughing suddenly. "Is that the only reason? Tell me truthfully, has anything else transpired to upset you that I don't know about?"

"No, nothing else." The hurt I had felt at Frau Mannheim's unaccountable coolness, her moods of withdrawal and lack of warmth, had been displaced by the degrading episode with the camisole. I could never hold a grudge or be angry for very long. *But how does Frau Mannheim feel about it? Is she still angry?* "You talked to your wife—maybe you know if there's something else."

"My wife has nothing but complimentary things to say about you. She recognized from the very first what a remarkable girl you are. She enjoys your company and wants you to stay. Forget that ludicrous incident. She has already forgiven you."

"Has she? Somehow I didn't think she ever would. The way she . . . she was so angry and upset."

"Of course she was. She reacted exactly as she would with our own daughter. Don't you realize that?"

My thoughts flashed back to my mother. How very angry she was when as a child I dressed up in her finery! "I guess I have no reason not to stay."

All too soon Karl Mannheim had to go back to Zaporozhye. He kissed his children, hugged the three of us, and helped his blissful wife into the coach. His eyes sparkled in the high noon sun.

Frau Mannheim saw her husband off at the station in Posen. The sun lay low when she returned. She sank into an armchair and leaned forward, her elbow on her knee, her chin in the palm of her right hand.

"Here we are"—she sighed deeply—"alone together again."

I couldn't see her face, but I caught the sadness in her quivering voice and knew she was weeping. I felt sorry for her, and I started crying too. I felt sad myself about Herr Mannheim leaving. He was, without a doubt, the best friend I had ever had. How awful she must feel to part with her husband. Who knew when she would see him again—another year and a half? I hoped the war would be over and that he would return home to his family long before then.

She raised her head slowly and turned to look at me. "Why are you crying?"

"Because you are. And because you want me to stay."

With the back of her hand she wiped her misty-blue eyes resolutely, as a child would, and then she smiled.

25

RED CROSS NURSE

Birkenhof soon recovered from the turmoil created by my arrival, which had disrupted Frau Mannheim's orderly existence and upset the entire household. It was peaceful once again. Frau Mannheim now regarded herself as my *Pflegemama* (foster mother). Her fosterling, a stubborn Russian, rarely now gave her cause to be irritated or upset.

Why, then, was I discontented? After a time I became excruciatingly bored. Birkenhof was unbearably monotonous. Some garden work, studying German, running errands, and swimming hardly filled the long days. The harvest season had not yet begun. Apart from reading at night, nothing stimulating or provoking happened. Not even a good argument or a pillow fight with the children was possible. Frau Mannheim—*the humorless schoolmistress*, I called her privately—would never put up with that. What challenge was there to an easy existence? Life should be more than a stomach full of wurst and Wiener schnitzel. I missed the companionship of young people, my kind of people most of all. The Germans seemed undemonstrative and self-contained. Frau Mannheim had no contact with anyone except the family.

A minor mishap added spice to my dull existence. Returning from a shopping trip with Gretchen, I was fuming over the unequal distribution of the packages. Sweet Gretchen had refused to accept her share, and almost everything was draped from the handlebars of my bike. I was pedaling fiercely, turned a corner too sharply, and with a full head of steam sailed into a ravine. The flurry of activity and concern on my behalf was the most exciting thing that had happened since Herr Mannheim's visit to Birkenhof.

Pflegemama ordered the coach to be harnessed, and I was taken to the only hospital in Pudewitz for X-rays. No bones were broken; I had only sprained an ankle and cracked a rib, and I was bruised and sore. It was a military hospital, Das Lazarett. The nurses in crisp Red Cross uniforms and the patients were all young. The air was vibrant. On the way home, an idea came to me, which I hoped would kill two rabbits with one blow.

I said to Frau Mannheim, "I'd love to be a nurse."

"Certainly, if that's what you want to be someday."

"I mean now."

"Not a German Red Cross nurse, surely. You seem to forget you are Russian."

I had not forgotten anything. I merely tried not to dwell on it. Anti-Russianism, anti-Semitism, it was all too upsetting to contemplate. This was the reason I wanted to become a nurse in the first place, to hide my true identity behind the German Red Cross uniform. And, too, I would be free to leave the boring Birkenhof.

"May I try, Frau Mannheim? I'd really love to be a nurse."

"I have nothing against your trying. As far as I know, there is no nursing school in Pudewitz."

I went to the German Red Cross headquarters in Posen and was promptly accepted for an accelerated course in wound dressing and bandaging. Frau Mannheim, whom I telephoned from Posen, was much surprised that a Russian would be accepted so readily. I didn't tell her that no one had asked my nationality. They couldn't tell by looking at me what I was and must have assumed I was *Volksdeutsche*, thus ethnic German.

"Stay with Luise for the duration of the course," Frau Mannheim suggested. I disliked Luise, the ignorant Posen woman who had met me at the station in Pudewitz, but I stayed with her. Worse still, Luise's divan was infested with bedbugs. During my first sleepless night I recalled German soldiers in Zaporozhye saying that they had never seen cockroaches and bedbugs until they came to Russia—I had seen cockroaches but never bedbugs, until I came to Germany. Cockroaches at home were nicknamed *Prussaki* (Prussians); in Germany they were the *Russen* (Russians). *What a unique way to show mutual respect*, I thought, while squashing the attacking bedbugs.

It was with a sense of accomplishment that I completed the short wartime course and as a *Verbandschwester* (bandage nurse) put on my nurse's uniform: white dress with powder-blue stripes, crisply starched white collar, apron, and headdress. A white enameled pin with a red cross completed the outfit. Not wasting a moment, I dashed to the photographer to record my victory, which was fortunate, as that was the beginning and the end of my nursing career.

When I returned home and reported to the Pudewitz hospital's wound-dressing station, it was belatedly discovered that I was not German, and my lovely uniform and the white enameled pin were promptly repossessed. The photograph and a tiny black pin with swastika and red cross, worn by nurses on the lapel of their suit coats, were the only remains of my glory.

★   ★   ★

There was not a cloud in the sky that August day. I swam across the lake and stretched out in the sun. Two tall girls came up to me and asked about the "insignia" on my swimsuit. To give my black tank top a lift, I had appliquéd my initials in white: SO.

"Your initials!" The girl with long dark hair rolled under at the back laughed gaily. "We wondered if perhaps you worked for SD."

Seeing my dumb expression, the girl whose hair shone golden in the sun explained, "SO looks like SD from a distance."

"What's SD?"

"It stands for the *Sicherheitsdienst* (Security Service)." At that point I didn't know that the SD was the intelligence branch of the SS.

"Nothing as glamorous as that. Just Sophia Orlovsky."

"I'm Christine Blaschke," said the blonde, whose dreamy eyes were brown. She was a year or so older than I. She had a lovely smile. "This is my sister, Monika." Monika was younger, seventeen, a striking brunette with blue eyes. We shook hands.

"I would never have guessed you are sisters."

"No one ever does," Christine said. "Join us in the shade. I can't take much sun. My skin is too sensitive."

We lay on the grass under a tree. Christine asked, "You're new here, aren't you?"

"I came to Birkenhof three months ago."

"Where did you come from?" Monika asked.

"Kiev."

"Kiev! That's in Russia!"

"Ukraine," Christine corrected her younger sister. "I remember Father talking about Kiev. It's where the Wehrmacht had so much trouble. Fortunately very few of our soldiers were killed. But the Russians, they lost thousands, and—" She cut herself short. "How stupid of me! I wasn't thinking. I am sorry." Christine reached out and touched my arm.

"Obviously you've had far too much sun," said Monika. "Why talk of war when we could be talking about other things. Like boys, for instance. But first tell us what brought you to Birkenhof. Are you related to the Mannheims?"

"They sort of adopted me. The rest may take an hour to explain. Some other time?"

"Oh yes, we must meet again," Christine said. "There are soldiers in town now who have recuperated enough to leave Das Lazarett in the afternoons. Maybe we could meet some of them and all go out together." Smiling wistfully, she added, "I can't remember when a boy last held my hand."

I laughed. "If not, we could go for a nocturnal swim or to the theater in Posen. I'd love to see a good play."

Neither girl swam, but they were enthusiastic about the theater, and they cried, "Prima!" Then, "Come visit us and meet our parents."

We set a date to meet a few days later.

I swam back across the lake, then walked through the fields, letting the stubble tickle my feet, and thought about friends and friendship, an important part of my life; I could not be without them. My close friends were far away, somewhere on the other side of the Ural Mountains, probably. I could see no reason why Christine, Monika, and I could not be friends. I was delighted to have met them and rushed home to tell Frau Mannheim about it.

"You do need friends your own age," she said. "But don't build your hopes too high. Don't expect too much from a casual meeting with the Blaschke girls."

And I thought: *Killjoy!*

Willi let me use his bike, and I set off, far too early, to visit the Blaschke family. I secured the bike, fidgeting with the lock, untied the flowers I had collected from the garden, then walked around their two-story white stucco house to kill time. The shrubs along the fence were of the variety the girls back home turned to for an answer when in love. I pulled a stem at random, plucked one petal at a time, and with Otto on my mind chanted in Russian, "He loves me, he loves me not; he'll spit at me, he'll kiss me well; he'll press me to his heart, he'll tell me to go to hell." *He'll tell me to go to hell! Oh, well . . .*

I watched children jumping rope across the street. A clock inside the house tinkled the hour. I pressed the bell.

Christine greeted me with her sunny smile and a shout of "Ooh la-la!" She looked at my small bouquet. "That's for me?"

"For your mother, you silly goose!"

She pulled me by my hand into the cheery sitting room and introduced me to her mother.

"My girls have been talking of nothing but Sophia since they met you," Frau Blaschke said, and she smiled Monika's smile when she saw the girl pinch me. "*Ach, ja.* When I was young, I also was very impressionable."

"You still are," I said.

"Impressionable?"

I didn't know the meaning of this German word. To be on the safe side, I said, "Young, I meant." Frau Blaschke, blue-eyed like Monika, must have been a beauty when she was young. Her dark hair had lost its luster, but her figure was still slim and agile.

A tall man with sleek blond hair sauntered in. "I'm the girls' father," Herr Blaschke boomed. "So you live with the Mannheims. *Ja, ja*, fine family . . . I hear you're a good swimmer. That's what my girls need, someone to show them how to keep afloat." He poked Christine in the ribs and guffawed. "They panic at the sight of a full bathtub!" He then asked about Herr *Sonderführer* Mannheim.

Frau Blaschke inquired about my parents and how I happened to be separated from them. "You're a brave girl," she said. "If my daughters had to go through what you've been through, I'd go out of my mind."

Christine, Monika, and I retreated gracefully after a coffee interlude and went upstairs to Christine's room, where we talked and made plans until it was time for me to go home. Frau Blaschke invited me to come again. "We'd love to see you."

In spite of the differences in our upbringing, our social and cultural background, nationalities, and political outlook, a great friendship developed between Christine and me. It was, with the benefit of hindsight, an amazing friendship. Herr Blaschke was a member of the Nazi Party and chief of the Pudewitz police.

I was stunned and intimidated when I first learned about it. Frau Mannheim was not a killjoy after all. She had tried to protect me from disappointment should Herr Blaschke prohibit his daughters from having anything to do with me, a Soviet Russian. I knew that in the Soviet Union a friendship between Christine—a foreigner—and me would not have been possible.

★   ★   ★

Posen was all lights and traffic and pedestrians, an exciting, bustling atmosphere—the streets a kaleidoscope of color. Most German men wore uniforms and the women—obeying Hitler's order that no black be worn for the dead for the duration of the war—were colorfully attired. German women did not paint their lips—Hitler was adamantly against makeup.

All dressed up and feeling *trés chic* in picture hats, Christine, Monika, and I had lunch at a fashionable *Konditorei* and visited the Raczinski Bibliothek (library) on Wilhelmsplatz and the Kaiser Wilhelm Museum on Wilhelm Strasse. *Kaiser Wilhelm everywhere!* I laughed for the gladness I felt.

We took pictures posing on the lawn in front of the stately theater and hoped to see a play. What we did see, instead, was far more entrancing: a political rally, an assembly of some thousand Nazis in a variety of uniforms.

As we entered the theater, I could not understand what the speaker was shouting about and why everybody was screaming so. A few moments later I stood at the back, mesmerized. Christine whispered to me that the speaker was Joseph Goebbels. He was a small man with a big head, but so powerful he seemed larger than life. I could feel the throng being carried on the crest of their emotions, and they responded to Goebbels with shouts of *"Heil Hitler!"* and *"Sieg Heil!"*

Neither of the girls wanted to stay. Monika tugged at my sleeve and whispered, "Let's go." To me, any meeting of a political nature had always been a burden and a bore, but not this one. Wild horses could not have dragged me away until the last strains of the German anthem, *"Deutschland, Deutschland, über alles, über alles in der Welt,"* died away.

The spell was broken the moment we stepped outside.

I had grasped very little of what Goebbels said. It was the show, the wild enthusiasm, the powerful male voices, and the singing that I found fascinating in a macabre sort of way. I was glad I had insisted we stay. I had witnessed how mass hypnosis works, and I began to understand the magnetic pull the Nazi movement had on the German people. It was all too easy to get carried away.

26

THE TRUTH COMES OUT

The harvest season came, and with it the field work. Haymaking was the only job that I enjoyed. I heaved the bundles with a pitchfork onto the back of the cart, then climbed on top of the sweet-smelling cargo, and let thoughts of love and romance drift through my mind while the old mare made its way lazily to the barn.

Potato digging was a nasty chore. To get out of it gracefully, I decided to get sick. I went to the lake at dawn on an empty stomach—germs don't attack a full one—stripped and stood rigid in the cold water up to my neck. I turned blue and my teeth were chattering when I finally came out, but the attack of pneumonia failed to materialize. What did rescue me from my awful fate as a potato digger was quite unsolicited: an agonizing toothache.

The dentist's waiting room was crowded. Appointments could not be made. Fräulein Trauber, the dentist, treated her patients on a first-come, first-served basis. At the end of the day, many a toothache sufferer had to be turned away.

Fräulein Trauber was a cousin of Karl Mannheim. She was in her forties, charming and witty, and one soon forgot her physical deformity: she was a hunchback and she hobbled when she walked. Short, with strong facial features, she had the strength of a giant when it came to pulling teeth. She was competent and kind, devoting all her time to her profession, even Sundays.

Since she knew me personally, I foolishly assumed she would take me immediately. Fortunately for me, she did not. I waited all day, and quite happily, despite my tormenting toothache. I enjoyed observing people, talking to the Germans and Poles. Besides, the slow torture of the drill could be delayed. At noon, Fräulein Trauber invited me to lunch at her adjacent apartment. I felt completely at ease with this delightful lady. By the end of the day I had come to the conclusion that she needed help.

I asked her, "Why don't you hire an assistant?"

"I have not been successful. With the war going on, help is difficult to find."

"I'm available, and I'll work for nothing. Maybe part-time? Then I could still help my *Pflegemama* whenever she needs me."

Fräulein Trauber glanced at me over the rim of her pince-nez. "What makes you think you could give me the help I need?"

"I could work the foot pedal of your drilling machine. I'd keep the office orderly, sterilize the instruments, change the drills. You could teach me other things too. And I would give each patient a slip of paper with a number on it as they came in. That way they could leave and come back later, instead of sitting here all day."

Her quick brown eyes smiled. "Nothing would please me more than to have you, Sophia. However, we must talk to your *Pflegemama* first. If she has no objections, the job is yours."

"To be honest with you, I'm bored at Birkenhof."

"I understand the feeling." She put her hand on my forearm and leaned on it. "I'll train you on the job. By the time I'm through with you, you might forget about engineering and take up dentistry instead. I tell you what, though. Instead of a salary"—she grinned with a twinkle in her eye—"I'll pull your teeth without charge."

I laughed. "How did you guess I'd rather have them pulled than drilled?"

Frau Mannheim was used to my outlandish ideas by now and voiced no objections. "You can start in the fall, after the harvest," she said. "I wonder, though, how long you'll stay with it. You have no way of getting to work. I can't spare a bicycle. Half an hour's walk is fine in good weather, but think what it'll be like when winter comes."

"That's all right. I'm used to all kinds of weather. And I love walking in the rain."

★   ★   ★

The long-awaited letter arrived at last.

"*Meine liebe Sophia!*

"I was much surprised to learn you were no longer in Zaporozhye when I returned," Otto wrote. "When I knocked on your door, Helga Weiss answered! Then I found your letter on my desk when I reported at the Wi-Kdo. Write and tell me what you do in Birkenhof. I can't picture you on a farm, what with all the geese and cows. Are you still afraid of them? I laugh when I remember you telling me in your broken German about the goose that attacked your red-clad derrière. Was it on a dacha? And as I tried to tell you, don't ever run away from them.

"Now some good news. Your mother is well and working in a hospital. I didn't get to see her, as I wasn't able to stop in Kiev. I asked my Vienna friend to visit with her and he did. Your Mutti cried when she heard you were all right and still in Zaporozhye. I wonder what her reaction will be when she hears you're in Warthegau?

"I spent one week in Vienna, another in Tyrol. But like all pleasant things, my leave ended too quickly. Hope to hear from you soon. *Liebe Grüsse und alles Gute* [Warm greetings and all the best]."

I read Otto's letter again and again, searching between the lines for any hidden nuances. But this and all his subsequent letters were written in the same friendly tone, with never a word to betray his feelings. All the same, they brought me joy.

I shared the letter with Christine, my new confidante.

Civil postal service between the Ukraine and Germany was functioning, and for a brief period Mama and I were able to correspond. Because of censorship, sealed letters did not get through, but postcards with a minimum of information did. Mama's postcards with sights of Kiev said nothing other than that she was feeling well and that she missed me. And I missed her, more and more.

I worried about my papa, wondered where he was. When I asked Mama if perhaps she had heard something, anything, about him, she either hadn't heard or chose not to answer.

★   ★   ★

Walking to and from work through the woods ablaze with brilliant autumn colors was a pleasure. Soon the winter set in; the leafless trees were bending in the wind. The pleasant walk turned into an agonizing one in freezing rain, then blizzards and deep snow. I was getting soft.

Working for Fräulein Trauber was a gratifying experience. With my numbering system in effect, her waiting room was no longer crowded. She explained things to me as she worked.

"This is a reamer." She inserted the tiny needle with incised threads into the patient's cavity. When the reamer emerged, a tiny red worm dangled from it. "It's the nerve," she said, placing the reamer and the worm on my hand.

Some patients' breath smelled very nasty. I concluded that dentistry was not the career for me.

Now and then I stayed with Christine overnight.

"I wish you'd stay with us through the winter," she said.

"So do I. Pity you have no room for me."

"Why, don't you like my bed?"

"With you in it? You use me as a hot water bottle the way you sprawl out. Stop giggling. Move! Anyway, Frau Mannheim would not permit it. It won't be long anyhow. Spring will be here soon."

Another winter was nearly over and fierce battles continued to be fought in and around Stalingrad. *One winter was all it took to freeze Napoleon out of Russia—but no, not the Germans,* I thought dejectedly as I plowed through the snow-covered fields, a shortcut to Birkenhof.

Early February 1943 brought tremendous news. The German Sixth Army had been soundly defeated at Stalingrad. My joy could not be dampened by Frau Mannheim's optimism. She was convinced the defeat was "reversible."

★ ★ ★

In March, Christine met Corporal Hans Auer, an orderly at the Lazarett. She fell in love and was most unhappy because her parents forbade her to see him, let alone marry him.

"I won't stop seeing him. I can't!" Christine wailed. "If we can't get married, I—I'll kill myself!"

I tried to calm her. "If you love him that much, you can certainly wait until you're twenty-one."

"What if he doesn't wait for me? It's an eternity!"

"Fifteen months? Cheer up." I pushed fair strands of hair from her broad forehead. "If I were a boy, I'd wait for you for all eternity."

She broke into a smile.

"The trouble is, you don't appreciate what you've got," I went on. "You love a man who loves you, and instead of singing praise to God, you cry. If it were I, I'd dance in the rain for joy. Pity, no man has ever really loved me."

"Nonsense. You just can't see it. Aleksandr did."

"No, I don't think so anymore. If he truly loved me, he'd at least have tried to dissuade me from leaving Stalingrad."

"All right, then what about Herr Mannheim?"

"His is a fatherly love. I don't mean *that* sort of love."

"I think he's in love with you."

"He's a married man, Christine. He adores his family."

"Sometimes you can be so exasperating. He can adore his family and still be in love with you. He wouldn't be the first married man to love a girl with great passion."

Something snapped inside me, and I stared dazedly at her.

"Don't look so horrified. I'll never mention him again, if you'd rather. Here"—she handed me a lit cigarette—"try it."

I took one puff from the cigarette and gave it back to her. "What—what makes you think—" I stammered, afraid to voice the words floating on the surface of my mind.

"Call it female intuition, based on what you yourself have told me about him."

"He was not attracted to me physically, Christine. He never so much as tried to kiss me, touch me, take me to bed."

"I could be wrong. Hans wanted me to sleep with him the very first night we met," she said, and blushed profusely. "The only reason I said anything is because I don't want you to develop an inferiority complex. You underestimate yourself as it is." She looked at me quizzically. "God, I wish I hadn't mentioned Herr Mannheim. Now you're all upset and . . . Why are you leaving? We have no one to disturb us and the whole evening to talk."

"Not tonight, Christine. Maybe tomorrow."

I needed to be alone.

★   ★   ★

Christine's words kept buzzing through my head as I walked home that misty, dripping April night. *"I think he is in love with you."* Could it be true?

Images of Karl Mannheim flashed across my mind. I tried to recall the details that I had previously ignored: his waiting, watching for me from the shadows of the yard, his irritation, even anger, when I spent time with the soldiers from TK-1. His unexpected arrival in Birkenhof—was he afraid I would leave unless he smoothed things over quickly? This must be why he used the power of his persuasion to make me stay. And because I had wanted to stay, I again ignored the whisperings of my instinct when he embraced me, the way he looked at me under the cherry tree.

How artfully Karl Mannheim had disguised his feelings. I loved him as a friend; he loved me as a woman.

Bits and pieces of the puzzle were beginning to fall into place. I began to understand Frau Mannheim's initial reaction, plying me with questions, trying to decipher her husband's motives for sending me to Birkenhof. It became abundantly clear she had suspected her husband's love for me. Why then did she repeatedly insist I must stay? Her mood swings and irritability continued to surface, and I had made up my mind to leave as soon as I could gracefully get away. When I persisted, she called me a stubborn Russian, told me what it was like in labor camps for Russians and Poles, and left a picture booklet in my room. Was it meant for me to see? I will never know, but it served its purpose. The horrible photographs were of emaciated Russians and Jews, I guessed, probably in a ghetto, sitting listlessly in front of shabby dwellings. Others clung to a barbed wire fence. They looked like skeletons, some with ridges on their flesh, obviously victims of beatings. I can still remember their eyes, huge eyes, pleading, hopeless . . .

"Why?" I had asked Frau Mannheim. I could say no more. But she didn't answer. Was she satisfied?

I sensed her reason for insisting that I stay. It was not her fear of what might happen to me, but her fear of Herr Mannheim. "You can't leave until we hear from my husband." Now I believed I knew why she couldn't let me go. If she had, Herr Mannheim might never have forgiven her, depriving her of the one hope she must have had that, given time, her husband would return to his senses and all would be well again.

I felt ashamed and guilty for having caused so much unhappiness, and I pitied Frau Mannheim. *How can I possibly make it up to her?* I agonized. *Can I tell her? Would she believe that my relationship with her husband was undefiled? Would I ever be able to convince her that I had been young and insecure?* I had had many illusions, but that a man could be in love with me was not one of them. *How naive I was. A stupid fool!*

"Grow up!" I cried out in the dark and smote my forehead. I must leave Birkenhof. The photographs, my Jewish blood, were all engraved upon my mind. I had no identification papers and could be picked up on the street like a dog without a tag on its collar. But I could see no other choice. To stay longer would be selfish, cowardly, and despicable. *I have taken advantage of these good people far too long and must remove myself from the scene. Tomorrow. Herr Mannheim must not be given another opportunity to intervene. By the time he finds out, I'd be long gone.* Frau Mannheim would have some misgivings, but she would be relieved all the same. She would write and tell her husband, "Sophia ran away. She did not say where she was going or why. She simply disappeared." There would be no fault on her part.

Up at dawn the next morning, I packed before facing Frau Mannheim. "Do you have a minute, please? I must talk to you."

"What is it?" she snapped. "Can't it wait?"

She was making it easy for me. One of her cold-shoulder days, the days I had dreaded in the past and had wanted to escape twice before.

"I'm afraid not."

She looked at me as if to say: "Well then, go on and let's get it over with." This irked me, but I had resolved not to provoke her. I wanted to leave on a friendly note.

"I'm leaving," I said softly. "I feel that I must. As you know, it's been on my mind for a long time. Yesterday I decided today would be as good a day as any."

"What are you talking about? For heaven's sake, would you mind repeating what you just said? But slow down, please." She stretched the words to twice their size.

"I am leaving, Frau Mannheim. I would like to say good-bye."

"You can't be serious! You can't just walk out without giving me a reason. When did you say—today? And where, may I ask, do you think you're going?"

"To Posen, to the Labor Office first. And then," I replied grandly, "to wherever my destiny directs me."

"I won't let you go."

"I am nineteen. I'm old enough to think for myself and to make my own decisions." I was getting desperate. My voice shook as I thanked her for all she had done for me. No one had ever looked after me and showed as much concern as she had, I told her, and I had taken advantage of her kindness long enough. "If my decision is wrong, I'll have only myself to blame. You mustn't worry about me. After all," I added with a weak smile, "*Unkraut verdirbt nicht* [Weeds do not perish]."

She was irritated rather than amused by my feeble attempt at humor. "I think it's ridiculous."

Yes, it is ridiculous, I thought. *It's ridiculous to go on pretending. We are both ridiculous. It's time we quit the masquerade.*

"I'll find a job. Life requires quick action and a positive approach to get ahead," said I, thinking that there must be room for one more Russian in one of those labor camps. "Once I have a job, I'll be all right. Please don't worry about me."

"After all the discussions we have had! I wash my hands of you. You're so stubborn, there's no reasoning with you." She was quiet for a moment. "If you insist, then go. Go and find out for yourself," she said with an exasperated gesture. "I hope you won't regret it."

A wave of immense relief flooded over me—not so much because she gave me so little opposition, but because she did not persist in asking my reasons.

"I'll write to you."

"I'd expect that much."

"Some day I'll visit you. I know I will miss you."

While the coachman was harnessing the horse to take me to the railroad station at Pudewitz, I said swift good-byes to the maids, who looked at me with baffled expressions. I hugged Gretchen. Willi and I shook hands. I vaguely remember Frau Mannheim and me embracing, and her saying, "Good luck."

Part V

INSIDE NAZI GERMANY

27

NEMESIS ON HORSEBACK

As I walked blindly through the streets of Posen that April day of 1943, I wondered if it had really been necessary to give up the security of Gut Birkenhof. *Frau Mannheim probably feels relieved to be rid of me, but was my presence making her really unhappy? How can I be sure Herr Mannheim's love is real and not merely imagined?*

Nothing seemed real, except for the possibility of a German victory. Two winters had passed, and though the Wehrmacht had lost a major battle at Stalingrad, they were still deep inside Russia. If the Soviets lost the war, I could never go home. I would have left Gut Birkenhof in any case, sooner or later. And I convinced myself that sooner was better.

Nothing seemed certain, only my anxiety about what lay ahead.

Before entering the *Gauarbeitsamt* (District Labor Office), I asked my guardian angel to intervene with the fates on my behalf. Then I wondered where the fates might take me.

The first clerk I approached had nothing to offer. Another said, "Your case is unique," and referred me to Herr Sandau, the man in charge of foreign labor.

Yes, I thought, *my case is unique. Surely I'm the only idiot to volunteer for work in a labor camp—deep inside Germany, no less. And just as well. No one with Jewish blood and in his right mind would ever go to Nazi Germany by choice. So who would ever suspect?*

I took a few deep breaths and entered Sandau's office.

Herr Sandau, a pleasant-looking man in a tailored gray suit, greeted me: *"Heil Hitler."*

"Heil Hitler," I said boldly, and exhaled.

"What can I do for you?"

"I'm looking for a job."

"What kind of job?"

"An office job," I answered quickly. "I'm a secretary. I also worked as a clerk for *Wirtschaftskommando* in—"

The phone rang. Herr Sandau lifted the receiver. "*Menschenskind!* [Oh, boy!]" he exclaimed. "You've just crossed my mind . . . I might be able to come up with a few . . . Come on up, I have found what you were looking for . . . *Ja, ja,*" he repeated at intervals and put the receiver back on its cradle.

"So. You're a secretary," he said jovially. "A good one?"

"I think so." I smiled when I said that.

"Quite a bit of confidence for a young girl. How old are you?"

"Nineteen."

"*Na, ja,* the man who called has been looking for a clerk. He'll be here shortly. His name is Gottlieb Brune, a good man. What's your name?" I told him. "*Volksdeutsche?*"

"No, I'm Russian."

His jaw dropped. *There goes my office job,* I thought, telling myself not to be disappointed and feeling let down all the same.

Moments later, Herr Brune came through the door. The sturdy, ruddy-cheeked man didn't flinch when told him I was Russian. He promptly hired me.

While the two men discussed their business, I studied my new boss. He was about thirty-five. His round, boyish face with ruddy cheeks made him look like a cherub, and my instinct told me he was a decent, simple sort of man. He talked in quick, short sentences. From their conversation I gathered that Brune had some kind of factory and that he needed many workers.

"At the moment, I can provide you with only four Polish girls," said Herr Sandau.

Herr Brune shrugged. "I'll take what I can get."

I longed to know where we were going, but I dared not ask that, nor how much I would be paid. I too would take what I could get.

"Speak any Polish?" Brune asked me.

"Yes. Also Ukrainian, some French, and of course Russian."

"Excellent. How about bookkeeping, know any?"

"I'm good at figures."

"*Wunderbar!* Just the girl I've been looking for. You are coming with me this afternoon, I hope."

"I came prepared," I said, immensely relieved that I did not have to sleep in the railroad station waiting room.

Herr Sandau accompanied us to a camp where Poles were held in virtual captivity prior to being shipped off to Germany as forced labor. They had been rounded up on the street, snatched from the fields or their homes. The four girls assigned to Brune were wholesome country girls; all had been forced to leave their homes and were frightened. In Polish I told them what I thought of Gottlieb Brune, assuring them as well as myself that with a boss like that we had little to worry about. "Our guardian angels are on the alert today," I added. Their uneasiness subsided somewhat.

Sandau and Brune led the way to the Central Station, while the five of us trotted behind them. The Polish girls, carrying large bundles across their shoulders, could barely keep up with the men. They asked me, "Where are we going?" I wished I knew.

As we boarded the train leaving for Berlin, the girls were whisked off somewhere. Brune disappeared, leaving me alone in a second-class compartment. When the wheels of the train began to grind, I was gripped with an uneasy anticipation, as at the start of a roller coaster ride, both excited and afraid to enter Nazi Germany.

Brune returned to the compartment. "Talk to the girls and keep an eye on them. They have a habit of slipping away. I don't want to lose them."

The girls were in a third-class carriage, their spirits neither elated nor depressed. I came back to report that all was well. "Why should they run away from you, Herr Brune? We have decided you are a very kind man."

"I'm nothing of the sort," he responded gruffly, reddening with pleasure.

As the train sped smoothly through farming country, I remarked casually, "Aren't these fields good-looking, Herr Brune? That rye is growing much too thickly, though."

"It is indeed. Glad you know something about farming. Wannefeld is a farming community." And he became quite talkative.

Rich farmlands and magnificent forests surrounded Wannefeld, a village in Gardelegen county eighty-odd miles west of Berlin. Brune was an ardent hunter, and his hunting lodge was a meeting place for his friends, among them several high Nazi officials. Brune was *Bürgermeister* (mayor) of Wannefeld; he owned a farm and a fruit- and vegetable-canning factory.

"How many people work for you?"

"At the moment only seventeen. I'm trying to build up to about forty. I've only one man working in the office, though. That's why I'm glad to have you. Herr Zucker can't cope with the hundred and one things there are to do. In any case, he'll be retiring soon."

★   ★   ★

Wannefeld was a prosperous village. Its inhabitants were urban in appearance, unlike the peasants I had known back home. People along the broad *Dorfstrasse* (village street) looked friendly.

A tractor rolled by. The driver, shouting above the roar of the engine, greeted Herr Brune, *"Heil Hitler!"* A woman leaned out of the window, *"Heil Hitler."* An old lady, sitting at the doorstep of her house, croaked, *"Heil Hitler."* No one said "Good morning" or "Welcome back, Herr Brune." The grocer, wearing a canvas apron, standing in front of his general store; youngsters on their bicycles—everyone smiled, *Heil Hitler*-ing. It was spoken so fast that it sounded like *"Halitler"* and, as far as I could tell, did not convey any meaning, beyond an automatic greeting. Before too long, I began to use this peculiar greeting myself—but not quite: I'd lisp a quick *"Halb Liter,"* meaning "half a liter," and no one ever noticed the difference.

At the far end of the wide *Dorfstrasse* was the cannery, a long structure extending into the garden beyond. Adjacent to the cannery, a two-story stucco house crisscrossed with thin strips of wood contained a dormitory for the Polish girls and the office, both on the ground floor.

Brune introduced me to Herr Zucker, a kindly old man whose glass eye attracted me like a magnet. Herr Zucker showed me upstairs to my room. I dropped my luggage and returned to the office, a busy place. People came in and out; new faces popped up; the telephone rang. I felt dizzy trying to understand the vernacular spoken in this part of Germany. By the end of the day, my jaw hurt from smiling, my hands were sore from shaking others' hands. At supper, a smorgasbord of new faces swam before my eyes: Hungarian, Polish, Czech, and French.

I shared a room with two delightful sisters from Hungary who worked at the cannery. Resi, a blonde with brown eyes, and Heli, a lanky brunette with blue eyes and an impish face, were as much of a contrast and of the same ages as Christine and Monika. I felt at home. Crests of happy laughter rose from their end of the room, and the sound of their chatter was like a lullaby. The shift from fear of the unknown to relief had been too sudden; exhausted, I drifted off into a deep sleep.

The early morning sun shining on my face woke me. I looked around and saw bleak walls, three iron beds, a kitchen table with chairs, a plain wardrobe, and in a dark corner a writing desk. A naked bulb hung from the ceiling. It was a room that had evidently never been used as a residence before.

Neither of my roommates stirred. I walked over to the open window and rejoiced at the sight of the dark green forest sharply outlined against the blue sky.

While we were having breakfast, I suggested to Resi and Heli, "With a little effort and a bucket of paint we could brighten the room and make it a bit more homey."

Heli clapped her hands. "When do we start?"

Within the next few weeks, the "three merry pranksters," as we became known in the village, turned the room upside down, painted walls and the wardrobe. Frau Brune donated a tablecloth; Frau Zucker gave us a vase, and we filled it with garden flowers. From scraps of donated material, I made a lampshade and two floppy cushions, as my mother might have done. There were holes in the floor; after I complained enough about mice scurrying around and crawling on top of me at night, Brune ordered linoleum.

Among my souvenirs I had found Guido Schneble's invitation to the river outing on the Dnieper the year before. His Munich address was printed on the top. I had never seen stationery printed with a letterhead and was so impressed that I saved it. But I had almost forgotten about Guido. I sent him a postcard and wrote letters to Christine, Otto, and Helga Weiss, who had left Zaporozhye and was living in Dresden now. But I would not start a correspondence with Frau Mannheim for some time. Nor did I write to Herr Mannheim.

★ ★ ★

The one-room office was large enough to accommodate three desks and a long counter with shelves for files. Herr Zucker and I sat facing each other at desks placed near the windows. Above Brune's desk at the far side of the room hung a picture of Hitler. Herr Brune was a member of the Nazi Party, as were many of the visitors who frequented the office and picked up cartons of goodies from the cannery.

Brune took me on a tour of the cannery and of his pride and joy: the field where the fat and juicy white asparagus, protected from the sun, grew inside mounds of sandy soil. Brune wore a cotton shirt, a faded blue vest, and pants tucked inside his boots. His visor cap looked as if he had slept on it. Though I liked my boss, he did not impress me as being clever—but successful, yes, and very popular with city officials now that food was rationed.

Herr Zucker retired late in May, and I took over the payroll, bookkeeping, and distribution of ration cards for food and cigarettes, coupons for clothing, and vouchers for textiles and shoes. I also maintained an inventory of all the farmers' produce, eggs and pigs among them, to ensure delivery of their assigned quota, and made myself popular reminding the villagers when taxes were due.

Remote as the village might have been, it never seemed far away from civilization. I adjusted to life in Wannefeld, made friends with local girls, and loved my work. For the first time since leaving Kiev I found myself fulfilled. We worked six days a week, ten hours a day, and sometimes on Sundays. The busier I was the better I liked it. This pleased Herr Brune, and he treated me well.

"But oh, how unreasonable he is at times," I complained unreasonably in a letter to Christine. "It's irritating to be interrupted in the middle of a task to be sent off to Gardelegen to see his Frau Mutter. Last week he sent me to Haldensleben to deliver a heavy carton of canned stuff to some official selected for his favors. And yesterday I spent the entire day in Magdeburg—waiting for a prescription medicine! I don't just sit and wait, of course. I do some shopping and see a movie or two. I enjoy these outings. All the same, it's unfair for Herr Brune to make me work late at night to make up for the time I spend running his personal errands. They should send him to the front. With a man like him in the Wehrmacht, the war would be over in no time."

Herr Brune, whose contribution to the war effort was canned goods and fresh vegetables, was exempt from the draft.

Our meals consisted mainly of vegetables (very little meat) and were prepared by a Polish cook in the style peculiar to this area—tasteless to our non-German palates but healthful and plentiful. The Polish girls and the men—one Czech, two Poles, one Frenchman, and a Ukrainian—ate in the dining hall, which served also as a common room. Public places, inns, movie houses, and cafés were off limits for the Poles and the *Ostarbeiter* (workers from the East).

It was mandatory in Nazi Germany for workers from Poland and the Soviet Union to wear labels, which identified them as slaves to be treated as inferior human beings. Those from the Soviet Union, the *Ostarbeiter*, wore a blue diamond-shaped label with white lettering that spelled *Ost* (East). The Poles wore a yellow badge with the letter P. The Czechs and Hungarians, nationals of friendly states, wore no labels. Our Frenchman was a prisoner of war and identified as such; he did not stay in Wannefeld very long.

I knew there were Jews in Germany, but I saw no one anywhere I could recognize as one. I didn't dare ask questions and felt sick at heart, assuming they were all starving in ghettos, as in the photographs I had seen in Frau Mannheim's picture booklet.

People with labels sewn on to their clothes were not allowed to travel unescorted, so I took them to Gardelegen to be photographed and to be issued employment cards, or to see a doctor, a dentist, or a stage show organized for foreign workers.

I was on a local train with several Polish girls one day when a German woman thundered, "It's a crime to let these stinking foreigners ride our trains. Go out on the landing where you belong! Let us breathe." The girls cursed softly as they moved. Furious, I said to the woman, "If it weren't for the stinking foreigners, you'd *starve* to death." The woman gasped. She wasn't sure what to make of me. I was not labeled, yet I spoke German with a foreign accent and was clearly also a foreigner. Before she could come up with a retort, the train slowed for the station and I jumped off, grateful to be in one piece.

Though I was an *Ostarbeiter*, I balked at the idea of being labeled. Brune never mentioned it. Nor did the locals, who seemed to view me with a kind of bemused affection, as an oddity.

The one person who refused to let me get away with it was the *Wachtmeister* (police sergeant) from neighboring Letzlingen. Wannefeld was too small to have its own police. The *Wachtmeister* used to ride his horse over, on patrol.

"How come you don't wear *Ost?*" the man in the green uniform growled the first time he laid eyes on me.

"You mean that thing they wear on their chest?" I asked in a sweet, innocent voice.

"You know perfectly well what I mean," he snapped. "If you don't, I"—he pounded his chest—"*I* am telling you. The *Ost* label must be sewn on to your dress and be clearly visible at all times. Do I make myself clear?"

"Yes, Herr *Wachtmeister*." He turned on his heels and stomped out. I stuck my tongue out at his back. *To hell with you!*

I burned to see as much of Germany as possible while I still could. Labeling would mean adieu to the few freedoms I valued and the travels I enjoyed.

28

FOUND!

The mid-June morning was quiet. I was alone in the office when the faint click of boots broke the silence. The footsteps grew louder, like a giant clock approaching zero hour. *The Wachtmeister!* I panicked and dived behind the counter.

"If you tell me what you're looking for, perhaps I can help." I knew that voice. I knew it so well. *But it couldn't be!*

"Herr Mannheim!" I cried, and I stared at him, speechless. *How could he possibly have known where I was?*

He stood at the open doorway, radiant and tall in his trim, impeccable white summer uniform, hat at a rakish angle, and contemplated me with patient good cheer.

"You are going to welcome me, aren't you?" He stepped in and extended his hand across the counter.

I placed my hand in his, still stunned, and stammered, "You really caught me by surprise. How did you know where to find me?"

"Nothing ever escapes me. Haven't I told you that?"

"Yes, but . . . you could've spared me the shock by letting me know you were coming."

"I didn't know until the last minute I'd be able to. You know what trains are like, the many transfers . . . You are glad to see me, aren't you?"

"Well, yes," I said, and I knew at once I had hurt him with my casual attitude. My offhand manner was a feeble attempt to discourage him. *It's wrong for you to come*, I thought. *So wrong, you shouldn't have.* Yet I was so very happy to see him. Karl Mannheim was my friend. Surely a friend coming such a distance deserved a warmer welcome, no matter what.

He still held my hand. I freed it and gently touched his arm. "So good to see you, Herr Mannheim. I'm very glad you were able to come." I came out from behind the counter and bowed.

"For a moment I thought I wasn't welcome."

"You and Frau Mannheim will always be welcome in my home, wherever it may be. How are you—and Frau Mannheim?" He nodded his head and did not answer. "Did you have difficulties finding Wannefeld? Such a small speck on the map."

"I'd find you no matter where you went. Or did you think you could disappear without a trace?" He sat down and crossed his long legs. "Guess who told me where you were."

"I have no idea. Otto Schubert?" I wondered out loud.

"So you found time to write him. No, not Schubert."

"Then who? I can't stand the suspense."

"Your mother."

"Mother!" He must have arrived here directly from Kiev. I had only recently found a way to let her know that I had moved to Wannefeld.

The civil postal service between Kiev and Germany had been stopped. I had racked my brain trying to figure out how to get a letter to my mother when a "brilliant" idea came to me: the military channel! It was prohibited; offenders were prosecuted. All the same, I wrote on the envelope the Wi-Kdo's Feldpost (APO) number 46114 as though it were my return address. Mother was petrified when she received the letter, delivered to her by two armed officers from the occupational authorities who came to investigate. No doubt my dear mama beguiled the men with her hospitality; charges were dropped and, moreover, one of the officers, named Otto Axner, promptly forwarded her return letter to me.

"Tell me, Herr Mannheim, how is she? Tell me everything! Did Mama tell you how I got in touch with her?" No, he said, and I was grateful. *He'd be aghast at my audacity.*

Karl Mannheim told me little I did not already know. He had arrived in Kiev around noon and spent several hours with a neighbor waiting for my mother to return from work.

"Your mother is a delightful lady," he said. "She received me warmly and with a great deal of excitement. She placed some food on the table and apologized sotto voce that she couldn't do more. I feel good about meeting your Mutti, Sophiechen. I know now from whom you inherited your green eyes and the beautiful timbre of your voice. You resemble your mother. And yet, you don't. You're quite a bit taller than she is."

"Then I must've grown. Mama and I were the same height when I left."

"Yes, you have grown. You were growing before my very eyes. Also growing more impatient, more obstinate. I told your mother about it, and she laughed. 'My Zosik has always been like that,' she said. 'She has no patience with people who can't grasp things quickly. Just like her papa.'" Mannheim leaned forward, bracing his elbow on his knee. "What else have you inherited from your father?"

"Oh, I don't know," I said slowly, wondering whether it was or was not a leading question. *What else did Mama tell him? The neighbor?* "His optimism, I think. Also, Papa could be quite sarcastic, and I know I can be sarcastic, too."

"Try not to be. Sarcasm is not a nice tendency to cultivate." He stretched his legs. "My visit with your Mutti was short but rewarding. I was able to answer many of the questions she asked about you. She has lost a lot of weight, apparently, but that's understandable, the food situation being what it is. She feels fine, though. And of course she loves you dearly, also understandably." He said it with a smile. Then a frown crept between his eyes. "Why didn't you write me?"

I said nothing.

"You were stubbornly determined to leave Pudewitz. Why?"

"Looking for another adventure, I suppose. A sudden urge."

"A risky escapade these days," he said, as Brune walked in and immediately went into a stiff Nazi salute, jerking his arm forward, as always when facing an impressive uniform.

"Heil Hitler," Mannheim responded with his arm bent at the elbow.

I introduced them. They shook hands, exchanged a few pleasantries, and sat down to talk about farming.

"Are you familiar with serradella?" Brune asked. "I tried but haven't been able to get the seed around here."

"It's the type of rye we grow in Warthegau. I'll see what I can do to get you the seed."

I hungered for watermelons and corn on the cob, and I said to Herr Brune, "Of all the vegetables you grow, why don't you grow corn?"

"The type of corn we grow in Germany is not fit for human consumption. We feed the cattle with it."

I looked at Mannheim. "If you'd send us some seed from the Ukraine, I'd grow the corn myself, in the back of the cannery. You wouldn't mind, Herr Brune, would you?" The two men laughed, Brune saying he did not mind.

It was still only nine o'clock in the morning when Brune gave me the rest of the day off. I thanked him, and Mannheim and I went for a long, leisurely walk in the forest.

"Remember your glum predictions, Herr Mannheim, of what would happen to me if I left Pudewitz?" Taking my clue from Mannheim, I avoided any reference to Gut Birkenhof. "You talked of horrible conditions for foreign workers in Germany, and it isn't all that bad. We're treated well. Herr Brune is a benevolent dictator. He really is a very nice man."

"I suppose conditions vary from place to place. I can't tell you how relieved I am you have stumbled upon a decent community with a benevolent dictator for a boss." He was smiling, and I laughed.

"He piles more and more responsibilities on my shoulders and lets me go anyplace I want. Only two weeks ago I was in Dresden, visiting with Helga Weiss, the Zaporozhye girl. We took a stroll along the Elbe and Saturday night listened to music by Haydn in the fabulous Zwingerhof. Dresden is a beautiful city." The thought of how I couldn't even buy a train ticket back home when my passport was stolen popped into my mind, and I said, "In all my trips I was never once asked to produce identity papers. I'm not sure that I am free, but I feel free."

"As long you don't stray too far from Wannefeld, you'll be all right, I suppose. Just don't get restless again. Stay here until the war is over. Please, promise me that."

"I'm content with my present lot and intend to stay."

After a lovely lunch at Hoppe's Inn, we went up to my room. A picture of Guido Schneble on the desk caught Mannheim's eye. He lingered over it and glanced at the inscription: "This is to remind you of our meeting deep in Russia."

"The staff sergeant is rude and disrespectful. I hope that in the future you will be more discriminating in choosing your friends," he remarked, and I remembered that the two men had met in Zaporozhye at the river in circumstances that were humiliating to Mannheim.

Soon the time came for Mannheim to depart. He was taking the last train from Wannefeld. He hadn't said and I could not ask if he was going home before returning to Russia. I only knew he had not been to see his family because he had arrived in Wannefeld directly from the front.

The parting was sad. He was part of my life, the life that I probably owed him. I knew now that he was in love with me, and I felt sorry, very sorry for him, for all that could not be. Somehow I knew we would never see each other again. He pressed my hand and did not say good-bye. "I'll write," he said. And though he smiled, there were tears in his eyes. When the train pulled in and he jumped aboard, I also cried and waved good-bye until the train disappeared from my sight, and with it the man I had looked up to as a father and loved as a friend.

★ ★ ★

Otto Axner, the officer who had delivered the letter I sent to my mother via the military channels, wrote again and again. Mother's letters and photographs were enclosed. She had lost a lot of weight and with it her voluptuousness. Her eyes appeared sunken, her cheeks hollow. It was painfully obvious how hungry she was, how hungry Kiev was during the German occupation. Mother considered herself more fortunate than most because those who worked were fed a bowl of thin soup. Mama, besides, worked in a hospital where the soup was thicker. It hurt me all the more because in Wannefeld there was food to spare.

She wrote about Karl Mannheim, how happy she was to have met him. She raved about his distinguished good looks, his fine manners, and his warm "Russian heart." "He wanted to see everything that's yours—your corner, your books, your photographs. When he saw the picture you sent me in the German Red Cross uniform, he said, 'Incredible! It cannot be!' He was amazed. I told him that if he knew you at all, he shouldn't be surprised. He smiled and said he knows you very well. Does he? And then he wept. I have never seen a man cry as he did. He loves you so much, Zosik. He told me that life without you wouldn't be worth living. He will keep in touch with me, and he promised to send for me to join you after the war . . ."

★ ★ ★

I wrote to Frau Mannheim. She promptly replied: "So good to hear from you! I'm glad you were able to find a job to suit your taste and temperament. We're all well, busy as usual. Harvest looks promising . . . The children join me in wishing you the best." I wrote another letter and sent a carton of canned white asparagus. So we began to correspond.

Herr Mannheim and I also corresponded for a time.

My correspondence grew. Some days I would receive as many as ten letters, and many received and appreciated my parcels with goodies from the Gottlieb Brune Cannery.

29

A PROPOSAL

I hadn't been troubled by the *Wachtmeister* for some time and began to think he had forgotten me when he came again, riding into the village on horseback like some righteous god.

He charged into the office. "Why don't you do as you're told? I'm warning you," he barked, "the next time I catch you without the *Ost* badge, you'll be charged with breaking the law."

I shook with frustration. I hated him, and I was afraid of him. But my fear of losing my freedom by wearing the badge was greater. *"The next time"—anything could happen by then*, I consoled myself. *A stray bomb might hit him and kill him. He might be sent to the front and die of a bullet wound. The war might be over next time.*

Brune remained impartial. Clearly he preferred not to get involved in my dispute with the law. I did not rely on him for support, but on the other hand I knew he needed me. If I were suddenly to wear the badge, I could not go anywhere, and he would have to run his out-of-town errands himself.

Emboldened by Brune's impartiality and his growing dependence on me, I continued to defy the *Wachtmeister* and to crisscross Germany without papers or permits of any kind. I was reckless, enjoying today as if there were no tomorrow.

★   ★   ★

Early in August 1943, I received a telegram from Guido Schneble announcing his arrival. When he came and greeted me with a warm Bavarian hello, it was as if we had been friends for years. He smiled a winning smile, revealing his sparkling white teeth. He had grown lean and looked quite dashing in his Luftwaffe uniform. Though he was only twenty-five, his smooth dark hair was receding—"from constantly wearing those damned forage caps."

He flung his forage cap and tunic on the bed and removed his black tie. "I've been looking forward to seeing you. It's been a long time." He lit a cigarette and began blowing slow smoke rings. "Oh, I'm sorry." He offered me one. "You smoke?"

"Occasionally." I accepted a black French cigarette and nearly choked on it. We smoked in silence for a time. Then, "Remember—" we both said and laughed.

"All right, Guido, you start."

"I was going to say, remember that outing on the Dnieper?"

"That's just what I was going to say. How could I ever forget? Remember that time when—" And so it went.

"Then suddenly you were gone."

"Yes, suddenly. But tell me about you, Guido."

After a year on the Russian Front, his unit had been moved to France. They had left Zaporozhye in the summer of 1942, riding a cattle train to Germany and carrying with them the pigs and chickens and cases of eggs they had stolen from the Ukrainian peasants. "Fruits of war," Guido added with a timid smile.

"You knew that pretty hairdresser in the shop on Main Street, didn't you?" he asked.

"Vaguely."

"A tragic thing happened. Her baby was shot, in front of her. She's Russian, but the baby's father was Jewish. Some Ukrainians must have reported it. I was near the shop when one of the *Einsatzgruppen* fellows grabbed the baby from her arms and shot it . . . right on the sidewalk. The poor woman collapsed, unconscious." His voice trailed off.

I shuddered. *Had I stayed in Zaporozhye much longer, I would have been shot like that hapless little half-Jewish babe,* I thought, and clenched my fists to keep my hands steady.

"There must have been an awful lot of Jews in and around Zaporozhye. The *Einsatzgruppen* couldn't cope with their gruesome task, so they looked for volunteers among us soldiers to help them shoot the Jews. Only one man volunteered from TK-1, our first sergeant. When Hauptmann Glockzin found out, he got rid of him in a hurry! Seppi Irschik replaced that *Schweinehund* [swine] . . . I hear there were lots of Jews in Kiev too. They were mowed down"—his voice barely audible—"by the thousands."

I felt the skin on my neck crawl from the sheer horror of these revelations. Sensing Guido's compassion for the victims of brutality, I ventured to ask quietly, my mouth suddenly dry, "Why do the Germans hate the Jews so much?"

"I can't tell you that. The whole world has gone mad, that's all I can say." He lit another cigarette. "You wouldn't believe what's going on in Paris now. The French are getting fiercer every day. We never know where or when they're going to strike."

"France was free until you conquered it. Can you blame them?"

"No, I don't. But"—he spent some moments contemplating smoke rings—"let me tell you what happened to my friend." The two comrades had gone to a brothel in Paris. No sooner had they entered separate cubicles and undressed when Guido heard an agonizing scream. He ran to investigate and found his friend writhing on the floor, drenched in his own blood. His penis had been cut off.

Nausea rose in my throat. "I need some air."

Guido put on his tie and tunic, and we stepped outside. "And this," he continued, "right after I saved a French girl from being raped. I had to slug my own comrade! Not that I regret it, but the point is, where's justice?" He frowned, and his eyebrows shaded his eyes. "My friend who died—O God, what a way to go. He didn't hate or hurt anyone. Yet they killed him. While the *Schweine* who hate them will go on raping and killing."

"Swine? They're more like dogs gone mad with rabies."

"It's a dirty war we're fighting. But, like it or not, we're in it."

Guido was staying overnight at Hoppe's Inn. Gregarious and generous, he invited the whole assembly to partake of the French cognac he had brought with him. The innkeeper's two sons put aside their accordions and listened to Guido entertain the men with war stories. The boys' eyes glistened with awe when they heard of Guido's exploits in France, Belgium, Holland, Greece, Yugoslavia, and even Russia. The conqueror! The war hero! They couldn't wait to enlist, were afraid the war would end before they were old enough.

If only they had known what little fascination these conquests held for Guido. He had enlisted when he was eighteen. His father, a staunch Social Democrat, had been arrested soon after Hitler came to power and spent a year in Dachau concentration camp. The elder Guido Schneble, who foresaw Hitler's reign of terror, had long been predicting that the Nazis would start the war and urged his only son to volunteer while there was a choice of services. He did not want his son to die for the Nazi cause, which he opposed, and for the Führer, whom he loathed. Guido felt the same, and together they chose a squadron that served the Luftwaffe from the rear. It was a smart move: Guido saw action on both fronts without firing a shot, and he got through the war with nothing more than a couple of black eyes.

Sunday was hot, a perfect day for swimming. We cycled to the Polvitz Lake—Resi and Heli, the innkeeper's two sons, Guido and I—one bike per couple. It was thrilling to be close to Guido. Squeezed between his arms and the handlebars, I felt secure and inspired by the secret understanding that seemed to flow between us.

Later, Guido and I went to my favorite clearing in the forest of mixed woods scented with pinesap. I was happy to share this idyllic spot with him. Leaves rustled in the breeze, sunlight filtered through the branches. We sat on grassy ground, and I listened to him speak warmly of his parents and two sisters in Munich.

"My mother is a good woman," he said, "and what a cook! But so is my old man. He's an illegitimate son of an Italian noble, Count Guido Donato Santo di . . . something or other."

"Ah, now I know why your name is Guido. I wondered about that. This is why you also look Italian more than German."

"We all look alike, my dad and sisters and even Pia's two little ones. Pia is the oldest. Isolde is expecting her first one. Do you have brothers or sisters?"

"I wish I had. My mother never wanted to have children. I owe my life to the mistake my parents made conceiving me." I laughed. "They named me Sophia but never called me that."

He tilted his head. "I like Sophia—Sopherl." He smiled.

Guido was comfortable to be with and easy to talk to, so easy.

Although there was solidarity among non-Germans in Wannefeld— we all wished for the Nazis' downfall—no one shared my hope for a Soviet victory in the East. The Poles hated the Germans, but they had no love for the Russians either. They feared that unless the British and the Americans overpowered Germany, all of Poland would be taken over by the Soviets.

I had kept my thoughts to myself and was cautious in my conversations, on guard at all times, hoping to find an ally, yet realizing with sadness that not one of them could ever be my true friend. Then Guido came, and it was marvelous to be able, for the first time in my life, to talk about forbidden subjects and not to be afraid.

"How is the war going in Russia?"

"Our troops are having a hell of a time, spread as they are clear across the three-thousand-kilometer-long Eastern Front. Our soldiers are beginning to lose heart, Sopherl."

"And the Soviet soldiers?" I wondered about their morale.

"With the Russians, it's the other way around. Your people didn't fight very hard at first. Over a million of them crossed over to fight on our side to liberate Mother Russia from the Soviets. Poor devils, they had no idea what awaited them—a dog's life in prison camps! *If* they even made it alive to the camps. Now Ivan fights like the demon." *Ivan* was the name the Germans used for the Russians.

We moved to a clearing in the woods, and I drew a map. A winding line in the sand represented the Eastern Front. Rostov-on-Don had been liberated by the Russians, so we placed a pebble for Rostov, also Moscow, Leningrad, and Stalingrad, east of the line; pebbles for Kiev, Kharkov, Orel, and Zaporozhye west of it. We marked the Dnieper and outlined the Black Sea with twigs. Then we tried to decide how long it would be until the Red Army recaptured each of the cities west of the line, and how long it might take before the Wehrmacht was expelled from Soviet soil.

"Zaporozhye will probably be abandoned without much ado. *Wie gewonnen, so zerronnen.*"

"Easy come, easy go," I echoed.

We, the rear guard generals, concluded that the Red Army would wait for the winter to set in before storming the Dnieper and that Kiev would be liberated by the end of the year.

Guido had to catch a train that evening. I stood up and brushed off the pine needles stuck to my skirt.

"We'd better go now."

"I don't want to leave." He glanced at me questioningly. "I could stay the night and catch an early train tomorrow."

"Oh, yes. Yes, please!"

I marveled at the ease with which I had opened to Guido. We understood each other. He had bared his thoughts to me, and I had been able to respond to him in the same way. I felt a spiritual closeness to him, and I wondered if this was a kind of love—less physical, not deeper but more meaningful than the love I had experienced with Otto.

Alone in my room that night, I thought about Otto. I recalled my struggle to communicate with him, his inventive sign language that made me laugh and learn. I recalled the way we danced to the tune "Bandurist" on a scratchy record, and the day my curiosity propelled me to his room. His passionate kisses and the strange way he looked at me that day convinced me he'd wanted more than to kiss—why else lock the door? So I'd panicked, called him idiot. And I dreamed of him now standing in the mist, his arms outstretched, beckoning. I struggled to reach him but couldn't move. The mist thickened; his vision disappeared. I called his name. Behind me Otto's voice: "I'm here." I turned, and there was Guido.

I woke up with a start. *Guido. Was he my destiny?*

Guido called for me in the morning and we went to the station, walking with our arms interlocked and our fingers entwined. I was proud to be seen with Guido.

"Will you be going back to Russia after the war?" he asked.

"I haven't really thought about it. Probably."

"I wish you wouldn't."

"It's my country, Guido."

"How could you live under that system?"

"Is yours any better?"

"Ah, but it won't last."

"That's encouraging."

"And over there, it'll never change."

"If I go back, it'll only be because I love Kiev. As for the rest—" I shrugged my shoulders.

"*Na, ja.* I understand. I love Munich and Bavaria . . . Why did you actually leave? Were you rounded up and forced to go?"

"Now you're asking—there's the train." It hissed into the station. "I'll write."

"Stay in Germany, Sopherl. It'll be different after the war, better than it ever was. Sopherl—"

"Yes, Guido?"

"I want to see you again, soon. I'll be thinking of you."

"I will think of you, too. Don't let anything happen to you. Take care."

He put his arm around me and tried to kiss me. The locals waiting for the train were watching us. *What will they think!* Then suddenly I didn't care. I fell in love again, and it wasn't even spring. I stood on my toes and kissed him.

★   ★   ★

Guido wrote from Munich: his mother was dying of cancer and he was distressed. A card from Paris followed, and then another letter: "You're in my thoughts constantly. I love you, Sopherl. Will you be my wife when this nightmare is over? There won't be a man alive to prevent us from marrying then . . ."

30

BEETHOVEN'S FIFTH

The summer wore on. The war was constantly on everybody's tongue. The men congregated at Hoppe's Inn after sundown and talked of a brilliant German strategy "to lure the Bolsheviks into a trap" similar to that of Stalingrad, only in reverse.

"To reduce the enemy in number to equal ours, that's what we're after!" said one beer-mug-wielding general.

Another rubbed his hands. "*Ja, ja,* the Russians are now throwing all their men in, all at once. They're desperate!"

"And we haven't even used our reserves yet."

"First we must retreat, regroup, and then attack."

"No more retreats for us, *mein Herr*!" another village elder at the situation conference declared. "Our summer offensive has begun."

I listened with the superior air of one who knew something they did not.

Herr Brune had brought a portable radio to the office and placed it on the counter. Left alone, I was an inveterate dial-twister. Searching for some music one day, I came across a curious station. Following eight notes from Beethoven's Fifth Symphony, a voice came on the air announcing the BBC London. I couldn't believe my ears. Some static interference confirmed that it was indeed the forbidden station from London. *England, imagine that!* I turned the volume down and pressed my ear against the set. A German-speaking voice said, ". . . now confirmed that the Soviet troops have captured the Russian city of Orel." I shivered with excitement. Belgorod was also liberated that day—August 5, 1943.

The German summer offensive had failed.

A few days later I heard about the Anglo-American forces capturing all of Sicily. On the Eastern Front, the Soviets were sweeping forward, hard behind the Germans retreating toward the Dnieper. The entire Eastern Front was ablaze.

The High Command of the Wehrmacht announced: "Our armored units have successfully penetrated into the defense lines of the enemy. Kharkov was abandoned. The enemy made minor advances west of Taganrog," which meant of course that the Russians had recaptured Taganrog. I had heard about Kharkov and Taganrog on the BBC, and it was like music to my ears.

Listening to the BBC was dangerous for Germans. For me, it was suicidal. And yet, partly in an attempt to test Gottlieb Brune, partly in a spirit of defiance, I turned off the radio one day and deliberately left the scanner on the BBC. The devil in me even increased the volume. Brune came in, turned on the set to hear the news, and went briskly to his desk. Moments later, the awe-inspiring eight notes announcing the BBC reverberated. Brune's reaction was instantaneous. He jumped up, red in the face, and practically threw himself at the radio, twisted the knob off the BBC, which he obviously knew well, and mumbled something unintelligible. I chuckled inwardly.

All through August and September, terrible battles were fought in Russia. I had been following the reports with an inner eye on the map in my head but could no longer visualize the front line; it was jagged and changeable. To follow the progress of the Anglo-American armies in Italy was easier. Italy had defaulted from Germany's side in September, and the Americans had captured Naples. I was jubilant. The Germans were losing ground, slowly but surely, I had no doubt about that. But my conception of how the war was progressing elsewhere in the world was vague.

★   ★   ★

On the fifth of September, Guido's mother died. Guido was granted special leave, and after the funeral and a few days of mourning with the family, he again came to Wannefeld.

"She suffered so long, Sopherl. It's a blessing in a way that she's gone," he said as I tried to comfort him. And then, placing his mother's wide gold band on my left ring finger, he said, "If only she could've met my bride before she died." (In Germany, the same ring is worn on the right hand after the wedding.) We were officially engaged.

But I did not rejoice just then.

The man I loathed had stormed into the office two days before and after the usual preliminaries banged his fist on the countertop and roared,

"I'm warning you for the last time. The *Ost* label must be attached to your dress!"

"But Herr *Wachtmeister*," I said in a small voice, scared out of my wits. "Why do I need to be visibly identified? Everyone around here knows me already."

"Oh they do, do they? Let me call a small detail to your attention—you're missing documents. No one knows who you really are. You may be a spy, a Communist."

"I never did concern myself with politics," looking directly into his ice-blue eyes. "What would a spy be doing here in Wanne—?"

"Silence! I heard your story before, a likely story. Lost your passport? How convenient. What is it you're trying to hide? Your true identity—are you a Soviet Jew?" His eyes narrowed to slits. "I've always had my suspicions about you. But we have means of finding out the truth."

I was terrified, my knees felt weak. He stormed out of the office, and I retreated upstairs to my room. Kiev was still in German hands. *If they find out, they'll kill me!* To put on the *Ost* label now wouldn't help. On the contrary, he'd suspect I was indeed hiding something and was suddenly willing to cooperate, just to placate him. *I will not, cannot give in—now or ever! I'd rather be dead*, I sobbed. *I'd rather kill myself than be killed by them.*

Suicidal thoughts were foreign to my nature. But that dismal afternoon I did consider it. A life lived in fear and threatened constantly is a life not worth living. Overcome with a deep sense of futility, I ran to the railroad tracks with the idea of throwing myself in front of a train. As I walked along the tracks, waiting for the 4:15 from Gardelegen to come roaring round the curve, I got hold of myself. I thought of Guido, Mama, Papa, and Kiev . . . Kiev might soon be liberated and all the traces of my origin would be lost. I squared my shoulders and pressed my lips together. *I must stay alive, if for no other reason than to see the Nazis crushed*—with the *Wachtmeister* first.

Guido knew of my battle with the police. I had told him about it as though it were a joke. I didn't want to worry him. Now that the situation was more serious and I felt threatened, I hardly mentioned it.

I had also told Guido of my ethnic origin, but I did not reveal the Jewish half. The fact that I was a Christian *and* a Jew—and felt good about both, because I was both—was my secret and my burden to bear for as long as Hitler ruled Germany.

"You must meet my father," Guido was saying. "You'll love my old man. How about Christmas?"

"I'd dearly love to. But Christmas is too far off," I said, trying not to think about what might happen in the intervening months. "If I'm forced to put on the *Ost* badge, I'll be stuck in Wannefeld until the war ends. I'll try to get away sooner, though."

"I might be able to squeeze a few days leave and go with you. And I will, by God!" He whacked his thigh. "I'll pick you up, and we'll go to Munich together. I have an engagement present for you at home, a silver service for twelve." He pulled a small box from his pocket. "Here," he said, "I have something else." I opened the brocade box and gasped. It was a small watch with a black velvet band. I had always wanted to have a watch. "Do you like it?"

"Yes, yes I do. Oh, Guido—"

We melted into each other's arms. He kissed and caressed me, gliding his fingers over my breasts. The sensation was glorious. But when his hand tried to invade my inner sanctum, I stiffened. I was determined to remain pure until the wedding night. When he did not persist, I loved him even more.

★　★　★

"Herr Brune, look!" I called after him. He stopped along the *Dorfstrasse*, one foot on the pedal of his bike, the other on the ground. I proudly displayed my ring that had belonged to Guido's beloved mother.

"Well, well." He squinted in the sun, his mouth twisted in an uncertain smile.

I had expected him to be surprised—it all happened so fast. But I did not expect he'd react so dispassionately. *Maybe he's concerned about losing an office clerk? That must be it*, I thought. "We don't intend to marry right away," I assured him, and I was struck by another thought, a tantalizing idea. "You think it is possible for me to marry now, yes?" And I beamed.

"Stop toying with your ring," he said impatiently. "Who is it you're engaged to?"

"Guido Schneble."

"The Luftwaffe sergeant? He can't marry you. Impossible."

"Are you absolutely, positively certain it is impossible?"

"What do you mean 'absolutely positively'? It's against the law."

"Maybe this law isn't all that strict. Would you mind if I asked Herr *Landrat* about it?"

"Talk to him. He'll tell you the same thing." He glanced at his pocket watch. "I must run." I showed him my shiny watch. He smiled then and pedaled away.

The *Landrat* (district president) had been there recently and left with one carton each of canned asparagus, cherries, string beans, and peas. I hoped he had a large family so I wouldn't have to wait too long for his return.

In the meantime, we were busier than ever. It was harvest season, and the factory was spitting out cans in record numbers. More girls had been hired—more people and a bigger payroll for me to deal with. I also had to arrange accommodations for the evacuees who were dropping anchor in Wannefeld, also in record numbers.

Frau Magda Ahring, one of the recently arrived evacuees, was promptly hired by Gottlieb Brune to share office work with me. She was a native of Hamburg, a friendly blond lady with a boyish, slim figure who wore sneakers. Her face was tanned and shiny, her eyes bright and blue. "Call me Magda," she said, with the simplicity I soon learned to appreciate about her. I told her about my engagement.

"I'm glad for you," she said. "What are the wedding plans?"

"We'll have to wait until the war is over. The present law is against us."

She thought about that for a moment, and then she frowned. "What makes you think you could marry a German *after* the war? You don't expect the law to change, do you?"

"It won't have to change. It'll be wiped out because"—*I nearly trapped myself. I must be more careful in the future about what I say*—"because after Germany has won the war, all of Europe will be 'one People, one Reich, one Führer,' " I quoted with pomp and in an overbearing manner, imitating Nazi orators of the day. "As Europeans, we'll all be citizens of this great Reich, sort of Germans automatically. Therefore, there will be no need for such laws."

I was not sure Magda was fooled by my attempt to extricate myself, but she did not argue. How could she? To disagree would be admitting that under Hitler, Germany could never become an enlightened nation. I congratulated myself, amused.

Magda had been in Hamburg during the massive raids of July and August 1943, when as many as fifty thousand people were killed.

"I'll never get over the horrors of it," she said, and continued in a low voice. "Thousands were killed instantly, thousands buried alive. Most people burned alive . . . The bombing started the fires, and a storm broke out. A firestorm. Sidewalks disintegrated from the intense heat, people were on fire." She lit a cigarette with trembling hands. "I still wake up at night with their screams echoing in my head. I escaped the flames by diving into the water. But even the water burned, from the oil spilled from the ships. The streets were littered with charred corpses. Our city burned for ten days. A horrible nightmare."

You started the war, you deserve it, I thought unsympathetically. To Magda I said, "That's a sacrifice you have to make toward an ultimate victory."

I was hoping to elicit the response "Who wants victory at this price?" But Magda remained silent.

Life in Wannefeld was not only work, it was also education. Apart from trying to learn English from a grade school teacher to whom I taught algebra, my sex education was broadened considerably. With no young men around, the local girls were hungry for love, and they talked without restraint about their exploits with older men and the rare soldier home on leave.

Three of us girls gathered for a *Kaffeeklatsch* (hen party) at Hoppe's Inn one Sunday afternoon when Heidi said, "I had it with a man here the other day." She grinned wickedly.

"Did Hoppe let you rent a room for *that*?" I was intrigued despite myself.

"Oh no. We did it right here." She tapped the bench we were sitting on. "I sat astride his lap, like on a horse, and he transported me into ecstasy. Mmm," she sighed, rolling her eyes, as though reliving the ecstasy.

I marveled at the nerve she had. *German girls are certainly uninhibited*, I reflected, vastly different in this respect from the Soviet girls.

"How is your Guido?"

When I risked confiding in them that I had never slept with Guido, they all but laughed at my old-fashioned idea of waiting for the wedding night.

"Then you're stupid!" Margot declared. "How can you marry a man without knowing what he's like in bed? *Kauf nicht die Katze im Sack* ['Don't buy a cat in a sack']. Suppose you're not suited together?"

"How would I know?" I chuckled. "All cats are gray in the dark."

"You'll know. The sparks will fly and light up the room, if he's able to satisfy you."

31

HOPE

Gottlieb Brune was the proud owner of an aging two-door sedan, a weird contraption that ran on gas generated by a charcoal burner. He drove to Gardelegen on a rainy October afternoon, and I went along to see the *Landrat*.

Herr *Landrat* was a tall gentleman with silvery-white hair. He listened to my plea and was sympathetic, but his answer was the same as Brune's: "A German cannot marry a Russian."

"Then it is hopeless. I was afraid of that."

He leaned over his desk and in a clear voice said, "I did not say it was hopeless." My ears pricked up, and I listened carefully to what he had to tell me.

The *Landrat* spoke in a formal language, using unfamiliar words and terms, such as *Staatsbürgerschaft* (citizenship), *Eindeutschungsfähigkeit* (suitability to become a German national), and *Heiratsgenehmigung* (marriage permit). It was difficult to follow, but I understood that there was a possibility. A marriage permit from the *Kreisleiter der NSDAP* (the Nazi Party leader of the district) could be granted if and when I was declared suitable to become a German national.

"To accomplish this, you would first of all need to apply for German citizenship with the *SS und Polizei Führer* [SS and Police Headquarters]. You may or may not succeed, but you're well advised to try." The *Landrat* added that he would uphold the *Wachtmeister*'s position (meaning, of course, that the *Ost* label must be attached to my dress) if my application were denied after an investigation.

"While the application is being considered," the *Landrat* concluded, "you will be exempt from wearing the badge."

Exempt! That was all I needed to hear. Whether the Nazis would grant me German citizenship was in itself irrelevant, although the idea of achieving what appeared impossible was tantalizing. To go through the seemingly tedious and complicated procedure would be worth my while, I decided, a matter of gaining time. To stop the *Wachtmeister* from terrorizing me, that alone would be worth the trouble and give me the satisfaction I craved.

Highly satisfied with the outcome of my mission, I returned to Wannefeld by train and told Herr Brune of my conversation with the *Landrat*.

"Are you sure you want to marry the Bavarian?"

"Sure I'm sure."

"You hardly know him. He might not be what he seems."

"How can you know another person? By the time I know what's in his soul, I'll be old and gray."

"What kind of education does he have? Any idea what he wants to do after the war?"

"Not yet." I meant to ask Guido about that. "Anyway, we love each other. That's all that matters." I believed that everything else would take care of itself.

"When are you going to apply?"

"As soon as we're not so busy," I said, knowing that I would wait until the BBC reported Kiev liberated, to make sure all traces of my origin had been lost.

And then the *Wachtmeister* came again. Before he had a chance to unglue his lips, I took the plunge.

"I'm applying for German citizenship."

"Ha," he snorted. "You will never get it."

"We'll see."

"*We* shall see. You're a long way from being above suspicion."

Magda Ahring remarked later, "What an unpleasant man. Aren't you afraid of him?"

"I'm petrified. But *he* doesn't know it."

★   ★   ★

Early in November 1943, the voice came over the air: "This is London calling—" Static interfered but not enough to drown out the news that, after two years of occupation, Kiev was liberated.

Goose bumps ran up my spine. It was a very happy moment for me—but also painful. My roots had been cut off. The same impenetrable barrier that had existed between Russia and the rest of Europe before the war had sprung up again. *Will I ever be allowed to visit Kiev? Will I ever see Mama, Papa, friends, and family again?* I missed my people, so demonstrative and emotional, never afraid to cry when the mood moved them, to sing and dance spontaneously. I missed the sound of the mandolin and songs in my native tongue. I longed for the Dnieper and the smell of the black soil after the rain.

Sometimes late at night I wondered how things might have been had I not flunked French during the entrance exams at the Institute of Aeronautics. My life turned upside down when as a consequence I went to work for DURP and met Aleksandr Platonov. *If it hadn't been for him,* I thought unhappily, *I would not have left Kiev. Ah—but had I stayed as I'd wanted to, I'd be dead today.*

I went to file my application on the kind of clear and crisp autumn day that makes you feel wonderful to be alive. My application was accepted. Stage One was a success.

Soon I was summoned to appear before the *Rassenpolitisches Amt* (the Racial-Political Authority). The man who interviewed me wore a Nazi uniform. Aware he was testing my ability to express myself in German, I answered his questions with measured precision. Frau Mannheim's tutoring served me well. As did my ballet training, when I was told to walk across the room, turn around, and sit down again. He scrutinized my profile, checked my forehead, and looked into my eyes. While keeping a straight face, I chuckled inwardly. Many Germans, who knew me as a Russian, had told me that I looked German. How could this superficial examination determine that half of me was Jewish? I felt confident that it could not.

The interviewer was stern but not entirely robot-like. He even smiled at the conclusion of the interview.

"Good—Aryan," he said. "You will soon be notified about fingerprinting and a blood test."

Oops! Is my blood different from the Aryan? I didn't know and it worried me—the entire few seconds it took to close the door after me. *Ridiculous! The whole thing is ridiculous,* I thought as I stepped outside into the fresh, open air. *But if that's what it takes to stop the Wachtmeister from terrorizing me and get a marriage permit, it's all right with me.*

★   ★   ★

A few days later I met Guido's father and saw Munich for the first time, a beautiful and exciting city even in those grim days of blackouts and air raids and bombing attacks.

"Greetings, *Kinder* [children]! Welcome, welcome home." Herr Schneble shook our hands, his eyes warm and vital. I squeezed Guido's arm to tell him his father was wonderful. I could have kissed them both there and then. Father and son had the same almond-shaped dark eyes, full sensuous lips, and the same winning smile. The father was stocky, his sparse hair and trim mustache gray, his eyebrows dark brown—a kind, caring man, a gentleman. "How long can you stay?"

"Two days. Before taking Sopherl home, I want her to meet Pia in Ruhpolding. Isolde might want to join us. How about you?"

"No, I think you young people would rather be alone. How was the trip?"

Guido cocked his head and pursed his lips. "It's getting worse every day. I've been in transit for over forty-eight hours—Paris to Berlin, Berlin to Gardelegen, Gardelegen to Wannefeld. I picked up Sopherl and back to Berlin again. We had to stand on the train between Berlin and Halle. But so what! Right, Sopherl?" I agreed wholeheartedly.

"Ah, that's youth for you. It takes no account of such inconveniences when the end promises to be exciting."

The apartment on Pettenbeck Strasse, near Marienplatz, where Guido grew up, was spacious and spotless. From the high, ornate ceiling in the main room hung a crystal chandelier. An appetizing aroma wafted in the air from the white braided bread Herr Schneble had baked that morning.

"Guido tells me you stay in touch with your mother," he said as we sat down to eat at the kitchen table, which was scoured to a creamy white. "I can imagine how she feels to be separated from you, her only child. It must be hard on her."

"I'm sure it is. I miss her too." He shook his head sadly when I told him that my parents were divorced and that I left Kiev without my mother when the war broke out. He listened pensively when I described my trek across the steppes to Stalingrad and back again. "I got stranded in Zaporozhye and hated it," I said, remembering every detail of my precarious existence in that town early on and the lingering uncertainty beyond. "Now I'm glad for it. Else Guido and I would never have met."

Herr Schneble wanted to know how I was treated in Wannefeld, and he agreed that it was a good idea I had applied for German citizenship. "Knowing how slowly civil matters are decided by the government agencies these days, this will eliminate your problems with the *Wachtmeister* for some time."

"He doesn't scare me as much anymore," I hastened to add. Since the *Kreisleiter* and the SS had ignored the fact that I had no valid documents, I felt less threatened by the *Wachtmeister*.

"From your description of the interview with the SS, it is not inconceivable you might succeed. Imagine, an illustrious Nazi warrior marrying a Soviet Russian under the flag of the Third Reich!" He laughed heartily. "You must, you positively must succeed."

"If not," the hardly illustrious warrior interjected, "we'll just have to wait for this bloody war to end before Sopherl can be mine."

"How did you manage to get another leave so soon? God forbid you're absent without leave."

Guido's eyebrows converged over the bridge of his nose, and it made him look menacing. He muttered, "It wasn't easy."

The father knew his son. Guido *was* absent without leave, and he would serve a sentence of three months in a military prison in Paris. When he wrote to me about it, I took it as a sign of true love. To think that he would risk imprisonment just to spend a few extra days with me!

There was so much gladness in my heart. Herr Schneble said, "I would be very pleased if you'd call me Vater." And I did, even though I was not yet his daughter-in-law. He gave my cheek a moist kiss, and that did not seem to me strange either.

Guido's sister Isolde and her husband, an engineer, came to meet me. After another day with Papa Schneble, we took a train to visit their older sister Pia, who had evacuated with her two small children to Ruhpolding, a resort town in the Alps.

How intelligent they are, I thought, *such fine people, so warm and sensitive. All of them!* Greatly impressed, I anxiously looked forward to marriage. I had never had a real family—no brothers or sisters. There was only Mama today, Papa tomorrow. I longed to become a member of Guido's family, longed to have a home, a home filled with the laughter of happy children, all in a new Germany about to be reborn.

★   ★   ★

In June 1943, a month after I arrived in Wannefeld, I had a prophetic dream. The interpretation came to me after I woke up. Along a wide cobbled road going north, people (the Germans) were scurrying back and forth in mute panic, as if not sure which way to turn. Two large bodies of water (the English Channel to the west, the Soviet Union to the east) flanked the road, which was blocked by a building of some sort. I faced that building. To the west on a rocky island (beyond the Channel) stood an enormous lion (England). People near me were thrusting spears at him (the weaponry the Germans were so proud of), but the spears broke on contact; the lion remained unharmed. On my right was a calm ocean (the Soviet Union); not a ripple disturbed its surface. Then the ocean began to churn. The roaring waves rose higher and higher; each violent surge lapped up another and yet another part of the road until only a narrow strip of land remained; the waves engulfed those who stood near the shore. I saw my cousins Valya and Igor swept into the ocean. Their heads bobbed above the water as they floated away. I turned to the south and took the only opening in the road, away from the obstruction ahead, away from the ocean.

I felt so sure the Red Army would reach Wannefeld that I left a note of welcome for them in Russian, on the underside of the linoleum being installed in my room in June 1943. "*Priviet!* [Greetings!]" I wrote in chalk. "*Dobro pozhalovat* [Welcome]."

That fall, the beer-mug-wielding general at Hoppe's Inn quoted from a bulletin: "We're holding on to the Dnieper. The Bolsheviks won't pass beyond that line, and in the spring we'll push them back beyond the Volga." At the dawn of 1944 the mood at the Inn was growing more optimistic. The men talked about a new weapon, a mysterious weapon that "will destroy England." And I thought to myself, *England is immune to your weaponry, and the Soviets will defeat you. It won't be long before they come.*

I hoped I would not be there when the Soviets marched in. I was not about to be swept into that ocean.

32

HALF-CRAZY, OR IN LOVE

At seven in the morning on January 5, 1944, an unexpected caller rapped at my door. "Come in," I said automatically. People dropped by all the time, though rarely at such an early hour.

The door swung open, and in walked Otto Schubert.

"Happy New Year!"

I stood before him as if paralyzed. "Good luck and gladness to you too," I murmured.

"Actually, I was hoping to be here January first."

"What a beautiful thought."

"It didn't work out as I planned."

"Seldom does. It certainly is a surprise to see you."

"This is my first leave in well over a year."

"It doesn't matter. I'm glad to see you." *But what is he doing to me?* The joy I felt at the sight of him was followed by an almost physical blow to my heart. I felt numb with happiness and anguish, torn between my love and loyalty to Guido and the strong attraction I still felt for Otto. I hadn't written him about my engagement. The thought of having to tell him now tormented me. I wished I had written him and was glad I had not. He would not have come. "For how long?"

"A week."

"A week!" *He mustn't stay that long.* "I work from eight to six. The inns are filled with evacuees. Where will you stay?"

"I'll find something in Gardelegen."

To commute by train between Gardelegen and Wannefeld for a week! He must be half-crazy, or in love. "You're no longer with the Wi-Kdo, I see." He was wearing a smart black uniform.

"I'm now attached to Hermann Göring Panzer Division."

"The same clerical duties as before, I hope?"

"Possibly. I won't know until next week, when I report in Berlin-Reinickendorf. By the way, *Schatz*, your German is fluent. I am impressed. How is your leather, still dry?"

I remembered Otto roaring with laughter when I showed him my hands in Zaporozhye and said my *leather*, instead of *skin*, was dry. Nearly two years had gone by since then. Now, as he touched my hand, I wished Guido's ring were on my finger instead of on the desk. He'd know then what I couldn't bring myself to tell him.

Before leaving that morning, he asked if something was troubling me. "You're not your exuberant self."

"Just a cold I had all week," I answered evasively. "It's given me a headache."

"Sorry to hear that." He kissed me quickly and went. "Until tonight."

Otto was back shortly after six. "He jumped off the train before it slowed down," Frau Zucker later reported to me. "He could've broken his legs!" I myself had not been able to concentrate on my work, thinking about him and Guido, trying not to compare them. Although I loved Guido dearly, I felt strongly attracted to Otto.

He dusted snowflakes off his greatcoat, wiped his boots on the doormat, and smiled an alluring smile as he walked in.

"How is your pretty head, still aching?" He took my hands in his, and then dropped them as his glance fell upon my ring. He crossed the room. Rooted to the spot, I watched him look at Guido's photograph. "It must be wonderful to be loved," he said in a disheartened undertone, as if speaking to the photograph.

I moved my lips to say, "It would be wonderful to be loved by you," but I said nothing. I knew now that he did love me, as I had loved him. And I thought of the dream I had had when Guido came to visit me the first time: Otto, shrouded in fog, calling to me, "I'm here." *He was here. He did come, but too late.*

Each day Otto arrived on the six o'clock train and left at eleven. But he and I were rarely alone. If not my roommates, local girls dropped by. I chatted with lightness and gaiety, all the while resenting having to share Otto with these uninvited guests who stayed too long.

I wrote in my diary and to Christine: "How frustrating it must be for Otto. He didn't come to Wannefeld to see all these people—he came to see me. He was so quiet, never said a word to betray his feelings. And neither did I. I remained strong and loyal to Guido. He's still in prison, serving his sentence for having gone AWOL because of me . . ."

Sunday was the one full day Otto and I could be alone together. He came early that cold January day, riding a bicycle through the snow from Gardelegen, his face flushed from the fast ride. But we were not to be alone.

At nine that morning another surprise visitor knocked at my door. The man who stepped in was of moderate height; he wore a Nazi uniform. His hair was red, and my first reaction was that the stranger was Jewish and maybe didn't know it. In Russia, redheads were invariably Jewish—their hair was often bright red and curly, a rarity in Germany.

"Heil Hitler!" He clicked his heels. "Otto Axner." His amber eyes—the eyes of Inna Bregman, my childhood friend—smiled at me. The resemblance was startling.

Of all the people I corresponded with, the one I had never, ever expected to see was Otto Axner. I welcomed the man who had helped me stay in touch with my mother and who used to forward my parcels to her while he was still in Kiev. *Only why,* I groaned, *did he choose today to show up?*

This very likable, amiable man stayed all day, talking about Kiev and Russia, discussing the war and the new rocket bombs with "my" Otto—all the subjects that would have been of the greatest interest to me any other time. Hurriedly I arranged for a hearty breakfast, also dinner in my room. While urging them to eat, I myself could not.

Otto Schubert kept me in an emotional turmoil. I watched him closely when he was quiet and wondered what thoughts were going through his mind. My own mind agonized. *How is it possible to be in love with one man and feel so strongly attracted to another? If he reveals the depth of his feelings for me, will I break my engagement to Guido? What if Otto Axner hadn't shown up? Would I have dared to take the initiative?* But it was not in me to bare my soul to a man who had not bared his.

Of all the frustrating moments that accompanied Otto's visit, the worst was to be called downstairs on Sunday to be yelled at by the *Wachtmeister*. "So. Where are your papers?"

"I didn't get them yet. I'm still waiting to—"

"The waiting period is over. If you don't want to end up in prison where we know how to deal with obstinate Russians, you'd better stop stalling. You'll never get German papers," he hissed, and he slammed the door behind him.

Two days later Otto Schubert left to join the Panzer Division. The parting was poignant, neither of us sure of the other's feelings. Afterward I regretted that I had been able to disguise my feelings and emotions so well—deeply regretted having left so much unsaid.

Some months later Otto was wounded on the Eastern Front. His injuries and loneliness, probably, caused him to pour out his love for me in a letter, which arrived from a field hospital. By then it really was too late.

I knew, with sudden stark clarity, that I could never have married Otto. I loved Guido, believed in him, trusted him. The Nazis were still in power. Otto had never once discussed the war or politics with me, never said anything to indicate how he felt about the Nazis. Either he did not trust me, as Guido did, or he believed in the Nazi cause, as Guido did not. Either way, Otto was not the man for me, because with him I feared that I would have to live a lie for the rest of my life.

★   ★   ★

Following the latest encounter with the *Wachtmeister*, Herr *Landrat* asked how my application was going. When I told him I hadn't heard anything, he admonished me, "You must look into it immediately. Your exemption to wear *Ost* is at stake."

I retraced my steps: the Racial-Political Authority . . . the German Labor Front . . . the headquarters of the NSDAP . . . the SS and Police Headquarters in Gardelegen. My application, it turned out, had been misplaced. This, after I had waited for two months! The clerk assured me of quick action now that my file had been located. I thanked him with my fingers tightly crossed.

Another period of waiting began.

January ended on a sour note with Hitler's speech. *"Der Sieg wird unser sein!"* he cried. I sneered as I recorded his closing words, "Victory will be ours," in my diary. *How could anyone believe that twaddle!*

While I waited for my papers and watched the war get closer to Germany, the villagers watched and waited for the victory. Life was definitely not boring.

★   ★   ★

The citizens of Wannefeld were law abiding, and only a few times was the *Wachtmeister* actually called to the village on an emergency. Once was to subdue a boisterously drunk fellow from the Western Ukraine; he was put away for the night to cool off. Another time, a Soviet-Russian girl caused some trouble; she was the only other *Ostarbeiter* in Brune's employ and a new arrival. Her German was limited to a few curse words, so the *Wacht-*

meister was forced to use my services as an interpreter. This must have irked him as much as it thrilled me.

The girl was accused of assaulting the cannery supervisor, an unpleasant woman, and calling her a goddamn pig. It soon became obvious that a correct translation would land the girl in a lot more trouble. So when she said, "That bitch deserved it," I said that the girl didn't know what came over her. The *Wachtmeister* threatened to arrest her should she ever again raise so much as a finger against her German supervisor. Sullenly the girl replied, "Pushing me around. I'm not sorry. I'd do it again."

"She says she's sorry, Herr *Wachtmeister*. She'll never do it again."

The girl later said to me, "I hate that bitch. I don't want to work for her. Next time I'll squeeze the shit out of her."

"It will squirt all over you. They could put you in jail. It's called 'concentration camp' in Germany," I said. "If you want to give 'that bitch' the satisfaction, go ahead. Or do you think they'll give you another job elsewhere? They won't. You're far better off in Wannefeld anyway. So next time you had better hold your temper and your tongue."

★ ★ ★

Toward the end of 1943, following heavy raids on Berlin, Sarotti-Berlin, manufacturers of chocolates, evacuated several of its key male personnel to Kolonie-Mainz, a small settlement near Wannefeld, where Sarotti continued its production on a small scale using foreign workers, mostly Poles. Apart from chocolates, they brought with them gaiety and the Berliners' enjoyment of life. They had a marvelous sense of humor, laughing at themselves and at the current economic situation.

They ate at Hoppe's Inn. One man loved to play chess, and when he learned that I did too, he challenged me, and many an evening thereafter he invited me to eat with them after the game. To celebrate the New Year 1944, a wine bottle was uncorked. Wine was a rare treat for ordinary burghers in wartime Germany. Another cork popped when the Berliners celebrated their being alive.

The night air throbbed with the thunder of British and American bombers roaring overhead, full of lethal cargo for Berlin, Leipzig, Magdeburg, and Dresden.

The bombings of Berlin, Leipzig, and Oschersleben in February were devastating. We had a ringside view, and many Wannefelders stayed up half the night observing the spectacle. Flares and searchlights streaked across the black sky. Bomber planes hit by flak plummeted to earth in a ball of flames. The horizon was ablaze. Thundering explosions deafened us. We knew that the destruction must be horrendous, and that many people were being killed, yet it was impossible not to be fascinated; the display was magnificent. And I—knowing that every bombing mission was destroying more and more of Germany's war industry and bringing the Nazis closer to defeat—I tingled with excitement.

In broad daylight, March 8, 1944, darkness fell as the American Flying Fortresses blacked out the sun. I counted nine waves, each wave consisting of several hundred enormous bombers on their way to the saturation bombardment of Berlin. Dangerous as it was, everyone was outside and watching—some counting, others praying. The locals were frightened; the Berliners sang: "*Berlin bleibt doch Berlin.* [Berlin will still be Berlin.]" The foreign workers were as exhilarated as I was.

The Allies didn't waste their bombs on Wannefeld, but our electricity was disrupted, telephones went dead, and several planes crashed there. A British plane nose-dived into the blue waters of Polvitz Lake. A German fighter plane plunged behind the cannery, digging a deep hole in the garden and uprooting a linden tree.

A fierce dogfight between a German and a British fighter plane took place directly overhead. The duel ended in a draw: both planes crashed, both pilots bailed out and parachuted safely into Brune's fields. Everybody ran to where they were about to land, I ahead of everybody else. Brune ran hard behind me. When the British pilot landed, an angry crowd thrust forward, ready to dissect him. Brune managed to stave them off, yelling: "Don't harm him! He's a prisoner!"

Gottlieb Brune and a burly villager escorted the RAF pilot to our office. The crowd followed, shaking their fists and shouting. I doubt that the dark-haired Englishman was aware that there were a number of sympathizers in the crowd. He looked very frightened, his face ash-white, his hands shaking. He was only about twenty-two, so young. I kept smiling at him, like a village idiot, but he did not seem to notice.

A few moments later a cheering crowd ushered their German hero into our office, but Brune would not allow the crowd in. Physically, the contrast between the two pilots was marked. The German pilot was taller, a blue-eyed blond several years older than the Englishman. The two men looked at each other and then, spontaneously, approached one another and solemnly shook hands.

I glanced at Gottlieb Brune and through the mist in my eyes saw that he was also moved. After the angry scene outside, the handshake summed up the futility of the war.

33

CRISSCROSSING THE THIRD REICH

In March Guido was released from prison, and soon we were in each other's arms again. His transfer to an anti-paratroop artillery unit enabled him to stop over to see me for a day, one precious day.

Despite the cheerful tone of Guido's letters, I had been concerned that the three months in prison might subdue him and was glad to see they did not affect his spirits.

His transfer to a fighting unit, a penalty for his AWOL offense, was a new source of concern.

"Don't worry, Sopherl, I'll be all right. What's more, the transfer will allow me to spend Easter with you in Munich."

On Good Friday, after eighteen hours en route, I finally arrived in Munich. Traveling had become a hair-raising, bone-crushing experience. One had to force oneself bodily through a door or climb in through a window, my favorite sport. Once inside, one stayed glued to the same spot, propped up on all sides. Sleeping was not impossible. One simply closed one's eyes and dozed off without worrying about falling over—there was no room. The Leipzig-Munich stretch was particularly gruesome. That time I was not even allowed the luxury of standing on two feet—too many bags and parcels underfoot. Unflappable, I dozed flamingo-style.

Guido was to meet me in Munich, but he wasn't there, and Vater hadn't heard from him. What could have gone wrong?

Papa Schneble's new ladylove lived with him. We went for a stroll in the English Gardens, he and I, and he opened his sore heart. He loved the woman with passion and was very sad because his daughter, Isolde, did not approve of her.

"I shouldn't think you need anyone's approval."

"Ah, yes"—Papa Schneble nodded, eyes downcast—"I shouldn't, but I do. Isolde thinks I'm being deceived, taken advantage of. My instinct tells me Isolde might be right."

And so it was. No sooner was his home bombed out in summer 1944 than Ladylove abandoned him.

The girl who had preferred lifelong ignorance to getting involved in politics was now fascinated with Papa Schneble's politics. He talked to me about parliamentary democracy, the type of government he hoped would soon replace dictatorship in Germany. He spoke with enthusiasm about freedoms that only a democratically elected government could safeguard: freedom to establish trade unions, freedom of speech and thought, freedom to establish new parties and reestablish the old.

Friday drew to a close and still no Guido. On Saturday a telegram came: "Stuck in Gardelegen. Will arrive Sunday 11:58." I met him at the station. "What were you doing in Gardelegen?" It turned out he had gone to Wannefeld to pick me up the day after I left.

Easter in Munich brought us still closer together. Guido showered me with presents, among them silk stockings, a leather handbag, and khaki gabardine for a suit. He also had a red leather handbag for Magda Ahring and a bottle of French cognac for my boss. I felt happy knowing that the man I would someday marry was so thoughtful.

Soon we said *"Auf Wiedersehen"* to Father. Guido and I took a train to Berlin. We had a jolly trip with a bottle of wine, then amidst ruins and smoldering rubble I wished my *Schatz* goodspeed and sent him off to Gotha.

★   ★   ★

Christine Blaschke and I had been corresponding faithfully. Each of her letters sounded sadder than the last.

She had written at Christmas: "I wish you were still in Pudewitz. There's no one I can talk to, no one to understand. I feel so alone, so very unhappy. It's all so hopeless. I don't care if I live or die." Greatly disturbed, I wrote back imploring her not to give up hope. "It won't be long now before you're twenty-one. You can then marry Hans whether your parents like it or not . . ."

Christine did not answer this or my subsequent letters, though her mother continued to write to me. When four weeks had gone by and I hadn't heard from Frau Blaschke, I began to worry and wonder what could be wrong.

In March, Brune's two Nazi friends came to the office and related their trip to Posen to bring back ten Polish girls. En route to Gardelegen, five of the girls had escaped.

The men left, and I said to Brune, "No wonder half of them ran away. The poor girls were scared to death of these two . . . not-exactly-friendly-looking individuals. I'd be scared too. You did better by yourself. Even I could do better."

Brune gave me a patronizing half-smile.

"Why don't you send me to Posen," I suggested, thinking of Christine in nearby Pudewitz, Frau Mannheim, and Fräulein Trauber. "You do need more people, don't you?"

"Well, yes," Brune said. "But no, it's impossible."

"You always say 'impossible.' Nothing is impossible," said I. "Send me, and you'll see. The girls won't run away from me. I'll tell them what a kind and fair boss we have, and that nowhere in Germany could they find better working conditions."

The Polish girls, like thousands of my countrymen, were victims of a ruthless manhunt. They were rounded up on the streets and in churches, dragged from their homes, sent to assembly camps, and finally shipped to Germany as slaves. I knew that I would be doing them a good turn by escorting them to Wannefeld where they would be treated like human beings—not free, but neither as slaves—well fed and paid for their labor, and given medical care.

Brune hesitated for long moments.

"You need serradella." I bribed him with the variety of rye seed Karl Mannheim had promised to try to send him. "I'll see to it that you get some."

"I'll think about it."

Within a week my trip to Posen was approved. Brune had promised to drive me to Gardelegen but left without me. I had to take a train and missed my connection to Berlin. My joy and jubilation were not diminished by either the sleepless night sitting up in the station in Gardelegen, nor even by being caught in the heavy bombing of Berlin, which made me run for shelter to the Friedrich Strasse underground station and caused the train to Posen to be delayed.

I called Christine the moment I stepped off the train. No one answered. I called Frau Mannheim.

"Sophia! Where are you? Posen! I can hardly believe it. When are you coming to see us?"

"First I must talk to Herr Sandau at the *Gauarbeitsamt*. Then after I've seen Christine—"

"Don't," Frau Mannheim broke in. "Not until after I've had a chance to talk to you. Finish your business in Posen and call me. We'll be at the station to meet you." The urgency with which she spoke filled me with foreboding.

I attended to my business, extracting a promise from Herr Sandau that the girls Brune wanted would be available—but not until Tuesday. *Great!* It was only Saturday.

Frau Mannheim, Gretchen, and Georg Mannheim, who resembled his younger brother Karl, met me at the station in Pudewitz. They were all smiles. "What a pleasant surprise. Good to see you."

"Gretchen, how you have grown." Her flaxen braids had grown long and were interlaced with silk ribbons the color of her light blue eyes. "A little girl has turned into a lady."

Gretchen blushed. "You look prima. I like your hat, it's chic." (I liked the hat myself; it had cost me only a few cans of vegetables.)

Everyone was talking all at once, a heartwarming reunion. I hadn't dreamed it would be quite like this.

"Who would have thought you'd be back so soon?" said Frau Mannheim.

"Certainly not I." I told them how it happened, and they seemed pleased that I had gone to so much trouble to see them.

"We were all so worried about you." Georg Mannheim was a mild-mannered man, and he spoke in a soft tone of voice.

Frau Mannheim glanced at him. "She seems content," she said, and turned back to me questioningly.

"I am. I have many reasons to be."

"Was it difficult for you at first?"

"No. I did not exaggerate when I wrote you. Everything worked out well from the start. If Herr Brune hadn't shown up at the *Gauarbeitsamt* that April day, I don't know what might have happened . . . I wouldn't be here today, that's for sure. So I have much to be grateful for. My boss wants results, but he rarely interferes, and this suits me well."

"It's amazing how you have changed," Frau Mannheim said reflectively. "You've lost the weight you'd gained with us and are so slim. It's becoming. But more importantly, you seem to have matured. Tell me, what's this about your trying to get German citizenship. Are you serious?"

"Yes. I'm not sure I'll get it, but I did apply."

"One never knows what our Sophia will try next." She shook her head with a little smile. "There's no limit to your imagination."

"Don't give me more credit than I deserve." *It doesn't take much imagination when survival is at stake,* I thought to myself. "I'm striving to achieve my goals, the most important one of which is, of course, to marry Guido."

We sat around the dining room table and talked nonstop.

"By the way, where can I get serradella seed? I promised my boss to get him some, if only a handful."

"No problem," said Georg Mannheim, and two weeks later Gottlieb Brune was the happy recipient of not one but eight large sacks full of the seed.

What a gratifying experience to be the guest of honor, I reflected, *to have people hang on every word that passes my lips, to watch them glance at me approvingly, to linger over all the photographs I brought with me.* Even Fräulein Trauber tore herself away from her suffering patients to join the family reunion. She leaned on my elbow and said into my ear, "I'll be hurt if you spend the entire time in Birkenhof."

After dinner, I sank back into a chintz-covered armchair. The eleven months I had spent with Frau Mannheim rolled over in my mind like a reel of film. I had liked and disliked her intermittently. Overall, though, I did feel good about her, for she was fair and kind, considering the circumstances. I hoped this visit would bring us closer together. I especially hoped she had come to realize that I did not share her husband's feelings for me. If not, then my good intentions in visiting her and showing my respect should remove any of her doubts. The one thing I felt positive about was that she had no idea he had visited my mother and me.

Frau Mannheim joined me in the sitting room. She brought a tray with two glasses and a decanter with sweet red wine. Filling the glasses, she asked, "Have you heard from my husband recently?"

"I had a postcard from him," I answered truthfully. "But no, not recently."

"I hoped you might have a clue as to his whereabouts. His letters no longer indicate that." A worry line furrowed her brow. "He's not in Zaporozhye, I know, as I'm sure you do."

"I guessed as much." Zaporozhye had been abandoned by the Wehrmacht months before.

"You mean to say you've stopped writing to each other? I find it difficult to believe. You were so close."

Though diplomacy was not my strong point, I tried to be diplomatic. "I feel close to both of you," I said. "That's why I'm here today. As for corresponding with your husband, it's enough for you and me to correspond, don't you agree? It's enough for me. Please give Herr

Mannheim my warmest greetings. Surprise him with my surprise visit to see you. He'd love that."

"I certainly will."

"Tell me about Christine, please. What's wrong with her?"

"She's very sick, Sophia. There are rumors in town, but don't ask me to pass them on."

"I must see her first thing tomorrow."

"Don't be hurt if they turn you away. No one has been allowed to see her these past three or four months."

★ ★ ★

Frau Blaschke was surprised but did not show any pleasure at seeing me. Looking drawn, she asked me into the sitting room. Her voice was tired. "Christine is not well."

"May I talk to her?"

"No, Sophia. She mustn't be disturbed."

"Please, Frau Blaschke. I came all this way to see her."

"I'm sorry."

"Mutti," Christine's voice came from the adjoining room, barely audible. "I want . . . Sophia," she added with painful effort.

After some hesitation, Frau Blaschke allowed me to see Christine, pleading weakly, "Please, don't excite her."

I had expected my friend to be seriously ill, but what I saw shocked and dismayed me. I hardly recognized her. Bloated and discolored, she lay in bed, a heartbreaking sight.

"My dear Christine," I whispered, covering my mouth with my hand.

"Sophia," was all she said, glancing up at me with glazed eyes. I sat at her side for five minutes, an hour; I had no idea how long. We didn't say a word, just looked at one another in the total stillness of the room. Her physical pain must have been unbearable, but the mental suffering in her eyes was even greater. When Christine closed her eyes, I tiptoed out of the room. Weeping, I could only cling to Frau Blaschke and murmur some broken words of the deep sorrow and affection I felt for my friend.

Monika and I met at the cafe. "Please, Monika, tell me what's wrong with Christine."

"She is very sick."

"I know. But what is she suffering from? We're friends, close friends. I'm suffering with her."

"She's pregnant."

"Hans Auer?"

"Yes. The baby is due any day."

"Did they get married?"

"My parents refused to give Christine their permission."

"And?" There must be more. Surely a child out of wedlock was no tragedy. A girl in Nazi Germany was awarded the title of *Frau* after the baby's birth, and the child was not considered illegitimate. But Monika would say no more.

Talking to Fräulein Trauber that afternoon, I was able to piece together the story of my friend's desperation.

"I know the doctor. When he confirmed Christine's fear that she was pregnant," Fräulein Trauber said, "she apparently went to the hospital to talk to the orderly. What transpired between them is anybody's guess. The one thing I know is that the orderly already has a wife and four children in Bavaria. He probably told her he could never marry her."

"What a bastard!"

"The desperate girl tried to abort the child herself and got blood poisoning."

Three weeks after my visit, Christine died in childbirth. Her baby lived and was adopted by the Blaschkes. Christine was buried on April 16, the day before I arrived in Pudewitz for the second time. I went to the cemetery and put a wreath on the fresh mound, sank to my knees, and wept.

★   ★   ★

On Tuesday, eight strapping Polish girls returned with me to Wannefeld. The journey went smoothly, though it was nerve-racking when going through Berlin. The girls wrestling with their bulky bundles as we stampeded down the steps to the underground railway trains—with me leading the pack and watching over them like a mother hen—must have been a perplexing sight. The underground trains took off in a flash, and I was afraid one of the girls might get trapped between the doors or left stranded on the platform. So I squeezed and pushed them through the doors in the seconds allowed for us to leap on. It was tricky. I did not want to lose a single one of them, and not only because of the vainglorious statement I had made to Brune.

If one of the girls got lost, she would be picked up again and forced to work elsewhere in Germany. Whether the girls appreciated it at the time or not, I knew that it was to their advantage to be brought safely to Wannefeld. I had meant it when I said to Gottlieb Brune, "Where else in Germany could they find better working conditions?" If Brune did not take the girls, someone else would, and that someone else might be bigoted and cruel.

★   ★   ★

Fifty-five *Ostarbeiter* subsequently arrived in Gardelegen from Posen. Fifteen of them were assigned to work for Sarotti in Kolonie-Mainz, others in the agricultural enterprise of Lotti Brune, a relative of Gottlieb Brune, in Clüden.

I had wanted to share my good fortune with one of my own. But my hopes of meeting at least one girl from Russia were thwarted once again; none of the *Ostarbeiter* came to Wannefeld.

34

"IMAGINE, RUNNING INTO YOU!"

The population of Wannefeld had swelled from some four hundred when I arrived to about twelve hundred the next year. I was moved into an already fully occupied house belonging to Frau Platz. Above me, a cheery young mother of four made do with two rooms. My own room was small and so cluttered with odd pieces of furniture and bric-a-brac that there was no room for roommates.

I was alone, waiting for Guido, aching to be with him. I knew I shouldn't sulk; it had been only three weeks since we spent Easter in Munich together. But he had written to say he would come May 1.

It was past midnight when he showed up, soaking wet. He had missed the last train from Gardelegen, so he walked! He walked three hours in pouring rain, along a road that cut across deep forests, and in the dark, for me. Even Brune would appreciate Guido's devotion and why I loved him so.

Guido stripped off his wet clothes and snuggled beside me in the bed, kissing and caressing me. He slipped his hand inside my thighs. I closed my eyes and basked in the delicious sensations engulfing me. My inhibitions vanished, and I trembled with anticipation. But oh, what a disappointment! I felt nothing that first time. Was that all there was to it? Guido was an expert, so I knew it must be I who wasn't doing it right. Only later did warm tides of delight flood over me.

Now that we were one, I thought that nothing in the world could separate us. No problem seemed insurmountable.

Seven days later, for the seventh time in nine months, there he was again.

"How on earth did you manage to get another leave? Just couldn't stay away from me, could you?"

"I had to see you." The way he looked at me made me think of an old faithful dog with his tail between his legs. I knew something was drastically wrong. "I'm on sick leave."

"But you're not sick. Else you wouldn't be traveling."

"I have VD."

I gasped.

"It takes a while to know for certain. But I had to forewarn you. If I have what I think I have, you'll have to see a doctor immediately. I am sorry, Sopherl."

I was frantic. The shame of it! I was not married, I was no longer a virgin, and now I might have syphilis. I didn't have sense enough to ask and assumed Guido had, or thought he had, syphilis. I knew of no other venereal disease.

Nine long days later I received a telegram: False alarm.

On his twenty-sixth birthday, May 31, Guido was again sent to prison, this time for insubordination. *No dull moments with Guido!* The reason seemed trivial, and though I knew Guido had a problem with authority figures, it did not disturb me at the time. What upset me was that upon his release, because of this and previous offenses, he was promptly sent to France to fight—to fight, moreover, our liberators.

It was June 6, 1944, the day the Allied Forces landed on the beaches of Normandy.

★ ★ ★

Mid-June saw me in Posen for the third time. I arrived weighted down with a dozen bottles of wine for Herr Sandau, and a promise of more wine for his daughter's wedding if he provided the wine cellars, Weinkellerei Klötze, with twenty-five workers. Herr Sandau was obliging.

My mission finished with the delivery of the bribe, and no time for Pudewitz, I decided to have a leisurely lunch at my favorite *Konditorei* before returning to Wannefeld.

As I approached the café, I heard a voice from the past.

"*Sophia!*" Karina yelled. My shy neighbor at the *Damenstift* in Zaporozhye didn't sound so shy anymore.

I had kept in touch and visited with several Zaporozhye girls now in Germany. I already knew that Karina lived in Lublin, in the General Government, the German-controlled part of Poland.

Karina joined me for lunch. "What are you doing in Lublin?" I asked.

"I work for the SD," she revealed.

It was the SD, allied with the Gestapo and controlled by the SS Führer Heinrich Himmler, that was carrying out the extermination of Jews, the Final Solution.

When Karina mentioned that most of the girls working with her were ethnic Germans from the Ukraine, I asked if by any chance she knew Liza Krause. Tetya Valya's son Svetik had dated Liza; she was a next-door neighbor.

Incredibly, my eyes at that very moment collided with those of Liza Krause. We ran up to each other. Still standing in the middle of the crowded café, Liza fired the question: "How on earth did you get here from Kalach? Imagine, running into you like this."

"One chance in a million, if that."

"When Valentina Sergeyevna [Tetya Valya] returned from Rostov, she told me you were on your way to Kalach-on-Don and on to Kazakhstan, most likely. Strange that our paths should cross in Posen."

"Very strange indeed." I asked about Tetya Valya.

"She left Kiev when the Wehrmacht was pulling out—about the same time I did," said Liza. "I think she's in Lvov now."

"And my father, did she not wait for him?"

"Oh Sonya, I wish you hadn't asked. He was killed. Killed in action," she added. "At Poltava, in September '41."

When I recovered from the shock, I realized that precisely at that time I was about to make my pilgrimage from Kharkov to Kiev, through the battlefields at Poltava.

A lump in my throat was choking me, but I willed myself not to cry. *I never told Papa how I loved him; now he is gone and he will never know just how much. I never asked and will never know about his life as a boy. I wanted to know where my grandparents had come from and about our Jewish roots, but I never asked, and now it's too late.* I recalled his parting words, "I'll fight for Kiev and our homeland to the last drop of my blood," and felt tears sting my eyes.

Liza and I exchanged addresses with promises to write. I looked at her address and felt my stomach lurch. She also worked for the SD. *Will she give me away?* My old fears returned, mounting into an anxiety even more agonizing than fear.

★   ★   ★

The Weinkellerei Klötze gave me a case of wine when I returned. "For your wedding," they said. Sarotti men presented me with a dozen each of wine and liqueur glasses. "For your wedding," they said. "When will it be?" I asked my diary. "Will I ever get my papers? The uncertainty is tormenting me."

Seven days later, on June 22, I wrote: "It's been three years since my country was forced into the war. When will it end? I'm tired of worrying about what might happen if . . . Why, oh why, did I have to run into Liza Krause?"

Mid-August, Guido arrived in Wannefeld for the eleventh time. He had volunteered to join the *Fallschirmjäger*, the Parachute Corps, to be near me while training in Wittstock. The news added to my desperation.

"Why did you do that? Why risk your life, you lovable idiot? Parachutists face far too many dangers. I'm afraid, Guido. I'm afraid you might get killed. You could be shot out of the sky or killed at the front. *If* you land alive."

"Don't worry about me," said he, "I've got it all figured out. By the time I'm through training—and believe me, I'm going to make it last—the war will be over."

I was not convinced. This, plus my concern at having received no news about my papers, the *Landrat's* accelerated pressure to resolve the matter, and no word from Liza Krause, was intolerable.

"O Lord, grant me the wish to get the papers," I prayed. "I'd be free then, free to leave and hide out in the Alps. If the baby in my womb and I survive the war, I'll never trouble you again."

Ten days later Guido reappeared, his face black and blue. Parachuting from an aircraft at night, he had crashed upon the rifle of a comrade in front of him and landed unconscious. "Don't let it scare you," he said, gazing at me through the slits of his swollen eyes. "This at least earned me another sick leave."

Guido couldn't wait to tell me he had secured a wedding permit from his commanding officer.

"I'll be happy if I can get mine before the baby is born," I said, hoping my news would bring him joy.

"Are you trying to tell me you're pregnant?"

"Yes! Yes, I am."

"Are you sure? How do you know?"

"I just do." My inner monthly monitor had told me so. "I knew it soon after you were here the last time, during the battle at Monte Carlo in Italy in August 1944. The baby is due around mid-May."

"Terrific!" He lifted me off my feet, hugged me and kissed me, and then he said, "It better be a boy."

"Whatever will be, will be, my love."

"Father would love to hear our happy news." He whacked his thigh. "Let's go to Munich."

Brune grumbled but gave me three days off. I wished I were going to Munich never to return. But Papa Schneble was out of town. His home had been destroyed in July. Munich lay in ruins. Innumerable buildings looked like nothing but heaps of stone.

Immediately upon my return, I went to the *Polizei Führer*'s headquarters. And there, on top of the desk, lay my application.

On September 5, I talked to the *Kreisleiter der NSDAP* himself. I approached him with almost insane self-confidence born from frustration and the determination to get the matter settled one way or another, once and for all.

Two days later my application was approved. The near impossible had happened. I was declared *Eindeutschungsfähig* (suitable to become a German national) and could apply for German citizenship, which I didn't bother to do. But I did apply for a provisional *Kennkarte* (identification card) immediately, which Herr *Landrat* would sign on September 13, 1944, and forward to me by mail. I did not wait for it.

Although I was now legally free to leave, Brune would not release me. "Not until I find a replacement," he said.

The marriage permit issued by the *Kreisleiter* was already in my hands. So when Gottlieb Brune checked into a hospital for some tests, I left without his knowing. With Soviet troops already in Poland and Czechoslovakia, it was high time I got out anyway. I did not want to be trapped in Wannefeld.

35

OFF TO THE ALPS

I can still feel the tremendous sense of relief I had when the departure whistle blew and the train carrying me to the safety of the Bavarian Alps began to roll.

Two weeks later Guido and I were married in Ruhpolding, a picturesque town in the Bavarian Alps: first in a civil ceremony, then two days later in a church where after Mass four young men in Wehrmacht uniforms and their brides in their Sunday best were called to the altar. A few words spoken by the priest, and four couples were simultaneously pronounced man and wife before God. I looked down on rows of impersonal faces, strangers at my wedding, and I smiled.

All too soon Guido had to leave, and I would not see him again for six months.

Ruhpolding had accepted yet another homeless evacuee. A room in the Fuschlbergers' farmhouse on Unterberg Mountain was my refuge. Below the steeply sloping fields, where placid cows with bells on their collars ruminated, Guido's sister Pia and her two small children were staying in a cottage the family rented every summer. Her home in Munich had been gutted by the bombs, as was Papa Schneble's.

My gentle sister-in-law Pia and I became close. I loved this intelligent, tall, stately woman with big brown eyes, the "Schneble eyes" inherited from their Italian grandfather. Pia was rather heavy in those days. In her youth, she had studied music and aspired to be a Wagnerian opera singer. She named her firstborn Richard, after the composer; the two-year-old was named Isolde.

It was during that time that I received my last letter from Karl Mannheim, a deeply moving, soulful letter beginning with a poem and recalling our meetings from the first to the very last. He wished me happiness in marriage.

"The only picture I have of you," he wrote, "is a copy of the one once displayed in the photographer's window in Zaporozhye. It was presented to me by one of your former coworkers." Dunya Kovalenko, the clerk from DURP, instantly came to mind, and I knew Mannheim was alluding to her. "It will always remind me of the remarkable girl who retained her sunny outlook on life in the face of bitter reality," he continued. "The war won't last much longer, Sophia. Be proud you managed to survive," he wrote, confirming that he knew I was a Russian Jew and that he had saved my life.

★   ★   ★

When deep snow covered the Alps, Pia and I retired to our private worlds. My world was quiet; I was alone but not lonely. The scenery surrounding my mountaintop retreat was magnificent. I talked to my unborn child, who was beginning to stir within me, read everything I could find, and listened to the war news and Charles Dickens's *A Christmas Carol* on the BBC.

Pia had given me a 220V radio, which I reserved for BBC broadcasts. Because Ruhpolding was still on 110V and transformers were not available, I strung wires between an overhead light and the radio, with a lightbulb in series with the radio, to adjust the voltage from 220V to 110V. The contraption worked, but for how long? I held my breath each time I strung the floating wires to listen behind closed doors to the BBC.

Papa Schneble came struggling up the hill one day and advised me to stop listening to the BBC. "One cannot be careful enough. Rest assured the war is rapidly approaching its final stages. The days of the Third Reich are numbered."

American bombers, on their way from Italy to raid Munich, Augsburg, or Regensburg, flew over our heads, dropping empty fuel tanks and foil strips, which served as an anti-radar device. Walking clumsily through the crunchy snow, I collected these sparkling streamers and used them as tinsel for my Christmas tree.

"It's sacrilege!" The unemotional Frau Fuschlberger, my landlady, was appalled.

At the end of 1944, Guido's unit was engaged in fierce front line fighting in the west, retreating toward the Rhine. The Soviets were closing in on Germany from the east. The Allied Forces in Italy were approaching Germany from the south.

Guido's now rare letters were depressing; the war was grating on his nerves. Morale in the ranks was low, and many were surrendering to the Anglo-American forces rather than go on fighting for a lost cause.

I hadn't heard from Guido for two months when in March he showed up, sneaking into Ruhpolding after dark.

"I deserted the Wehrmacht," he said.

"You needn't have done that, darling. The war is nearly over." I couldn't bear to think of my husband as a deserter, which to me had always been synonymous with cowardice.

"Why risk getting killed on the eve of peace?" he said. And when he stroked my stomach and listened to the baby's heartbeat, I agreed.

The night darkened as the moon disappeared behind a cloud. Guido rose from the bed, ready to depart. Yet again.

"Will I be able to let you know when the baby is born? Where are you hiding out?" I asked, holding on to him, kissing him.

"In the Alps," he said, afraid to say more lest I might be questioned and forced to give away his whereabouts. "I'll keep in touch and meet you in Traunstein when I think it's safe."

We met in Traunstein on April 18, 1945. Despite the snow that covered the mountains, Guido had emerged from his hideaway on a bicycle. He could not travel by train since the military police were making scrupulous checks for deserters. As we were having lunch near the railroad station, the air raid sirens wailed.

"Let's get the hell out of here," Guido said, and I obeyed though I wasn't a bit nervous. Neither Traunstein nor Ruhpolding had ever been bombed.

We had scarcely crossed the railroad tracks when the American bomber escort planes began dropping flares, outlining the area to be bombed. We were inside that area, and the Flying Fortresses were close behind them.

"Down on the ground!" Guido shouted.

I hugged the ground where I stood, careful not to crush my belly. Facing the tracks—still irrationally convinced that I was in no danger—I turned my head to look for Guido, but he was nowhere near. I craned my neck at the darkening midday sky and realized to my horror that the huge four-motored planes were directly overhead. I can still see very clearly the first hatches opening up, the first bombs hesitating and vibrating for a split second before whining through the air.

"Dear Mother of God, have pity on my child," I prayed, as the planes began to rain clusters of bombs. Thunderous explosions rocked the earth. The air was thick with black whistling death. Flying debris and shell fragments splattered all around me. I lay only about a hundred paces away from their target, the railroad.

In the quiet that followed, Guido's voice ordered me to run. "Another wave is on its way!" I scrambled to my feet, astounded that I was in one piece, and waddled like a duck to join Guido in the shelter of some trees. Only then did my eight-months-pregnant body begin to shake and shudder, and I noticed that the hair on my arms was standing on end. Guido's eyes were wide, his face pale.

The heavy throb of the bombers and the thunder of bombs once again filled the air. I pressed myself against Guido as we watched the vital railroad artery between Munich and Austria being smashed.

When the planes flew back to Italy from where they came and the sirens sounded the all clear, Guido took off on his bicycle to his hideaway. I walked a mile or so to find and board the little train stranded halfway between Traunstein and Ruhpolding. Then I trudged and struggled for nearly two hours up Unterberg Mountain through snow so deep that I sank in it up to my knees each step I took. I finally got home and collapsed into bed.

The baby had been kicking merrily throughout the ordeal.

At night my water broke. *An accident*, I thought. I changed the linen and went back to sleep. The baby was not due for another three weeks.

At seven in the morning I knew it had not been an accident. The baby was on its way. I had never been to a doctor, I was unprepared for the delivery, and we were quite a distance away from Ruhpolding.

"Frau Fuschlberger!" I called. "The baby's coming."

"Oh my God!" My landlady panicked momentarily. "I'll get a midwife in town right away. Try not to push. Hold on!"

It was so still in the house that I could hear my heart beat. *It will take Frau Fuschlberger two hours to get there and back. A midwife might not get up the snow-covered mountain in time. Or she might not come at all.*

Mother Nature proved stronger than my will to hold on. Just as the midwife burst into the room, Sylvia arrived with a bubbly cry.

I looked at my baby tucked into a fruit basket and laughed happily. As the Chinese say, "There's only one beautiful child in this world, and every mother has it."

★ ★ ★

Despite all the coupons issued to expectant mothers, I had been able to buy only a few bare necessities for the baby. Germany's economy was shattered, the stores virtually empty. So I unraveled Papa Schneble's moth-eaten sweaters and began to knit a tiny pair of panties, booties, socks, and a bonnet. From little Isolde, Sylvia inherited a blanket and six or seven diapers, gray from use. There were no soap flakes, no baby oil. I boiled each soiled diaper and spread it out in the sun to bleach and dry. My baby's bottom was sore, and she cried.

"You must let her cry, otherwise you'll spoil her," Pia had advised. But it was heartbreaking to hear my baby cry. She didn't thrive and had no color in her cheeks. What was happening to my Sylvia?

I remembered my mother telling me that I was a blue-skinned, puny baby. It was her fascination with horses and horse racing that saved me from the grave. The groom took one look at me in my mother's arms and declared, "Your baby is starving." "I have enough milk for two," Mother countered. "Yes, but it lacks nutrition. Give your baby the oats I feed my horses, and you'll see." To feed babies anything but mother's milk was unheard of in Russia. All the same, my mother fed me the oats the groom had given her, and I thrived. So now I got a bag of oats, cooked them in water for hours, strained the mush, and fed it to Sylvia. It worked like a charm. Soon my baby with the Schneble eyes blossomed, and her cheeks turned a healthy rosy red. For this I thanked the wise old groom and my heterodox mother.

Food rations were barely adequate. The God-fearing, churchgoing peasants had little compassion for city dwellers and were stingy with the evacuees. They parted with their produce only if an evacuee had something valuable to give them in return.

Papa Schneble often came by train equipped with a bicycle and a rucksack, to trade with the peasants and to visit Pia and me. Pia's little ones clung to their *Opa* (grandfather), whose smile grew broader and brighter.

The war was rapidly coming to an end.

Part VI

POSTWAR GERMANY

36

LIBERATED BY THE AMERICANS

May 8, 1945, brought peace to this part of the world. On this greatest of all days I kept running between my room and the balcony that spanned the front of the farmhouse with an unobstructed view of Ruhpolding below, watching for Guido.

Peace at last. But on our mountainside only Pia and I rejoiced with tears, laughter, and more tears. Frau Fuschlberger witnessed our emotional outburst with a dispassionate curiosity. Pia's landlords, like the unemotional Fuschlbergers, showed neither joy nor grief.

Germany's capitulation coincided with the arrival of American troops in Ruhpolding, one of the last areas in Germany to be liberated—or occupied, depending on how one looked at it. They did not march in but nonchalantly drove up in army jeeps one by one. Expecting trumpets and fanfare, I was amazed at the Americans' casual approach. They seemed to have taken their remarkable victory in their stride and, from my perspective, far too modestly.

The first Americans I saw were two great big black men. They came up to the Fuschlbergers' house, rapped at the door, and in deep baritones asked if they might come in.

"Aren't you curious about the Americans? Go on, open up," I coaxed Herr Fuschlberger. "Don't be afraid."

The heavy door squeaked ajar and in pressed the two black men. The Fuschlbergers drew back and froze. I also stepped back, involuntarily. I had never seen black men, except in the Soviet film *Circus*, which attempted to promote racial tolerance. The Fuschlbergers were frightened enough to quickly part with a dirndl dress and a pair of lederhosen; they received two packs of Camel cigarettes in exchange. Thrilled with the souvenirs, the grinning soldiers looked like overgrown boys. I smiled at them and was rewarded with a Hershey bar.

Life under the American occupation was no hardship. The American servicemen were friendly and easygoing, and I liked them because they smiled a lot. They were notorious providers of cigarettes, coffee, whiskey, and nylon stockings (all highly prized on the black market). The children appreciated their chocolates and chewing gum.

The occupational authorities established their local headquarters in Traunstein. The moment the doors were flung open, burghers besieged them with various requests. When my turn came, I asked for a baby carriage. The American with close-cropped hair laughed and said in German, "That's the funniest request I've ever had."

I felt my face turn red. "I heard people say the Americans try to help everyone. My baby has no carriage, nor a crib. She sleeps in a fruit basket."

The man smiled and said, "Okay." He wrote out a slip of paper and sent me with it to a warehouse, confiscated from the Nazis, where another friendly, gum-chewing American wheeled out a brand-new, white baby carriage.

★   ★   ★

I saw Papa Schneble cut across the pasture above Pia's cottage. A man in lederhosen was running up the hill ahead of him.

"Guido!" I dropped the wet diapers on the lawn and ran to greet him. He lifted me into his arms, and I clung to him for a long lingering moment. "Thank God you're home. At last."

"Yes, at last." Guido let me slide to the ground, adding gloomily, "Germany is kaput."

Sylvia was in her carriage on the lawn, flailing her tiny arms as if in contemplation. Seeing her for the first time, Guido said, "It's a good thing she was born on the nineteenth. I'd hate it if she'd waited another day and were born on Hitler's birthday."

I presented Sylvia to her daddy. He looked at her with pride. "This time I'll forgive you, wifey. Next time if it's another girl, I'll strangle her."

"That's a horrible thing to say," Father interjected.

I laughed. "It's only a joke, Papa. He wants a son."

"Nonetheless, it's most inappropriate." Father cradled the infant in his arms and asked his son, "What are your plans? Any ideas for a job? I trust you've given it some thought while in hiding."

Guido appeared irritated. "No, I haven't," he said. "Not while strug-gling to survive." Then self-pity crept into his voice. "I kept moving from one peasant's house to the next, shoveling snow, milking cows, dodging military police."

"It's been rough on you. I suspected that much. But you did come through in robust good health. Your future is what concerns me now most of all. This is why I urge you, Son, start looking. The entire Wehrmacht is on the loose and jobless." He stood up. "I'll be expecting you in Munich soon. In the meantime, I'll look and see what possibilities there are."

Father returned to Pia's house, and Guido and I talked a bit about our future. As we talked, the nebulous future began to gain shape and form.

Guido had joined the Luftwaffe soon after graduating from high school and felt barely qualified to be an office clerk. My bright and spirited husband seemed to have lost his self-assurance now that he was stripped of his uniform. It surprised me that a man who couldn't wait to shed his uniform could feel lost without it. I tenderly put my arms around him.

"I'd make a good mechanic, though. In my long years with the TK-1, I've learned all there is to know about cars."

"Then what's the problem? Get a job as an auto mechanic. We've made it through the war. Just think of it! We've made it, Guido. And we'll make it now." I felt optimistic about the future and trusted that Guido's former belief in himself would return. "Cheer up, my love."

A smile erased the gloom from his face. But as we clung to one an-other lovingly in bed, I still felt tension in his limbs.

The next two weeks we lived in bliss. We hiked the mountainside, climbed the Unterberg, and made love on the summit and among the pines. We celebrated our marriage and caught up on the eight months dur-ing which we had been apart.

Afraid to rupture the silk cocoon we had spun around ourselves, I nev-ertheless felt driven to rid myself of the secret I had lived with all these years. I had no idea how a German might react when he learned his wife was half Jewish. But I believed that the man I had married was a different breed.

We were behind the farmhouse, stretched out on the grass studded with flowers. Sylvia, four weeks old and no bigger than the alpine cow's bell, lay sleeping on Guido's shoulder.

"I bet you never suspected your loving wife is a Roman Catholic Jew," I said, as if in jest.

He gave me a side-long glance. "What are you trying to say? Are you Jewish? You can't be a Catholic and a Jew."

"Yes, you can, " I said, and I went on to explain. "You know me as a Russian of Polish and German ancestry, and that a Catholic priest baptized me. What I didn't tell you is that my father was Jewish and that my Soviet passport identified me as a Jew. Soviets don't consider 'Jewish' as a religion but as one of many ethnic groups in the USSR. My father saw my passport and said: 'Only in the Soviet Union is it possible to be a Roman Catholic Jew.'" I expected Guido to ask how I managed to survive the war, but he didn't.

He whacked his knee. "What a mix! I'd never have guessed. Can't wait for Dad to hear about that. He'd love it! Come to think of it," he continued, "my background is not much different from yours." I pricked up my ears. "My grandfather, the Italian noble who fathered my Dad, descended from the Moors." Before I could digest this revelation, he burst out laughing. "So, we're both mixed up." And then, "Why didn't you tell me this before?"

"I was afraid."

"Afraid of what?"

"Hitler was very much alive until recently. To Hitler and the Nazis, a half Jew, a Christian Jew was still a Jew. Or have you already forgotten that?"

"No, Sopherl, I haven't. I thought you were afraid I wouldn't marry you." He plucked a yellow flower and presented it to me. "You're the only one I ever wanted, the only one I ever loved."

It was the nicest thing he had ever said to me.

I looked at him, at the slumbering baby, and sighed for the happiness I felt.

★ ★ ★

Guido followed his father to Munich and through him got a job as chauffeur to Herr Doktor Wilhelm Högner, who in September 1945 became the first prime minister and minister of justice of postwar Bavaria. Papa Schneble and Doktor Högner were old friends and fellow Social Democrats.

Papa Schneble, who had spent a year in Dachau concentration camp for his open opposition to Hitler, was now offered a high position in the Bavarian government. A powerful public speaker but hard of hearing, with the problem growing steadily worse, he regretfully declined.

Munich, damaged and scarred by the bombs, was a sad sight. Parts of town had been flattened; ruins and rubble littered the streets. Houses with blown-out, patched-up windows and temporary roofs were occupied to overflowing. The city was crammed with evacuees and soldiers returning home; German refugees from the East and foreign workers who chose to stay in the West flocked to the city. Survivors of concentration camps began to filter in.

Doktor Högner's chauffeur and his elated wife were provided with a solid roof over their heads. Our apartment was converted from an office in the Ministry of Justice, adjacent to the magnificent old Palace of Justice, which lay partially in ruins.

It was invigorating to live in the heart of town, to feel the pulse of activity as I explored Munich with Sylvia in my arms. Skeletal remains and piles of brick made the city look grim. Yet there was optimism and something cheerful in the air. Maybe it was the warm sound of the Bavarian dialect, the natives' gemütlichkeit, the vigor with which they went about restoring the *Kunststadt* (City of Fine Arts) to its prewar glory. As a city of music and fine arts, Munich was one of the first European cities to have concerts in the bombed-out university after the war. Whatever it was, I fell in love with Munich and felt at home among its people.

On his days off, Guido would strap Sylvia onto his bicycle, and we'd ride to Starnbergersee, one of many scenic lakes in Bavaria, where our friends had a summer cottage. Or he'd take us along in his official car when he drove to the country for food supplies.

Guido was on the road a great deal, driving Doktor Högner to Bonn. It was a good job, and Guido loved to drive. Every time he returned, he brought back Rhine wine for his own consumption and some with which to do shopping. He traded the wine for various household items. The black market thrived; bribery was commonplace. Even Guido was approached with various requests: some people needed help to find jobs, others asked him to intervene on their behalf with the prime minister. These were uncertain times, when even minor Nazis trembled with fear of losing their homes and businesses. Doktor Högner would not be influenced, but the kind man, whose doctorate was in law, was free with legal advice to some of those Guido brought to his attention. Meanwhile, Guido was plied from all corners of Bavaria with flour, butter, basketloads of apples, and a goose for our Christmas feast, which we celebrated with Papa Schneble and Pia and her family. When driving alone, Guido gave lifts to thumbing Americans, who reciprocated with cigarettes, another valuable commodity.

I often visited with the family. Pia's husband finally returned from a prison camp; their apartment had been restored. Papa Schneble lived in Munich-Laim, on the street that would later bear his name: Guido Schneble Strasse.

★   ★   ★

Guido loved to entertain his wartime comrades, and everybody loved my generous Guido. Six of them sat around our kitchen table, drinking Rhine wine, smoking American cigarettes, and talking of nothing but the war. It seemed more like a strategic conference than a meeting of friends.

They were all glad that the war had ended and spoke of Hitler as "that raving maniac" or "that blundering fool." They all agreed with Guido when he said that the Nazis received their just deserts, that the massacre of Jews was criminal, and that the Nazis' race discrimination policies in general, apart from being absurd, had cost them the war.

In the course of the evening they would cover all the fronts, relishing the memories of their exploits, as if the brutal war had been far more exciting than the prosaic peace.

On their vicarious marches through Russia, I'd naturally march with them. Then I'd listen again, amused at some of their suppositions.

"If the war had lasted another day, we'd all have lost our balls . . . Excuse me, Sophia." The gallant Franz Fischer bowed from the waist.

"If those slant-eyed *Japaner* hadn't double-crossed us by attacking Pearl Harbor, the Americans would have stayed put on the other side of the globe. Dragged into the war, it was *they* that got us into trouble. The Bolsheviks alone could never have done it," said a corporal, blowing out a thick stream of smoke.

"You're an imbecile! If not Ivan himself, his deep freeze would have finished us. You weren't there. I was, I know." The man with the wooden leg knocked on it. "Without the help of the fierce Siberians, you'd probably be deep inside Russia yourself today, freezing off your . . . you know what," he added with due sarcasm.

"You'd better believe it." Guido took a quick drag on his cigarette. "The Russians fought like demons. The Americans helped them, all right, but only after Ivan got to us at Stalingrad. Now, comrades, if that blundering fool hadn't dilly-dallied elsewhere and had taken Stalingrad—"

"If that lunatic had only attacked England first—"

"If you'd treated the people you conquered the way the Americans are treating you today," I said, "you might not have lost your . . . you know what." Satisfied with my contribution, I went to bed long before the strategic conference broke up.

Their discussions left me with the feeling that despite the way these men felt about the Nazis, they were sorry, very sorry that the lunatic had caused them to lose the war. I understood how they felt; I, too, wanted my country to win, regardless of how critical I had become of the Stalinist regime. And while I felt a sense of pride that the Soviets had taken Berlin, I was disappointed that the Americans had let them take it. While I was glad that Russia had won, I felt regret that the Americans did not continue their advance to the east to stop the Soviets at their own frontier.

I was ashamed of the way my countrymen behaved when they entered Germany. I could understand their craving for bicycles, watches, and radios. But it hurt me to hear of women being raped and of minor officials arbitrarily killed. Gottlieb Brune was a *Bürgermeister*, a harmless man—did they kill him? Gretchen, Monika—had they been raped? I had worried about how vindictive the Soviets might be and hoped they would use restraint; I wanted them to show the world that they were not the barbarians the Nazis had been. Instead, they could not wait to repay the Germans "an eye for an eye." Now and then came heartwarming tales of compassionate Russian soldiers, but unfortunately, these were overshadowed by the stories of their comrades bent on vengeance.

I was further dismayed by alarming reports that the former slave workers, the *Ostarbeiter*, were forced to return to Russia. Most of them wanted to stay in the West. They fled from the encroaching Soviet troops and toward the Anglo-American military forces, which by the terms of the Yalta Agreement promptly turned them over to the Soviets. The penalties upon their homecoming were harsh: quick arrests and long sentences of hard labor in Siberia.

Of course, I reflected, in one way or another we had all been contaminated by the West. If a wayward traveler were allowed to go free in the Soviet Union, he would most certainly contaminate the rest by spreading outlandish ideas picked up in the "decadent West." Who could blame the Soviets for deporting the vast number of uprooted humanity beyond the Ural Mountains? Never mind that the vast majority had been *forced* to leave the Soviet Union to work like slaves in Nazi Germany.

I often wondered how I got through the war. *Why did I survive when countless others did not? Was it because of my determination to stay alive? Everyone had that same determination. Was I more daring and imaginative than most? Perhaps. Or was it a matter of divine intervention? Maybe God—if there was a God—and my guardian angel did have something to do with it.*

When I was cast adrift at the shore of Zaporozhye, I believed myself to be a victim of unknown conspirators. Who wrote the script? I did not appreciate the plot. Now that the horrendous details of the Nazi concentration camps and gas chambers began to filter in, only now did I believe in the existence of God, only now did I appreciate his and my guardian angel's efforts to protect a foolhardy soul.

Being stranded in Zaporozhye helped enormously, I thought. But so did my interpretation of the dream I had in June 1943. Had I stayed in Wannefeld until the end of the war, I would have been swept into the ocean, and my countrymen would now be welcoming me as well—with open arms in the Stalinist concentration camps, the gulags.

I shuddered.

And then, looking at my baby cooing in her crib, I smiled and said to her, "I cheated *Batiushka* Stalin and tweaked the Nazis' noses, darling. Now I'm safe and warm, at home at last with you and your papa."

★ ★ ★

Years later, when I learned that most of the hundred thousand Kievans killed at Babi Yar were Jews, I recalled Guido telling me that Jews in the Ukraine were "mowed down by the thousands" on the spot. I realized then that Karl Mannheim had helped me escape from the Holocaust on Soviet soil. No concentration camps and no gas chambers for Soviet Jews: the Nazis and their collaborators massacred the Jews—men, women, and children—soon after German troops invaded the Soviet Union in 1941.

I thanked God for preventing me from reaching Kiev in 1941. I thanked him for helping me navigate the treacherous waters of the war and stay afloat.

37

A CHANGED MAN

Now that Hitler was dead, people's attitudes were changing and women began to wear lipstick again. I was probably the only young woman who didn't. My husband would not allow it.

"Get that stuff off your face," he demanded when he saw me wearing it for the first time. "Take it off!"

"Why should I? If you stop yelling and tell me nicely what's wrong with it, I might obey."

"I know what goes through men's minds when they see a woman with red paint on her lips. You attract enough attention to yourself without it. That's all I need . . . to worry about my wife when I'm on the road."

"Have you been bitten by a jealous bug? That's crazy."

He bared his teeth so that his mouth looked square. He grabbed a newspaper from the kitchen table and roughly wiped my mouth with it.

"You are mad," I blurted, and he slapped my face with the back of his hand.

I left the room feeling angry and hurt. *What's got into him?* I wondered. *He never treated me so harshly, never lost his temper before. We hardly ever argued. How he had changed—since the gallant Franz Fischer came to live with us,* I thought. *It's his* influence.

Guido followed me into the bedroom. Sylvia was asleep in her crib, her thumb in her mouth. I lifted her to take her potty. She murmured, "Ma-ma," her first word. I kissed her chubby cheek and tucked her back in the crib. She fell instantly asleep, sucking on her thumb. I pulled it out gently, and her mouth made a funny little sucking plop.

Guido closed the frosted window, left ajar for fresh air, and followed me back into the kitchen. His eyes were mild again, and there was no harshness in his voice when he said, "It's about time we had another one. What do you say?"

The sight of Sylvia melted me like a cube of sugar in a cup of tea, and I said, "Yes, Guido." Nothing could please me more than to hold and cuddle and care for another child.

★   ★   ★

Franz Fischer, Guido's wartime pal, had stayed with us until Guido found him a job as a chauffeur for a government official and a place to live near us. Franz was amusing and we enjoyed his company, but soon I recognized him for what he was: a scoundrel—a charming scoundrel but a scoundrel nonetheless. He siphoned gasoline from the tank and stripped the tires from his official car, sold them on the black market, then reported the theft to the police as if someone else had stolen them.

A smooth talker and womanizer, Franz thought he was irresistible. Indeed, a flick of his long black eyelashes seemed enough to persuade any girl to spend the night with him. The Lothario often coaxed Guido away from home. When he was otherwise unoccupied, he would entice Guido to uncork a bottle or two, and they would simply and deliberately get roaring drunk.

Waiting for Guido till the wee hours of the night, I lay in bed furious at him and Franz. Franz's influence on Guido dismayed me.

The day after a drinking bout, when he was sober, I told Guido, "I hate Franz. I hate him for what he's doing to you, to me, to our marriage. Have you fallen under his spell that you can't see what's happening?"

"What kind of talk is that? What is it?"

"If this drinking and carousing doesn't stop, I'll leave you." It was an empty threat born from frustration. I had been stewing over this for weeks and finally decided to use a bit of cunning to get my point across. "It's Franz or me—make up your mind." I was trying to stay calm yet forceful. "I never complained before, not even when you hit me."

"Oh come on, Sopherl. What man doesn't slap his woman now and then? It's part of bringing up a wife."

"I am serious. So don't be flippant about it."

"*Kruzifix, Kruzifix!*" he swore, Bavarian-style. "Get off my back. I'll never let you go, and don't you ever forget it. So you'd better get used to me."

"And you, you married the wrong woman if you think you can bring me up, as you put it. You can't cow me into submission." I flared up. "I can't stand it when you're drunk, and quarreling about it makes me sick. Very sick."

He tilted his head and smiled at me. "Don't be cross, wifey. I'll stop drinking. I swear I will." And because I loved and trusted him, I allowed myself to be convinced.

A few days later, he crawled to bed at dawn, drunk again and slobbering, and began to fondle me roughly.

"Don't touch me!" I exploded. It was all right for him to turn away from me when I wanted him to hold me, kiss me, make love to me—but he could never be denied.

His reaction was instantaneous. He began to shake me by my shoulders like a maniac. His face, dimly visible in the early light, was that of a frenzied man, twisted and contorted. It did not belong to the man I loved. I closed my eyes and rolled away from him, fear sweeping over me.

"Don't turn your back on me!" he roared, and gave me a blow to the head. He then forced himself on me. "Try to leave me now," he muttered, again and again, "just try . . . If you're not pregnant now," he gloated afterward with self-satisfaction, "I'll eat a broom."

Could a husband rape his wife? Of course not. Guido merely took me by force, against my will . . . while drunk.

It pained and grieved me to see this warmhearted, loving man turn into a monster overnight. I tried to tell myself that it was only an isolated incident, a nightmare I had to forget. *Once Guido stops drinking, as he promised, everything will be all right*, I thought, *and we'll be happy again*. I was determined to keep my chin up even if my spirits sagged, for Sylvia's sake and for the sake of our unborn child, whom I already so dearly loved.

★ ★ ★

Franz-the-Lothario announced he was getting married, and I rejoiced. Finally, I would be rid of him. At his wedding I gave Guido the opportunity to see how his drinking repulsed me. I drank myself full of champagne, and my disgruntled but sympathetic husband drove me home, drenched my head with ice-cold water, and tucked me in bed.

Champagne did not sit well with me. I was horribly nauseated, but it was worthwhile: Guido drank far less throughout my pregnancy. My hopes rose when he found an apartment for us near Perlacher Forest, a good distance away from the Lothario and his influence, and we moved only a few days before our second child was due.

Our new apartment, previously occupied by a Nazi, had five rooms and a kitchen outfitted to Guido's specifications with peasant-style furniture crafted from oak.

Looking out the large kitchen window I felt happy, visualizing our children playing in the sandbox in the yard. I'd be able to keep an eye on them while I cooked and ironed and knitted sweaters for them. "I love this kitchen, Guido. So gemütlich," I said, recalling with nostalgia another kitchen that smelled of rich Ukrainian borscht, gefilte fish, chicken soup, and onions . . . I squeezed my big belly between the table and the corner bench, plopped down and stroked the back of the bench, smiling at the memory.

"Did you notice the intricate carving on the chandelier? The woodcarver outdid himself."

"Oh yes, I did. It is beautiful," I said. "I was just thinking about Mama's borscht, thick with meat, navy beans, beets, and potatoes. She served it with sour cream. Delicious! I'll make it for us someday."

"I'd like that. Come here, wifey. Look at the leaded windows." The upper section of the breakfront had three such windows. As I stretched to inspect the shelving on the inside, Guido slapped my bottom playfully.

Despite my size, I flitted joyfully from room to room, cleaning and polishing the hardwood floors and sponging the walls in the nursery. Our home, my first real home, had to be ready to receive our son. Guido wanted a son, and though another girl would have made me just as happy, I hoped it would be a boy.

On the morning of November 24, I heard a baby cry. But there were no babies above or next door to us. Sylvia was not a baby anymore; she was nineteen months old, blond with large brown eyes and a disarming smile. She jabbered away in German and delighted me with a few Russian words: *nosik, glazki,* and *poopik* (little nose, eyes, and bellybutton).

The baby's cry was within me, in my mind and heart. Our new one was anxious to be born; I knew it the moment I woke. Still, it waited all day, patiently, almost as if it did not want to arrive while its daddy was away. The moment Guido returned from Bonn, he had to rush me to the hospital.

But he did not stay, and he would not come to the hospital to see our newborn. As I sat in the empty predelivery room, listening to the wall clock tick away the seconds, anger and resentment expanded and contracted rhythmically inside me. This child was only another way for Guido to hold on to me, to tie me down. It had nothing to do with his wanting to share in the joy of creating a beautiful new life.

The triumph and delight of hearing the baby's first cry, and the doctor's "It's a boy!" were for my ears alone.

We named our son Guido; his daddy called him Burschi, Bavarian for "a little guy." To me, he was Guidoli.

It was a hard, cold winter. Gas was rationed and used for cooking alone. Because firewood was scarce, the wood-burning oven in the kitchen made this the only livable room. As I stacked the wood in the yard and hung the daily laundry in the freezing outdoors, I recalled the days I had struggled with the coal, and of all the help I had gotten from Herr Mannheim . . . Not from my husband. I didn't need his help to run the household, but I did need it when I was running a fever.

"The children might catch my cold. Would you mind changing their diapers tonight?"

"No self-respecting man would do that." He lit a cigarette and started blowing smoke rings.

"Would you at least feed Guidoli? The baby falls asleep while sucking. It takes him forever to finish his bottle."

"That's a woman's job." He stubbed his unfinished cigarette in a coffee cup.

Were all German men like that, or did I marry a heartless son of a bitch? My gentle sister-in-law, Pia, and several couples among our friends had their share of marital problems, but none of the husbands were quite as selfish and insensitive. I had to face the fact that my Guido was indeed a different breed.

But I was blessed with two healthy children. It was with joy and fascination that I watched them thrive and turn into individuals. Sylvia and little Guido resembled their father, but Guidoli's eyes with the serious expression in them were my father's eyes. Both children were bright and bursting with good spirits, but their personalities were worlds apart. Guidoli, a strong, handsome boy, his hair golden blond and wavy, was circumspect; he had inherited some of his father's temperament along with my stubbornness. Sylvia was sensitive, her disposition cheerful. When I gave them an equal amount of sweets, Guidoli would square his lips; he wanted more. Sylvia loved her little brother and would happily surrender her share, saying to me, "Let him have it, Mutti, so he'll stop whimpering."

Guido was good with the children, played with them, and was as proud as I was of the rich mixture of blood that coursed through their veins: German, Polish, Jewish, Italian, and Moorish. "No wonder they're so smart," he'd say. He provided for his family like no other man I knew, and he was a reliable hard worker.

So what if he was disgusting when drunk? His sprees happened rarely now, since he had developed bleeding ulcers. When he gambled and lost playing Sheep's Head, his friends' favorite card game, he was furious. His generosity was legendary, but so was his temper. He exploded like a firecracker, then calmed down just as quickly after he had spent himself. Afterward he rarely remembered what it was that had upset him so. To avoid the brunt of his rage, I would escape to one of our neighbors until he had a chance to cool off.

But I could not escape his stifling possessiveness or his mercurial temper, which erupted against me at unpredictable intervals. I tried not to provoke him and kept my own emotions under control as best I could, but I did not always succeed. I did not possess the kind of humility and patience that living with such a volatile and unjustifiably jealous man required.

One Sunday a ridiculous argument over *Kartoffelknödel* (potato dumplings) sparked a fight. Try as I might, I could not get them as light as his mother's were.

I let Guido's stream of insults pass over me. When he was through, I said angrily, "You make me want to vomit the way you carry on about nothing. *Kartoffelknödel!* Fix your own damned dumplings if you don't like mine. Your temper tantrums are childish. If it weren't for the children, I'd be long gone."

"You want to go? Go!" he exploded, knocking two plates off the table. I backed away and out of the kitchen. Fists flying, he came after me. And before I could dodge, he struck me repeatedly.

Sylvia was rocking her little brother on a swing at the other end of the hallway. She came running to us, crying. Guido kicked at her and sent her skidding down the hall.

Enraged, I fought him then, as hard as I could, scratching, kicking, and pounding his chest. But I was no match for the burly Guido. Another blow on my head, and I was down.

All I could hear then was the children crying. I felt Sylvia's little hands on my face and heard her calling to me, "Mutti, Mutti." I wanted to open my eyes and rise but couldn't. And through the fog that seemed to have enveloped me, I heard Guido's voice, "Calm down, Sopherl. Who the hell cares about the potato dumplings anyway? Come, give me a kiss."

I thought about Otto Schubert with longing in my heart. I felt regret that I had been able to disguise my feelings for him so well, deep regret at having left so much unsaid. Now the Nazis were gone, and so was my love for Guido, my abuser. Karl Mannheim's words came back to me: "The staff sergeant is rude and disrespectful. I hope that in the future you will be more discriminating in choosing your friends." Yes, Herr Brune, you were also right when you remarked: "You hardly know him. He might not be what he seems."

I finally understood that I had married the wrong man.

38

TEN CENTIMES SHORT

Sylvia accidentally stepped on a woman's toe in the streetcar. The young woman cringed in pain and cried out in Russian, *"Neukluzhiy porosyo-nok!"* I apologized for my "clumsy piglet" in Russian, and a warm friendship ensued.

Vera was also an only child, born in Dnepropetrovsk. As a young girl she danced the *Gopak*, as I had, sang the same patriotic songs, was a Young Pioneer like me. Unlike me, she had been snatched off the street and driven to Germany by force to work in heavy industry; she hadn't heard from her mother since. I had lost touch with my mother in 1943 and would not hear from her again for several years after Stalin died in 1953.

Forewarned by a sympathetic British soldier of the forceful repatriation of Soviet citizens, Vera had fled to the American zone of occupation, where the situation had eased by 1946.

"I've had my share of hard labor here in Germany. Why go home for more? Even if I were sure to escape punishment, I couldn't live under those conditions anymore," she said, expressing my sentiments precisely. "Did you ever have to stand in line for a bag of rotten potatoes?"

"Frozen or rotten, depending on the time of year," I elaborated jocularly. "Sure, all kinds of lines. Even to the toilet."

"We didn't have a toilet. We had to pay the debt to the Tatars in the outhouse," she said, alluding to the Mongol Tatar overlords of the eleventh through thirteenth centuries, who extorted high taxes from the Russians. "We used buckets at night." Vera smiled, and suddenly the girl with golden curls and round face with brown eyes looked like a sunflower. "There was a man next door to us, he was my alarm clock. I could hear him urinating in his bucket at seven o'clock sharp."

"And when you sneezed upstairs, no doubt someone downstairs always said *'Gesundheit!'* "

We had a good laugh.

Vera often came to visit me in our apartment. It was wonderful to hear the melodic sound of Russian again, to share memories of childhood days. They were happy, carefree days, the days when laughter came easy, when fear and terror, love and pain, hurt and jealousy, were just words without meaning, the days when there was no one to bully me.

Vera was living with Andrei, who wanted to marry her. "I'm not sure that I will," she said. "He makes a good living trading American goods on the black market. Still—"

"Do you love him?"

"Oh yes. And he's mad about me. Trouble is he's mad about vodka too."

"How lucky you found out before you married him."

"You're the lucky one. We're both twenty-four, and you already have two blond angels and this large apartment. I'd be so happy to settle down in a home like yours."

"Vera, Verushka. Four walls won't make you happy. It's the quality of life inside the walls that counts."

"What dreams I had . . . I wanted to be an actress in the movies. I was so sure that as a famous actress I'd be given my own apartment. Maybe even a car someday," she added with a wistful smile. "Instead, Andrei and I are crammed into a crummy room with three other Russians."

"All I ever wanted was to be an engineer," I said. "I never fantasized. Even as a child I was a realist, with a pragmatic approach to life. We're all lucky, though, if you stop and think about it—all of us who have escaped Stalin's tyranny."

Like most refugees from the East, Vera and her Russian friends dreamed of emigrating to America, Australia, or Canada. All roads, which used to lead to Rome, were now leading to America. The United States was everybody's first choice. As displaced persons they would all be eligible to apply. Vera eventually settled in Canada, Andrei in Milwaukee, Wisconsin.

★   ★   ★

Bright sunlight poured in through the wide-open windows. The balcony was lined with potted pink geraniums. Guidoli was contentedly sitting on my lap or playing with his toys close to me. Sylvia and her boyfriend Dieter were in the sandbox.

Vera and I were sipping tea in the living room. "Where did you get all this furniture? It looks brand-new. Was it very expensive?"

It was not unusual for a Russian to ask such tactless questions. "It depends on how you look at it," I answered, not taking offense. "Would you say five pounds of butter was too much for an armchair? Our friendly neighbor, an upholsterer, made it for us. For extra butter and some gasoline coupons, he also reupholstered this old sofa."

"You have a car? That must have cost a lot of butter."

"Not even one pound. Guido paid cash for every bit of it, and not much cash at that. He assembled the car himself. From scratch."

Guido had found a stripped-down chassis of a Maybach limousine, one of the best cars produced in Germany before the war. Then he searched all over West Germany, including West Berlin, until he found all the parts he needed.

"Guido's very clever that way," I added with a touch of pride. "If he sets his mind on something, there's nothing he can't do. Unfortunately, he's an irresponsible show-off and drives like a maniac, especially after a few drinks. He's a poor drinker, Vera. Two beers can push him over the edge. But he never drinks during the day. He'd lose his job with the prime minister if he did."

Vera and Andrei came to dinner to try my borscht, and from that day on Guido and Andrei were like one, their friendship lasting for years to come.

The four of us were in a quaint *Biertaverne* one night. We'd had a glass of dark beer each, when a Russian pounced on Andrei.

"You mother fucker!" the man swore in Russian. "You ripped me off!" *Probably on the black market*, I thought, as a fight broke out between the two Russians. Immediately Guido was at Andrei's side, fighting in defense of his friend's honor.

Another time Guido and Andrei volunteered to drive a truck to Essen with highly explosive nitroglycerin. And the two "lunatics" always embraced when they met.

"That Guido, I swear he's got a Russian soul," Andrei declared at one of the parties we gave for all our friends, Russian and German.

Guido was in his element that night, entertaining the guests, serving drinks—a perfect host. Looking at him, a drink in his hand, I thought that, yes, he was joyously social and hospitable like a Russian, insisting our out-of-town guests sleep in our bed. He was generous, fiery, and explosive like a Georgian. He was stubborn like a Ukrainian *muzhik*, wild and unbridled like a primitive steppe-dweller, Tartar or Mongol. He had the soul of all these peoples rolled into one. Everything he did—eating, drinking, making love—he did on a large scale. It was as if he were born and bred on Russian soil, on the land endowed by nature with large inland seas, deep lakes and wide rivers, the taiga, the tundra, and the endless steppes. He could be inflamed or very sad one moment, deliriously happy and laughing the next.

★   ★   ★

In the spring of 1948, Guido came home with the news that Herr Doktor Ehard had succeeded Doktor Högner as prime minister of Bavaria, while Doktor Högner remained minister of justice, and that the prime minister wanted to buy Guido's Maybach limousine.

"How much could you get for that black hearse?"

"He offered eight thousand."

"Don't sell it, Guido. What good is eight thousand now? It's worthless."

Sure enough, when the currency reform occurred on June 20, 1948, and the Reichsmark was declared nonnegotiable, the prime minister bought the limousine and paid eight thousand new deutsche marks. Compared to the forty marks each and every person in the Bundesrepublik (the Federal Republic of Germany) received from the government that day, eight thousand marks was an enormous sum. Guido wanted to keep it in the bank.

"Money in the bank won't do us any good. We'd use it up and have nothing to show for it. How about investing it in our own business?"

Guido cast a skeptical glance at me. "What business?"

"I don't know. Maybe a store of some kind, why not? Germany has been at war too long. People lost so much and need just about everything. I could go to Switzerland—"

"Are you crazy?"

"I am. Haven't you gotten used to it yet?"

"If they catch you, you'll be in deep shit."

The only way I could cross the border was illegally. After Germany's capitulation and until the end of 1949, when the Allied High Commission permitted Germany to establish consular relations abroad, no one could leave Germany. With my usual bravado I had decided that I could sneak into Switzerland without being caught, and I tried harder to persuade Guido.

"Please let me go. I'd try to pick up ideas for a store, find out what sells best. After all, Switzerland today is what Germany will be tomorrow. What do you say?"

Finally he agreed. "Under one condition: if Frau Hug goes with you." Frau Hug had lived in Basel during the war. She and her husband were now living upstairs with her family; they were a fun-loving, friendly family.

The prospect of owning a store stirred my imagination. I visualized Guido as a successful, sedate businessman and I a businesswoman working at his side in harmony. The best nursemaid we could find would look after the children; her room would be at the end of the hall. Why, she'd even help me do the nasty household chores! I laughed for happiness at the optimism I felt as I rang Frau Hug's bell.

Two days later, the attractive and energetic Frau Hug and I journeyed to the edge of Germany: via Freiburg to Lorrach. From there we walked through vineyards, feasting on succulent grapes. We crept furtively over the cone-shaped hill overgrown with thick shrubs, crossed the border, and went on to Basel by streetcar with our heads high. No problems at all.

The contrast between Switzerland and Germany was staggering. Here was a country that had remained neutral throughout the century; it had been spared the destruction and tragedies of war. The stores were overflowing with merchandise and reflected the prosperity of the well-dressed inhabitants.

I wondered how long it would take Germany to reach such heights. Surely, without free enterprise, Russia never would.

I had fun looking around town and gathering ideas, but it was also frustrating. German marks could not yet be exchanged for Swiss francs, so I couldn't buy anything. Frau Hug kindly offered all the francs and centimes she could spare, and with them I went shopping for yarn with which to knit sweaters for my children. Such luxuries were still unavailable in Germany. As it turned out, I didn't have enough money for even the least expensive skeins.

In one small store I simply put my money on the counter and asked the shopkeeper for the cheapest yarn she had. The shopkeeper counted it and said, "You are short ten centimes."

Red in the face, I scooped up the coins from the counter. "I'm sorry, that's all I have." I left, thinking, *I will never be like that when I have my store!*

Later I related my unsuccessful shopping mission to Frau Hug in the presence of her well-to-do friends. I had hoped they might offer me the ten centimes (less than five cents), but they did not. And I thought to myself, *People with full stomachs cannot know what hunger means.* My mama would probably have said, "You can have a heart and still feel nothing."

Instead of the yarn, I returned home with two multicolored rubber balls for the children—and with an idea to open a glass-fronted store I had admired in Basel, a store that sold refrigerators, washing machines, and electric stoves.

39

PEDALING THROUGH THE SLUSH

The store opened its doors on December 16, 1948, in the midst of the Christmas rush. Ours was one of several business enterprises in a temporary structure erected on a bombed site in the heart of the city, near Sendlingertor Platz. A camera shop, an optician, a newspaper publisher, and Café Loya were all under one roof. I liked our business card, and I was very pleased Guido had secured the dealership of NEFF electric stoves for us.

Guido was not in the store for the opening. He had said he would continue working for Doktor Högner, the minister of justice, until the business was well on its way, and I agreed—quickly and probably too enthusiastically.

My idea of a store that sold nothing but sparkling white refrigerators, washing machines, and electric stoves had to be modified, and we started with the retail of small electrical appliances: toasters, coffee percolators, irons, electric plates, waffle irons. Germany had only just begun production of refrigerators and gas and electric stoves; these were in great demand, and retailers could get only a few at a time, even if they had the necessary capital, which we did not. Our immediate problem was that the cost of building and outfitting the store with shelves and counters had soared from the estimated two thousand marks to five thousand marks, leaving us with barely enough cash to buy merchandise. To get the maximum discount, we paid all our bills cash on delivery or within thirty days.

To learn the basics of the trade, the technical terminology, names of suppliers, and the wholesale and retail price structure, I worked four weeks as a salesgirl for an established electrical firm without pay. When our store was ready for occupancy, I left, never dreaming that our store would in one year's time become that established firm's biggest competitor.

Our opening inventory consisted of about twenty-five electric irons and toasters, some electric plates and immersion heaters, and a number of cords, plugs, and lightbulbs. We had so ridiculously little to start with that I sold all the appliances the first day. And more.

"I'm sorry," I said to a customer, "I'm sold out of irons. If you don't mind waiting, I'll deliver it to you tonight."

"How very kind of you. Are you sure it's no trouble?"

"No trouble at all," I assured the customer, as I told another, "I'm sold out of 220-volt toasters. I'd be happy to deliver one to you later today."

Before the first memorable day was over, I had called the wholesale house several times, giving them a big order to be ready when I came at closing time to pick it up. Then I got on my bike and with a singing heart pedaled through the slush from one end of town to the other to make the promised deliveries.

Our competitors made no deliveries of any kind in those days. But for me, no purchase was too small or too large; I was glad and eager to pick up and deliver anything, and it paid dividends. We built up a steady and loyal clientele who came to us from all over town, if only for a lightbulb.

When trade was slow, I prepared various lengths of extension cords and repaired small electrical appliances, replacing heating coils and disks inside the appliances, which I did for customers without charge.

Apart from buying, selling, and repairing, I decorated the window, changing its display once a week. I took great pride in it. Instead of the red runner I had envisioned for the store, I lined the large window with red velvet and for greater effect placed only chrome-plated items on it. Guido installed a rotating three-tiered platform in the middle of the window. This, also covered in red velvet, was a great eye-catcher. It delighted me to see people stop by to admire it.

In the spring, Egbert Wagner, the owner of a wholesale business who frequented our store, came by.

"Frau Schneble," he said, "I have about two hundred waffle irons, very cheap. The problem is, they're all 110 volts. Can you use some of them?"

"I'll take them all," I said without hesitation, even though Munich had mostly 220V. "I'll fix them myself and will be able to sell them all for a low price."

"Your competitors might not like being undersold," Herr Wagner observed with a smile.

I laughed. "That's their problem. My customers are entitled to share a bargain with us. They'll appreciate it."

Even before credit became standard practice, I was selling on credit to customers short on cash. It seemed only fair to trust people who trusted us, and we were disappointed only once.

It was our superb location in the center of town that was mainly responsible for our quick success. Within six months, we hired a salesgirl and bought a Ford panel truck. We had already begun to sell electric stoves and small refrigerators, and I delivered them, driving the Ford to many parts of Bavaria. Guido helped me load, and the customers helped me unload. Guido also took care of the bookkeeping and prepared our first income tax return.

The neighboring Café Loya, furnished with upholstered armchairs and low tables with white cloths, had a cozy ambiance. It was a delightful place to meet friends and wholesale representatives for coffee and a chat. Guido and I became quite friendly with the café owners, and they began inviting us to their sanctuary at the back. In the room stood a camouflaged roulette table. When a group of their intimates gathered, the table was bared and gambling began, which was against the law. Gambling held no fascination for me, but Guido, who shouldn't have gambled at all because he was such a poor loser, loved it.

The last time he played roulette, he lost not only money but our next-door neighbors' friendship and respect. In a fit of violence at having lost, Guido overturned the heavy roulette table, smashing the wheel. And he was sober.

Peace and quiet reigned when Guido was out of town. Sylvia and Guidoli were at my side at night. "Read *Struwwelpeter* to me, Mutti." It was Sylvia's favorite, and she'd break into peals of laughter when I recited the pranks of the mean-spirited boy whose hair was never cut or combed and who wouldn't let anyone touch his ten-inch-long fingernails. Guidoli nestled in the crook of my arm holding on to his teddy bear, a gift from an American.

The children were in the good hands of a live-in nursemaid who had been employed in Hermann Göring's household; she was a cousin of Papa Schneble. On winter Sundays I took the children to a playground for sleigh rides and snowball fights. In summer we frequented the zoo and a swimming pool. Four-year-old Sylvia was a fearless water rat and already could swim. Guidoli preferred the swing on dry land. He was two-and-a-half years old that summer of 1949.

Quite often I took my little ones along when making deliveries in the country, and we picnicked at the foot of the nearest mountain or frolicked at Tegernsee or Schliersee lakes. Seeing a boat for the first time, Guidoli cried: "Look, Mama, look! The boat is taking a bath!" To be alone with them was joy and happiness.

★   ★   ★

After long years of austerity, *Fasching* (carnival) had been revived in Munich and in 1950 was celebrated as never before. The fun-loving folk plunged into the pre-Lent festivities soon after New Year's Eve. There were many house parties and balls. The doors opened at nightfall to merrymakers dressed as Marie Antoinette and Louis XVI, Pierrots and Dominoes, gypsies and turbaned sheikhs. Dancing and celebrating went on all night, every night for weeks. Many a make-believe romance blossomed on the dance floor to fade into memory by dawn.

I was enchanted with this fantasy world. I wanted to dance and laugh and flirt without constraint. That's what *Fasching* was about. But Guido would not let me romp and frolic with the rest. I had to dance with him or not at all. The only man with whom he allowed me to dance, even at the costume party we gave at home, was Egbert Wagner.

Egbert was a Berliner, an ambitious and able man, tall and lean with chiseled features. The contrast between his nearly black, shiny hair and his aquamarine eyes was quite striking. He came daily to our store, and we became good friends. Egbert and Guido were both excellent skiers, and the three of us enjoyed the fun of skiing in the Alps and the convivial aprés-ski atmosphere. Egbert didn't have any male friends, and Guido, his opposite in all respects, was the only one with whom he associated.

Egbert was a good influence on Guido; a sloppy dresser, Guido began to pay attention to his appearance and to acquire some of Egbert's courteous manners. The handsome bachelor was dating Hella, a Greek girl.

Guido tried to coax Egbert into marriage, and I was tickled to hear my husband say, "Life is like a stepladder to the chicken coop: full of shit from top to bottom. But let me tell you, my friend, to live a single life is worse. Hell, it's like eating raw meat without salt and pepper! What you need is a woman like my Sopherl."

Egbert smiled as he said, "I take your word for it."

"But if you are looking for perfection, you had better forget it. You won't find it in any woman." Guido made a sound that might have been a chuckle or a sneer, removing the crown he had put on my head moments earlier.

"Perfection? I'd settle for a girl who is clever, ambitious, and stimulating; a good mother and a cook—"

"A lady by day and a whore at night," Guido finished the sentence, epitomizing the German male's idea of a perfect wife.

Their friendship never ceased to amaze me. Guido did not have the qualities I'd imagined the suave bachelor would look for in a friend, while Guido disliked sophistication, especially in men.

But there was nothing puzzling about my own feelings for Egbert. I found his company invigorating. We danced well together and flirted on the dance floor during the masquerade ball at the luxurious Regina Palace Hotel. Egbert, as a Domino, whispered make-believe words of love into my ear while the orchestra played "La Vie en Rose." I was a gypsy. Guido, a bedouin, actually looked and acted like one with his intense dark eyes and wild demeanor. He danced with Egbert's girlfriend Hella. The tall, exotic-looking Greek girl was appropriately dressed as Helen of Troy. Confetti showered in abundance, streamers entwined the dancing couples, uniting them. Magic was in the air. I felt young and alive and loved by this man who stimulated my sensuality, if only for that one night.

40

A TWENTY-MARK FINE

In July 1950, Seppi Irschik, the TK-1 staff sergeant I had met with Guido in Zaporozhye in 1941, arrived from Vienna by motorcycle with his wife Hilde to visit us. We took our friends to the Hofbräuhaus, ordered HB tankards of foaming beer, sizzling-hot bratwurst, and sauerkraut. Around our table were happy people, and we linked arms with them, swaying back and forth, laughing and singing traditional drinking songs.

Raising his tankard, Guido sang, *"In München steht ein Hofbräuhaus, eins, zwei—gsuffa!"* He took a thirst-quenching gulp, and then another. We all joined him in the song.

Across from us a mustached man in lederhosen was smiling at me. And I, forgetting how dangerous it was for me to show friendliness in my husband's presence, returned the man's smile. A flush of fury flooded Guido's face. He leaped to his feet, dashed his tankard of beer in the man's direction, spilling its content, and in a hoarse voice hurled insults at the bewildered man, creating an unpleasant scene.

"*Dirnenjäger!* [Whoremonger!]," blurted Guido—a double insult at the man and me.

Seppi grabbed Guido's arm. "It's enough!" he snapped. "Let's go."

"I hope you're satisfied," I said angrily to Guido as he drove us home. "You've made a fool of yourself in front of all those people."

"They can all crawl up my ass."

"Guido, for God's sake"—I castigated him in an undertone—"don't be so vulgar." He stepped on the gas pedal, and the car lurched forward at full speed.

Once at home, he served cognac and proposed a toast to our friends. The Irschiks, with a long journey to Vienna ahead of them in the morning, retired to our bedroom after the toast. I spread a sheet on the sofa in the living room and lay down on my stomach, pressing my face into the pillow. Guido finished his cognac in one gulp and stubbed out his cigarette, then lowered himself on top of me. No preliminaries, no sweet words or caresses, just an animalistic urge to satisfy his physical need, as always after an uproar.

He reeked of alcohol. I recoiled. "Get off my back."

My rebuff revived Guido's vile mood and goaded him into a frenzy. He wrenched me around, and I, twisting and kicking with my feet, managed to push him off the sofa. He cursed between gritted teeth and hit me broadside on the jaw. I cried out in pain and outrage. In one swift movement, he grabbed me by the throat and began to strangle me.

My voice, ordinarily soft, sounded raspy and garbled as I screamed for help. The screams brought our guests rushing from the bedroom. While Seppi tried to subdue Guido, I wriggled out of his grip and ran for the telephone in the hall to call the police. I was sure he had gone mad.

"My husband is trying to kill me," I pleaded urgently. The chilly voice on the other end of the line said, "We don't intervene in marital strife."

Like a tortured animal, arms flailing, Guido lunged after me. "I'll kill you!" His eyes were inflamed and his teeth luminous in the semidarkness.

The nursemaid ran out of her room. "*Gott im Himmel!* [God in heaven!]" She joined Seppi and Hilde in the hall, and all three were unable to restrain Guido. He tore the telephone from my hands, ripped the box off the wall, and was poised to pounce on me again.

While they struggled, I darted out the front door in my thin nightgown and hid in a clump of bushes down the street. I was paralyzed with fear; my teeth chattered. My legs were shaking so badly I thought I was going to collapse. I could hear Guido's screams, and Seppi shouting at him, the sound of windows opening, people's voices asking, "What's going on?"

A man in number twenty-three has gone berserk, I answered silently. *He'll pay for this! May his bleeding ulcers suck all the blood out of him!* I hated him.

My throat felt as if it were filled with blood. I touched my teeth; at least they were all still there. After what seemed like hours with no sign of Guido giving chase, I ventured back. Dawn would be breaking in an hour.

Guido and Seppi were talking in the kitchen. I went to the bathroom, spat out blood, rinsed my throat, and brushed my teeth. Quietly I crossed the hall and went into the children's room; both were asleep. I lay motionless beside Sylvia, and she snuggled in my arms. I eased off the bed without waking her and left their room.

Guido breathed evenly, sound asleep in the living room. It was quiet in the house, still dark, and everyone was asleep.

Except Seppi. He was at the kitchen table, sitting straight up, not slouching as Guido would. He had a kind face—he was an affable man with soft blue eyes. His native Viennese soothed the ear.

I made a pot of coffee, lit a cigarette on the gas flame, and inhaled deeply to calm my nerves. "So now you've seen your friend in action. What do you think?"

Seppi shook his head sadly. "Guido hasn't changed."

"Tell me about it."

"He nearly killed me once. In Zaporozhye, back in '41. We were arguing over some trivia when he grabbed a stiletto knife and hurled it at me. Luckily, I dodged in time to avoid the blade. It grazed my temple and embedded itself in the doorjamb. That temper of his! He was notorious for that among our comrades. And yet"—Seppi's eyebrows merged in a thoughtful frown—"he's a good-hearted fellow."

"To me he is not," I growled, moving to the window. I pulled the shutters up. "Just look at me." The left side of my face was swollen and bruised, an eye a mere slit; my upper lip was split, and there were purplish-red finger imprints on my throat.

Seppi looked at his friend's handiwork in horrified disbelief. We drank our coffee in silence then.

At noon Guido and I saw our friends to the Austrian border, as we had promised. Guido rode on Seppi's motorcycle with him; Hilde rode with me in our Ford Taunus.

Hilde brushed a strand of hair off my forehead. "How can you live with a man who treats you so abominably?"

I shrugged with a deep sigh.

"If my Seppi did that to me, I'd probably kill him first."

"It's easy to kill a lamb. Not a brute like Guido."

"My heart aches for you."

"Thank you, Hilde." My voice cracked.

On the way home, Guido took the steering wheel. I looked straight ahead, couldn't stand the sight of him, and did not say a word. And neither did he. Suddenly he turned to me and said, "What's the matter, Sopherl? Why don't you speak to me?"

★   ★   ★

Convinced his brutality must not go unpunished, I reported Guido to the police. For having nearly strangled me to death, they fined him a paltry twenty marks, reluctantly, and only after I had produced a doctor's certificate of injuries.

There was nothing in the world I wanted more than to escape from this crippling marriage. If it had not been for the children, I would have abandoned Guido then. I knew that if I tried to get away with Sylvia and Guidoli, he would come after us and kill me. He loved the children as much as I did.

A divorce was not possible. Adultery was the only legal ground for divorce in Bavaria at that time, and only if both parties agreed to it. Guido would never agree.

He was out working on an electrical installation contract when Egbert Wagner came by the store. As usual, his dress was impeccable. "What happened to you?"

"Your friend tried to tame a wild horse."

Egbert cast a look of caring and understanding.

"I hoped they'd arrest him," I said. "An insane asylum, that's what he needs. He's sick."

"No, it isn't that. It's more likely his Bavarian temper."

"Bavarians are meek by comparison. Guido's temper is all his own. He lacks self-confidence, and there's a lot of frustration bottled up inside him. That's what is fueling his jealousy and driving him insane."

"He's obsessed with you." Egbert lit a cigarette and came to sit behind the counter. "Have you talked to his father?"

"He knows. But what can he do? Guido kicked me in the stomach once, in front of his father. I don't even remember why . . . Father is such a grand old man. He was so very angry with Guido. They had a long talk afterward. And what good did it do?" I asked for a cigarette. He lit it for me. "I think I know what the problem is. Let's face it, Egbert—it's a man's world. That's why the police were reluctant to fine him—one of their own. The law is on Guido's side, and not only because he's a man. He is German-born, a native Bavarian, no less—and I am not," I added as an afterthought. "If I withdrew from the store, do you think that might help the situation? It should boost Guido's male ego, if nothing else."

"He'd go bankrupt," Egbert remarked.

"If worse comes to worst, I could always start another business—something that is less threatening to Guido. A custom-made dress shop for ladies, perhaps."

"You can do that anyway, as a sideline. In fact, I have a suggestion to make. But I don't agree with your idea of turning the store over to Guido. That won't change him."

"I can't change either. So there we are. A stalemate. He can't accept me as I am, and I can't accept his bullying me. And we argue and fight. We're wrong for each other. I bring out the worst in him, and he brings out the worst in me. Anyway, you have a suggestion to make. What is it?"

"My sister is coming from Berlin. She's a first-rate dressmaker and designer. If you're serious about a dress-making enterprise, she could help."

"It just struck me as a possibility. I haven't really thought about it. But I'll consider it."

"Whatever you do, Sophia, don't neglect the business. You have established it. Don't let him take that away from you."

★   ★   ★

With Guido and me both in the electrical business, it grew until the store had to be enlarged. We sold the panel truck and bought a brand-new Ford Taunus for Guido and a used red Fiat convertible for me. We also bought a tall trailer suitable for deliveries of refrigerators. We hired one of Guido's wartime comrades, a capable electrician, who with Guido fulfilled our increasing contracts from private customers, local building contractors, and the U.S. occupation forces.

Munich was throbbing with industry and activity. New apartment houses were springing up. A department store was under construction. The old Palace of Justice, the National Theater, other stately buildings and museums were renovated. Stores filled with merchandise. West Germany was on its way to prosperity.

Trade was good, our financial position healthy. Guido and I were effective as business partners; we worked in harmony. This had a soothing influence on our relationship, but I had no feelings left for him. Although Guido had gained some control of his temper, and indeed appeared to have become the sedate businessman I had hoped he would be, the change had come too late.

41

IN THE CARDS

"Okay, my little marvels, get your toys together so I can finish packing. Your daddy is driving us to the mountains."

The children skipped and squealed for joy and set out to scour the apartment for the toys that were strewn about.

I overheard Sylvia tell her little brother: "I'll take my tricycle and stroller for my doll, and you take your teddy bear."

"I want my train *and* my teddy bear."

"The train's too long! It won't fit in the car, silly," Sylvia said with authority.

"I want my train." Guidoli started wailing.

"That's all right, baby." I pressed him to me. "Of course you can take the train." It was disassembled, easily packed, and everybody was happy.

Guido drove up, loaded the car with the toys, and we were on our way to Törwang, a resort at the foot of Hochries Mountain. The children and I had spent two weeks there the year before, in June, when business was slow, and I looked forward to being alone with them again now.

We had a glorious time romping in the meadows, gathering wildflowers, and hiking. Both children were enthusiastic mountaineers. With pride I watched my little ones run free. I had made a resolution about how differently I would raise my children from the way my mother had raised me. Yet I wanted them to grow up independent, as I had, so that when the time came to walk out into the world, they would be prepared.

On the last day of our holiday, we were packed and waiting for Guido to take us home when Egbert drove up.

"How lovely to see you," I called to him from the balcony. "Pity we're leaving. Guido is coming to pick us up."

"No, he isn't." Egbert ran up the two flights of stairs. "You're in my hands now." He laughed softly. "Guido couldn't come so he entrusted you to me."

Well, well, what do you know? I thought. *Talk about letting the fox take care of the chickens! My jealous husband trusts me with the only other man I know who cares about me and with whom, given a chance, I could easily fall in love.*

"You could've brought Hella with you. She's good company, a lovely girl."

"Are you trying to marry me off?"

"Sounds like a good idea. I haven't been to a wedding in a long while."

"Hella is a lovely girl. But—"

"Yes?"

"She isn't you."

"What's that supposed to mean?"

"If I could meet a girl like you, I'd marry her tomorrow."

"You're *très* gallant. Too bad I'm not a girl."

"That's my tragedy."

"And mine." I laughed. I was fascinated with the game we were playing. "Now you had better take us home. Sylvia and Guidoli are jumping up and down. They're anxious to see their daddy and tell him about their adventures and mountain climbing."

Guidoli sat on Egbert's lap and "drove" the car. Sylvia knelt on my lap, her head out the window, hair flying, afraid to miss anything. She reminded me of myself at that age.

As we approached Munich, Egbert made a suggestion, which somehow did not come as a surprise. Guidoli by this time had fallen asleep on the back seat; Sylvia had settled down beside him.

"You're not happy with Guido, and I'm not happy without you," he said in a low, urgent tone of voice. "Could you find some time to be with me?"

"I wouldn't trust myself alone with you." The thought of what Guido would do to both of us if he ever found out was enough to cool my lust.

★   ★   ★

At home that night, Guido stumped me by asking if I would tell him his fortune. Since Zaporozhye days, when I was troubled, I had been laying cards for myself, looking for good signs to give me hope. In all the seven years of our married life, I had only twice spread the cards for Guido. *What does he want to know now, and why can't it wait?* The electrician we had hired to work with Guido was there; he was a gaunt man with a prominent Adam's apple.

"If you insist." I shuffled the deck. "Now concentrate. Make a wish and cut the deck three times, toward you. Well, well," I said slowly, looking at the cards surrounding the King of Hearts. Facing the King was the Queen of Clubs; on the "threshold" and in "his heart" were the cards belonging to the Queen of Clubs. "Well, well," I said again, glancing up at Guido with "all-seeing, all-knowing" eyes. "There is another woman in your life. I'd say her hair is dark."

The two men exchanged glances, a little too quickly. The electrician looked ill at ease. Guido merely sank back into his chair; his face showed no emotion.

A seed of suspicion grew within me. I finished the reading and volunteered to drive the electrician home.

On the way, I bluffed. "I know Guido is seeing another woman. How long has it been going on?" I asked, keeping my voice matter-of-fact.

His big Adam's apple went up and down in his scrawny neck as he gulped. "How . . . how did you find out?"

"You've just told me," I said, outwardly calm but inwardly shocked that I had been right.

"Oh my God. Guido will kill me!"

"I won't give you away. Don't worry." And the nervous Adam's Apple told me then what I wanted to hear.

Guido had been seeing the dark-haired Hanna steadily since they had met in the store some weeks before. They had just returned from a three-day retreat in the Tyrol. *Aha, so that's why!* I realized. *Guido asked Egbert to bring the children and me home from Törwang and then took off with his Queen of Clubs.*

Guido stayed out that night, and in the morning, when I confronted him, he didn't even lie. He saw nothing wrong in having a mistress. He, so jealous of me, seemed to look upon this affair as a perfectly normal interlude.

Angrier than ever, I came to realize that clinging to this sick, corroded marriage for the children's sake would do them more harm than good. I had to go. But I couldn't run or walk away. There was no place for me to hide with two small children. Guido would find us no matter where we went. I thought about Russia. He would never find us there. But for me, "contaminated" by Western culture, there was no going back. I felt at home in the West, and though I was not materialistically inclined, I thrived on the challenge of free enterprise. I must try to get Guido to agree to a friendly divorce. It was important to me that we part amicably.

"Would you marry Hanna if I were to give you a divorce?" I asked calmly, casually, afraid to antagonize him at this stage.

"Oh no," he said, "I haven't even considered it."

He began to take sizable amounts of money from the cash register, and we quarreled in the store. His weakness of the flesh and his conduct were difficult to ignore. He flaunted the romance; everyone knew about it. To get me to react, he started telling me about Hanna, how she'd wait for him with champagne and bubble bath for two. She gave him freely what he desired no matter what time of day or night, and asked for more.

But I didn't care.

For two weeks I watched, waited, hoped for him to ask me for a divorce. He did not, while I was afraid to press the issue knowing he could not be pressured into anything. He might give up Hanna, and my one chance for a divorce would evaporate. Or he might agree and later deny his guilt in court; I had no proof of his marital infidelity. Our friends would all claim ignorance. I knew that. They were all as afraid of him as I was, deathly afraid.

★   ★   ★

Early in July I had an unexpected visitor at the store.

"Frau Schneble, may I take a few moments of your time?"

"Certainly." To the salesgirl, I said, "Please take care of the customers. I don't want to be disturbed."

I knew instinctively who the woman was, even before she introduced herself. *But what does she want of me?* I wondered, showing her into the cubicle that served as an office.

Hanna sat down, lit a cigarette, and came straight to the point. She was in love with Guido and he with her, she informed me. "I came to beg you to release him." She spoke in an even tone of voice, but I sensed her nervousness.

For all Guido's tales of her sensuality, she looked rather masculine in a pleasant sort of way. Her facial features were strong; she had surprisingly mild gray-blue eyes.

"It isn't up to me," I said regretfully. "It's entirely up to Guido. As far as I'm concerned, the choice is his."

"Really. Guido tells me you refuse to give him a divorce."

Hanna quickly grasped the situation and took matters into her own hands. She left Munich. Several days later, a sizzling love letter to Guido came by post. I intercepted it. Inside were two photographs of her with Guido taken in Tyrol. Hanna was compelled to remind Guido how much she loved him, yearned for him; she missed his burning kisses and embraces, his electrifying touch.

Whatever Hanna's reasons were for writing it—for all I knew the letter was meant to be intercepted—she had given me the proof I needed, and the courage to press Guido for divorce.

At lunch the next day, I faced Guido with half of Hanna's letter (the other half, with her signature and the photographs, was safely tucked away) and was amazed how easily he gave in.

"Go ahead and divorce me. What does it matter anyway? Only don't try and make me pay for it, because I won't."

"Are you talking about alimony? I'm not asking for it."

"That would really be the limit. Imagine even mentioning alimony. The attorney's fee, I mean."

"I'll pay the fees. Let's find a lawyer and talk to him."

"Just a minute, please." He eyed me suspiciously. "What do you expect from this?"

"All I want is a divorce. Once this is over, you'll be free to do as you please."

"If you think you'll get to keep the store, or any part of it, forget it. I'm its legal owner. The cars and bank accounts are also in my name. And so is the apartment—it belongs to me."

I was prepared to give up the store, the money, and my car. But the apartment? This came as a shock. I hesitated, but not too long, before I said, "If you insist, so be it. Keep it all! Just give me a divorce."

"The children will stay with me, of course."

"I expected you to say that. Now, shall we go?"

The divorce court had nothing to do with the custody of the children; a guardianship court, *Vormundschaftsgericht*, decided the matter after a marriage had been dissolved. Since I would be divorcing Guido on grounds of adultery, the ultimate offense, I had no cause for concern. The children would be awarded to me. The children's court, however, was primarily concerned with the welfare of children, and I knew that in deciding custody they would favor the parent who could house them and provide for them. Apartments were still extremely hard to find.

Having accepted Guido's harsh conditions, I was about to lose everything and would need time to get myself established again. *It won't take long, though*, I thought. In the meantime, the children would have to stay with him.

Of course I didn't, couldn't tell Guido that this arrangement was only temporary, that I'd be fighting him in court another day.

★ ★ ★

On August 29, 1951, I was granted a divorce from Guido on grounds of adultery. The usual reconciliation period of up to one year was waived. The marriage was declared shattered, utterly and beyond repair. Guido, whose deposition had been taken in writing by the lawyer, did not appear in court.

While waiting for the papers to be delivered, which took two weeks, I dissolved my recently established custom dressmaking enterprise and did not go to the store. I wanted to be with Sylvia and Guidoli day and night before leaving them for who knew how long.

Sylvia started school on the third of September, and I took her there and picked her up. I had never forgotten my first day at school. First-graders were traditionally accompanied by their mothers or grandmothers. At least she would not be left with the memory of having had to walk alone.

The papers were delivered a week before our seventh wedding anniversary. But I did not rejoice. As I was packing the few things I was allowed to take with me, I was sadly aware that my home was not mine anymore. Hanna would soon have it all. No matter how many tears I had shed within its walls, parting with it was painful.

The children did not see me pack. Sylvia was at school; the nursemaid took Guidoli to the Perlacher Forest to romp.

I couldn't bear for them to see me leave.

But I did not cry. *I'll be reunited with them in no time at all. It won't be long. Come Monday, I'll start looking for a job. Jobs are plentiful.* To find a decent place to live would be difficult, I knew, but I would not allow myself to brood over it. I was practically penniless and couldn't pay the rent today. But tomorrow I would. *"Yes,"* my inner voice said, *"you will get through this obstacle in your life, just as you have survived so many others."*

Guido came home unexpectedly and shook me out of my reverie. "Where do you think you're going?"

"To Larissa." Vera and Andrei had stayed with her before they emigrated to North America. If not Larissa, Frau Gruber or the owner of Café Loya would give me temporary shelter. I knew they would.

"Now, if that isn't stupid. They only have that one room. Unpack and stay."

"That's really quite generous of you. But no, I won't. We're now legally divorced."

"Who cares about that? It's only a scrap of paper. You wanted it, you got it. As far as I'm concerned, you're still my wife."

"What?"

"Unpack, I said."

I picked up my two suitcases and crossed the threshold of my home for the last time.

42

BIRD IN A MAZE

My first job with the brand-new department store on Sonnen Strasse came to a quick end. When I arrived to work as an electrical goods buyer, the manager, who knew of me and had hired me, said that the position had been filled.

I was stunned, could hardly believe it. "How could that be? You hired me only yesterday."

"So sorry, Frau Schneble. We hired two people for the same job by mistake. No, there are no other openings at the moment."

In the street Guido ran into me, as if by chance. Smiling craftily, he asked, "How did it go at the department store?"

"So it's you! *You* made me lose this job. For God's sake, what did you say to them?"

"I told them you're unreliable and a whore."

"You're out of your mind! How dare you call me a whore—you, of all people."

"I've done it, and I'll do it again. It's crazy looking for a job when I need you in the store. If you don't come home, you'll starve to death."

Guido still saw himself as the undeniable head of the family. He regarded his wife and children, among other things, as his possessions. He could not accept the fact that we were divorced, that I was no longer his. Faced with the reality, he tried all kinds of ways to get me back. He was constantly at my heels, exerting steady and unyielding pressure. I moved almost daily from one friend's house to another. But I could not escape from him.

"Come back to me, Sopherl. On my word of honor, I'll change. Would you like to go to Venezuela or South Africa? We could sell everything and start anew."

"Why don't you marry Hanna and go with her to South Africa? We are divorced. *Ge-shie-den!*" I emphasized each syllable. "Why can't you get that into your head? Now go. Leave me alone."

"I'll never leave you alone, get *that* into your head. I'll make your life so miserable, you'll wish you'd never been born."

Two weeks went by, and I was still unemployed. Guido accused me publicly of deserting him and the children, and he kept calling me a whore. He also made it hard for me to see my children, and under the circumstances it was premature to demand my rights and fight for custody.

I was homeless, jobless, and penniless.

The owners of Café Loya remained my friends. Through them I got a job with a mail order company and was able to rent a room in an apartment house near Sendlingertor Platz.

I moved in on a drizzly October afternoon and was awakened that night by bright lights shining into my room. I looked out the window. Standing beside his car, Guido was directing strong spotlights into every window of the four-story building.

"Come home where you belong," he bellowed when he saw me at the third-floor window. "Come down, or I'll wake up the whole damned place."

I retreated from the window, sick at heart that he had found me so quickly. The glaring lights, his yelling and honking the horn, woke up the other tenants.

At last Guido left, and it was quiet again. But he came back the next night.

The following day I was evicted for disturbing the peace.

"The tenants are complaining," the manager of the building said to me. "Nobody can sleep with all the noise going on."

I was walking along a darkened street on the way to Frau Gruber's house for the night when Guido drove by; brakes slammed and tires squealed. He turned the car around and drove straight at me. And I ran, zigzagging, illuminated by the headlights. Suddenly he accelerated, jumped the curb, and drove onto the sidewalk. I pressed my back flat against the wall, gasping with fear. The car screeched past, barely missing me.

My feet felt like jelly. "You'll fry in hell for this!" My voice sounded hysterical.

Guido devoted more time to tracking me down than to Hanna or the store. He hired his sister Pia, recently divorced, to help him in the store part-time.

Hanna, loath to live in my shadow, had urged Guido to move. He complied, trading his large apartment for a much smaller one and furnishing it with all new furniture.

"Oh, incidentally," Guido said late in November, having cornered me at the Marienplatz. "I kicked Hanna out and got rid of the maid."

"Who's looking after the children?"

"I put them in an orphanage."

Even today I find it almost unbearable to think about that moment.

"I don't believe you!" Then I took one look at his eyes and I believed. There was spite in them, and gloating.

Guido did not follow me when I ran across Neuhauser Strasse and after the streetcar. I leaped on it for the ride to the orphanage, my eyes and heart crying. He could hunt me like an animal, he could make me a nervous wreck, he could drain me of my courage and destroy my faith in humanity, but how could he do this to the children?

And he claimed he loved them. "Bastard!" I cried. *You love them like my mother loved me. Hers was a selfish kind of love, and so is yours. If Mama had truly loved me, she would have released me to Papa's care. But she held on to me, held on to me even though she had no time to spare for me. I used to wonder why she would not allow me to see my father, let alone live with him. Now I understood. She was punishing my father the only way she knew—and Guido was doing the same thing, using the children to punish me, much as my mother had used me. If that is love, then the children can get along without it very well.*

They were outside when I got to the orphanage, playing in the yard with other children. I watched them from a distance for a while, then swallowed the sobs that constricted my throat and called to them. "Sylvia! Guidoli!"

"Mutti!" Guidoli outran Sylvia into my arms. I wiped his nose, pulled up his and Sylvia's stockings. They planted moist kisses on my cheeks, and then ran back to play, showing off and waving to me. They were having a good time; their spirits seemed high. But their stockings were drooping again.

My pain that night was so intense that it will never be fully eradicated. I lay on blankets spread on the floor of Larissa's room and sobbed. My mind lingered on the possibility of snatching the children from the orphanage and escaping with them—but where to? I tried to convince myself that the orphanage was the safest place for them to wait out the storm, that they would be far better off staying there for a while. Papa Schneble was personally involved with the orphanage and would make certain his grandchildren were looked after properly. Still, it hurt—hurt to know that in his desire for vengeance there were no barriers Guido would not crash, no moral codes he would not break, no dastardly act he would not commit to attain his ends, and that there was nothing I could do to stop him. I felt entirely at his mercy, with the threat of physical violence against me lodged in my throat.

I was trapped, trapped like a bird caught in a maze, hurling myself against the walls, desperately searching for a beam of light to point the way out. I could see none.

★ ★ ★

Papa Schneble was heartsick as he witnessed our marriage deteriorating and, finally, breaking up. He had tried not to intervene, but now that he had heard through Pia of his son's deplorable activities, he decided it was time he did.

Guido called me at work to say that his father wanted to see me. I, too, wanted to see him. "Come by the store and take the car. I won't need it," he said. When I got there at two in the afternoon, as agreed, the salesgirl told me Guido wasn't there, but that he had left his Ford Taunus for me.

As I drove along Landsberger Strasse, passing motorists kept honking. I pulled over to the curb and stopped to see if perhaps there were something wrong with the car. I could see nothing wrong. When I started the engine again, a passerby called, "Your trunk is open!" I stopped again. The lid was closed. I tried to lift it, but it would not open. I jerked the lid—and there, curled in that small space, wild-eyed and gasping for air, was Guido.

He pushed the back seat forward and crawled out of the trunk into the back seat of the car. "Drive!" he ordered.

I cringed into the seat.

"Get going!" he commanded through gritted teeth.

I drove off. Paralyzed, as though welded to the steering wheel, I could only wonder how long it would take before he strangled me. I was sure he meant to kill me. After all the struggles to survive the war, to die like this . . .

Father took one look at his son and paled. "You scoundrel! Get out of my sight!"

Guido instantly obeyed.

Papa Schneble sank to his knees before me and clasped my hands. "Sophia, I beseech you, leave Munich. Leave before he kills you."

"Why must *I* be sacrificed? Where can I go? He won't let me go with the children. He won't! He'd kill me first."

"You mustn't tell him anything. Just go. Go alone to Stuttgart, Frankfurt—"

"Alone?" I looked at him in blank amazement.

"You can't take the little ones with you."

"I won't do it. I can't!" I started crying. "I beg you, Father."

It was all so hopeless. And this wonderful old man, on his knees, pleading with me to leave, to leave without my children. He could not help me. He who devoted much of his time to the betterment of public institutions, the orphanage, and a school for hard-of-hearing youths, he could neither help nor protect me.

I sobbed convulsively, my face buried in Father's lap. He stroked my head and tried to comfort me, but there were tears in his eyes too.

"The children will be all right. I'll look in on them every day. Once you're gone, Guido will take them back home. Listen to me, Sophia—it's for the children's sake that I'm urging you to leave. Think of Sylvia and little Guido. Think of how they would feel if their father were hanged for killing their mother. Someday it's going to come to this. Think of them."

"Think of them, think of how they would feel" . . . *Is there anyone in the world who cares about how I feel?*

After several desolate nights, I began to appreciate Father's concern. The children would be orphans if I stayed. I must leave. Or go back to Guido.

I went back and tried again. But it did not work.

A few weeks of relative calm came to an abrupt end. Guido came home dead drunk, and when I refused to remarry him, he vented his rage on the new Chippendale furniture, smashing the glass-top coffee table and the chairs, and tore down the drapes from the window. I wished he were dead.

To escape from the remnants of bondage, and to stay alive, I began to think about leaving Germany, and my resolve to emigrate ripened fast. I made up my mind to leave the children in their father's care. I would make certain, though, that they followed me to a country where German law did not apply and where I would have a chance to win their custody. My chances of succeeding in Bavaria were nil. Guido would make certain of that. And the law was on his side.

The German Law of Domestic Relations violated the principle of equality insofar as it favored the father in decisions affecting children. The law was changed, but not until 1956.

43

A DOUBLE RAINBOW

Things happened swiftly after that.

At the IRO Resettlement Center in Munich, my inquiries led me to a knowledgeable, compassionate clerk from Poland. He was a sturdy man with a wart on his nose.

"I want to emigrate to the United States," I said.

"Are you a German citizen?"

"Yes, I am."

"You can apply for an immigration visa only if you're a German refugee."

The interview was casual; the clerk sat on his desk. He probed deeper into my background and came up with a fascinating interpretation of the facts. My German papers indicated that I had been a German citizen before May 1, 1945, but that I was born and domiciled in Kiev prior to January 1939; moreover, I had come to Munich from Gardelegen County, East Germany—hence, I was a German refugee. "What you must do now is apply for *Flüchtlingsausweis* [a refugee card]. When you get it, come back and see me. Do you know anyone in the United States?"

"Yes, a Russian girl who's now living in New Jersey. I could write and ask her to sponsor me."

"There isn't time for that. Fill out this application form and include your friend's name and address, just in case. You may not need a sponsor. It'll be up to the Americans to decide on that. Now see to it that you get those refugee papers."

The interview took place on December 23—one day before all business closed down for the holidays—and seven days before January 1, 1952, when the International Refugee Organization, the IRO, was concluding its resettlement operations. Had I waited another day, my desire to emigrate to the United States might never have been fulfilled. I was issued a refugee card on January 28. Meantime, my application had already gone through the proper channels of the IRO.

★   ★   ★

Over New Year's Eve I went skiing with friends who had a cabin in the Alps. At dawn on New Year's Day, I climbed through heavy layers of snow up to the summit and picked my way cautiously along the icy ridge toward the mountaintop chapel. I wanted to be the first in 1952 to ring its cast-iron bell. I wanted to be alone to pray.

The air on the mountain, the loftiest in sight, was so clear and pure that I had a feeling of being above the earth's protective atmosphere. I shut my eyes. "O God, forgive me for doubting." And I prayed, prayed hard, asking him to help me reach America. "Please, dear God, don't let anything come between me and my little ones. Grant me the wish to be reunited with them."

I tolled the bell. Its sound reverberated and filled me with faith, strength, and inspiration. I believed God would answer my prayers. For the first time in my life I believed in God.

★   ★   ★

It was much easier to descend the mountain. And it was infinitely easier to approach Guido with my plan now that there was faith in my heart. Guido could easily prevent me from getting a visa by going to the American immigration authorities and defaming my character. The Americans were thorough in their investigations and were known to refuse visas to persons of dubious repute.

I also knew that the only way I could take the children out of Germany was with their father. He would never surrender the children otherwise. I might have to promise to remarry him.

So I asked Guido if he would follow me to the United States of America. "I don't know yet whether I'll be accepted. But if I am—"

"What do you mean 'follow'? If we can't go together as man and wife, you won't be going either."

"You have so often talked about leaving Germany and starting anew somewhere else. Here's your chance. Do you want to go to the greatest country in the world, or don't you?"

"Yes, I do. But . . . how do I know you'll keep your word and send for me?"

"I will, Guido. You can depend on that. Or do you think I'd go off and leave the children behind with no hope of ever seeing them?"

"No, I guess not. And you will remarry me?"

"Yes," I said, the word choking in my throat.

Some three weeks later—after I had had the medical examination, had been photographed and interviewed by an American officer, who was all smiles and friendliness, and had passed everything with ease—Guido again brought up the dreaded subject.

"Let's get married now. Why wait until we're in New York?"

"It would screw up my visa. I told you so. It's too late to do anything about it now."

"I'll tell you what," said he, "I'll come to Bremerhaven and we'll marry there, just before your ship sails."

"Don't rush me into it, for heaven's sake."

"If you refuse, the kids will have no mother." His eyes bored through me.

I returned his gaze unflinchingly, though I hesitated one swift moment—the moment that could decide a lifetime—before surrendering to his final demand.

"All right," I said with a melancholy sigh, hoping that I could board the ship and sail before Guido reached Bremerhaven.

★ ★ ★

"Where are you going, Mutti?" my little ones asked when I came to the orphanage to say good-bye. They looked at me with trusting eyes, expectantly, when I said, "I'll see you soon, my darlings. I'll see you in New York."

I did not trust myself to say more without bitterness, without breaking down, without crying. And they would cry, too. At least, I knew Sylvia would. She had always been sensitive to my emotions, laughing when I laughed, crying when I cried. *And what more could I say? Could I tell them why we were being separated? Could I explain their daddy's actions without turning them against him? Would they understand?* They were still so young.

I left Munich by train and arrived in Bremerhaven on March 18. The huge camp was full of emigrants: single people young and old, entire families large and small. Some reflected healthy optimism; others were apprehensive of the unknown. All of them were waiting patiently for their turn to sail. Except me.

"Is there any possibility of getting just one more on the ship that is sailing tomorrow?" I looked pleadingly at the man with close-cropped hair in charge of embarkation.

"I guess one more won't sink the ship. You're on."

On March 21, 1952, the USNS *General Harry Taylor*, a former U.S. Army troop transporter, was boarded by 2,041 people bound for a new life in the New World. I imagined myself to be number 2,041.

As the ship pulled away from the pier, I stood on deck but didn't once look back at the Old World. Russia, my motherland, the land that I loved; Germany, the land I had learned to love and where I had felt equally at home—both were behind me now.

Sailing by the coast of England, shrouded in fog, I sent nostalgic greetings across the channel to my wartime friends: Big Ben and the BBC. Then the full impact of leaving all I had known and loved swept over me.

The sturdy ship heaved, rose, and fell during a storm in the midst of the awesome Atlantic Ocean. After the storm, not one but two perfect arches of color spanned the horizon. The double rainbow strengthened my hope that I would soon be reunited with my children, and it carried me on the crest of renewed optimism to the shores of the Great New World.

EPILOGUE

Kiev, 1962.

"Zosenka, you're so thin!" Twenty-one years since I heard that voice. "Don't you get enough to eat in America?"

I laugh heartily as I run into Mama's welcoming arms. Mama takes one look at the tall man approaching us; he is impeccably dressed in a charcoal-gray suit, undoubtedly an American, and she cries, "Jeemie!" Still holding me with one arm, she throws her other arm around my husband, Jim, and the three of us are locked in an embrace.

Mother is heavier and much shorter than I remember. At seventy-four, her complexion is still unblemished, unlined, her graying hair tinted blond, her lips and nails painted a dusty pink to match her summer suit. She bubbles with energy.

"A remarkable woman," my darling Jim says.

The rest of the family surges around us. "How you have grown." My gentle Aunt Yulia strokes my hair. "You're so tall."

I toss my head back and laugh. We were the same height when I left home at age seventeen. Now I tower over her. "Must be the food they feed us in America."

One by one other dear familiar faces come into focus: Uncle Vanya, Cousin Igor and Cousin Valya with their spouses, neighbors, friends, classmates—sixteen people in all, and all but the men present me with bouquets of flowers.

The happy maelstrom moves through the airport. Jim utters the only Russian words he knows, *"Kak pozhevayete?"* ("How are you?") and is overwhelmed with a torrent of explanations, of which he understands not a word.

The Intourist guide rescues him. Our car is waiting.

Dazed and bedazzled, Jim and I ride to our hotel in a chauffeured black limousine. Family and friends pile into three hired Volga cars and, waving and blowing kisses, follow us.

As we cross the bridge over the Dnieper, I cry, "Look, Jim!" High above the river, obscured by the lush green August foliage, is the city of my birth. The garden town—the air is sweet. I smell the rich black soil, and the smell is as I remembered it. The golden cupolas of Orthodox churches and monasteries sparkle in the sun. "A beautiful sight, darling. Isn't it?" Jim smiles without taking his eyes from a hydrofoil gliding on the surface of the broad Dnieper. We climb a steep hill and drive along Kreshchatik, a splendid tree-lined avenue; it was totally destroyed by bombs and partisans during the war and has been reconstructed in the rather ornate postwar Soviet style.

We arrive at the Hotel Intourist on Lenin Street. I am delighted. My school was only two blocks downhill from the hotel. A short climb up the hill and just around the corner on Vladimirskaya Street is where I grew up and where my mother still lives.

While Jim takes a shower in a deep tub, I dress for the reunion celebration at Mother's and chat with the floor matron who has brought jam jars for my flowers. She wants to know when and how I left the Soviet Union—but neither she nor anyone else asks why I have not returned since the war. *There's no simple answer to that question,* I reflect, and think to myself: *How amazing that only ten years after landing in New York with seventy-five cents to my name, I am able to return to Kiev and find so much the same, and yet the world so different.*

★ ★ ★

I landed in New York Harbor late in March 1952 with a buoyant feeling of freedom and fulfillment. I had small change in my pockets and spoke no English, but my heart brimmed with gratitude and love for the country that was giving me an opportunity for a fresh start in life.

I found America such a vibrant country, the New Yorkers cool on the outside, warm and welcoming on the inside, and full of energy. I was impressed and felt invigorated by the competitive, gutsy atmosphere. I took to my adopted country as though I had lived there in a previous life.

Three days after my arrival I landed a job as an elevator operator in a twenty-five-story office building occupied by EBASCO, an engineering firm. Remember the days when uniformed operators called out the floors and chatted with you about the weather? That's how I learned to speak English. Although traveling vertically in the daytime, I soon began to make a horizontal commute across the river to Hoboken, New Jersey, to study engineering, my childhood dream. About a year into the program, a professor suggested that I was now skilled enough to get a job as a draftsman. I applied to the personnel department of EBASCO, but the personnel manager told me bluntly that they did not hire women for engineering jobs.

I was on a subway a few days later, when one of my elevator acquaintances sat down next to me. "On your way to English classes tonight?" he asked. "I'm studying engineering, not English," I said, and recounted my job-hunting episode. He happened to be a vice president of EBASCO. I was hired the very next day—the first-ever female in their engineering department. I was first again to break into the traditionally male territory at Ford, Bacon & Davis, my next job.

In September 1955, word came to New York that Bechtel Corporation was hiring in San Francisco, the city I wanted to make my home. I sent my resumé, along with a note asking: "Do you hire women?" The return telegram said, "You are hired. Start immediately." I promptly reported to work on the West Coast. My association with Bechtel would span three decades and take me around the globe.

It was over a game of bridge with other Bechtel employees that I met and fell in love with Jim Williams. He was a project engineer at the time, I a piping designer. We were married in Santa Barbara in 1959.

Guido and the children landed in New York in May 1953. I only wanted Guido in America to be near Guidoli and Sylvia—it was the only way that I could be reunited with them. I had sent him the papers and let him know that I would not remarry him. Guido came anyway, as I believed he would, and took the children directly to Milwaukee, where a job as a welder was promised him and Andrei, his Russian friend from Munich, waited for him.

Every summer I flew to Milwaukee to spend my vacations with the children. But each time, incensed at my refusal to stay and be his wife, and crazily jealous as ever, Guido threw such ugly scenes that I had to cut my visits short.

I still did not have custody of the children. I was afraid to start legal proceedings because Guido had threatened to return to Germany with them the day I did. He was a German national, and he did not apply for U.S. citizenship for that reason, while I became an American in 1957.

In 1958, Guido married a girl sent from Bavaria by his father. Desperate for a wife, he had advertised in the European newspapers and hundreds of letters arrived containing photographs of equally desperate, hopeful brides-to-be. He chose a woman from Barcelona, but when she landed on the East Coast with her two small children, Guido was not there to receive them. He was already married to the girl his father had picked. What a bastard! I felt for the Barcelona girl when Sylvia told me about it. As for the second marriage, it was brief and ended with the second Frau Schneble hospitalized following a beating by Guido.

Sylvia asked me, "Why did you ever marry my dad, Mutti? You're so different."

"You're only fourteen, sweetheart. When you are older, you will understand. Your dad and I didn't give ourselves a chance to learn to live with our differences, to accept each other as we are." I didn't want to poison the children with my real opinion of their father. They had to live with him.

"I do understand why you don't want to stay. I love you, Mutti, and when I'm eighteen, I'll come to you." As I waited the four years for us to be reunited, I corresponded secretly with her and talked to her and Guidoli on the telephone.

Guido soon married for a third time; his marriage to a woman from East Germany was, at last, a happy one. He never returned to Munich; his father had disowned him.

Papa Schneble, elected chairman of the *Bezirkstag* (district assembly), was active until the day he died in 1960. For his many contributions to the community, the city of Munich bestowed a high honor upon him posthumously by naming a street for him.

Guido died of Lou Gehrig's disease (amyotrophic lateral sclerosis) in 1971, at the age of fifty-two.

★   ★   ★

Karl Mannheim was taken prisoner by the Soviets in 1944. After ten years in Siberia, he was released from captivity a broken man. He died in 1955, shortly after rejoining his family in West Germany. The oncoming Soviet troops had nearly trapped Frau Mannheim and the children in Pudewitz, but they managed to escape to the West before the Communists consolidated their hold in the East. I searched for and found them through the Red Cross. But Karl Mannheim was dead by then. Frau Mannheim wrote to tell me about it, and a powerful surge of sympathy and sadness stirred me. The sense of personal loss I felt at the time remains with me to this day.

★   ★   ★

I had written to my mother soon after the war but received no answer. I took her silence to mean: "Don't write to me—a letter from America could get me in trouble." As soon as Stalin died and was reburied outside the Kremlin wall, I wrote again, and after thirteen years, in 1956, Mama and I resumed our correspondence.

My burning desire to see my mother overcame Jim's fear that the Soviets would not let me leave. He called the State Department and was informed that no American national had been detained by the Soviets, at least so far. We decided to take the chance and visit Mama. I was seventeen when I left Kiev. Now I was thirty-eight.

★   ★   ★

Jim and I step over a pile of rubble in front of the cast-iron double gates; beyond them the courtyard beckons. Suddenly I am a child again. I chase a ball that rolls toward me and kick it back to the youngsters playing soccer. I exchange greetings with the women hanging out their windows.

In the garden beyond, the stage and the gymnasium apparatus are gone, no flowers grow there anymore, no names of boys and girls in love are scribbled awkwardly on our "bulletin board."

The beautiful building of czarist vintage is sorely neglected, the white marble stairs gray and chipped, windows between the landings broken, the walls dirty, paint flaking. I could swear it has not been painted since before my parents and I moved there in 1928.

It is not the same, and I feel sad.

Mother greets us at the door. She points to a heap of rubble on her landing. "It's embarrassing!" she says. "What will Jeemie think? The roof is leaking and the *Upravdom* (management of the buildings) is trying to fix it. It will take *years* before they do. In the meantime, they could at least clear away that rubble. I've complained and complained. I'll tell you about it later. Come in, children, everybody's waiting." In the entry hall, she tells me, "My room is not what it used to be, Zosik. Tell Jeemie that, so he won't think I don't know any better."

Poor Mama, she lost her possessions in the war after all: the Germans confiscated them. But she needn't have worried, Jim understands. In any case, she has improvised marvelously; her room is cheerful and bright. On the walls are several good paintings and a silk carpet, on which hang enlarged and framed photographs of little Guido and Sylvia, and of Jim and me.

The room is full of relatives and friends seated around the table, waiting thirstily for Jim to uncork the first bottle and for Mama to propose the first toast. The table groans with bottles of Georgian wine and cognac, two kinds of vodka (one a very hot and peppery *Gorilka*), mineral water, Soviet champagne, and *zakooska* (appetizers): a dish of beluga caviar, herrings and boiled potatoes with fresh dill, marinated mushrooms, dill pickles, and a basket of thinly sliced black and white bread

Mama sits down between Jim and me and lifts her glass. "God and you are my witnesses how I longed for this moment. Here's to my children, Zosik and Jeemie! May they always be happy and live long and in peace."

Water glasses (the only glasses available) click all around and the men down the vodka in one swallow. I nudge Jim. "Bottoms up, darling! Vodka left in your glass means hatred in your heart."

"Oops, I forgot." Jim grins, downs his glass and barely suppresses a shiver. He stands up and proposes a toast, "To the forever young and beautiful Mama." She beams when I translate.

Mother's carefully guarded secret of our arrival spreads like wildfire. Throughout the evening people keep ringing the bell. Childhood playmates, old family friends come to embrace me tearfully, to meet Jim, to join us in a toast, and to depart again because there simply is no room for another body. Youngsters come bearing gifts; they part with their precious envelopes of stamps, lapel badges, a whistling nightingale of clay. I search for a few things from America to give them in return.

The eating and drinking continues late into the night. Mama flits back and forth to the kitchen bearing platters piled with baked chickens and, especially for her Zosik, dumplings with cherries served with hot melted butter and cherry juice. When I think I can eat no more, Aunt Yulia carries in a large square of napoleon, the pièce de résistance.

I ask Mama, "How is your love life? Do you have a gentleman friend?"

"Ekh, Zosik," she answers with a nostalgic sigh. "My spirit is willing, but my window dressing is not as alluring as it used to be."

I laugh and explain to Jim: "Mama says she lost her beauty and with it her sex appeal."

"What did you want to tell me on the landing, Mama?"

"Ah yes. I complained about that shameful mess of rubble everywhere, told them I am expecting visitors. They ignored me, of course, so I said, 'Not just any visitors, my daughter and her husband are coming from America!' And one day later two officials show up and offer me a brand-new apartment."

"They what? Why didn't you take it?" I am amazed she didn't jump at the chance. Most of those present are still living in communal apartments, and many are waiting anxiously for completion of this, that, or the other new block of flats, known as Khrushchevki, in which they are promised an apartment of their own.

"One room is enough for me," says Mama. "Besides, I'd be lonely by myself. My neighbors and I get along." Isn't she the one, I remind her, who used to complain about sharing the facilities with others? "Well," she drawls, "the truth is, I'm afraid to give up this room in the center of town. They wanted to move me to the devil's side of town" [meaning the outskirts]. "When you leave, Zosik, they'd probably take the new apartment away from me—and there I'd be. I don't trust them."

Shocked to hear her say this in front of all these people, I kick Mama under the table. "Ha." She flings her arms. "What's there to be afraid of? We can say anything we want now, since Khrushchev."

"I'm glad to hear you're happy with Khrushchev," I say.

"Who says we are happy? Khrushchev is much better than Stalin ever was, but he is not good enough."

"You're not being entirely fair to Khrushchev," Uncle Vanya, Aunt Yulia's husband, says. "He's doing a great deal to solve our housing problem. And another thing, if it were not for Nikita Sergeyevich, Zosia and Jim wouldn't be here with us today."

Uncle Vanya doesn't say it, but neither he nor Cousin Valya would be among us if Stalin were still alive. Uncle Vanya was arrested shortly before the war and released after Stalin died. Cousin Valya spent seven grim years in Kamchatka, a penal colony in the Russian Far East. She had worked as a slave in Germany during the war. *And was foolish enough to return to the Soviet Union*, I think to myself. I remember the dream I had in June 1943 of seeing her head bob above the water as she was pulled into the ocean. And Cousin Igor—he was in that dream too. I had no idea either of them was in Germany, and they both were pulled back into the Soviet Union.

What I discover in the Kiev of 1962—or rather, rediscover—is still the world of apathy, inefficiency, and waste. Mama takes us to see the new apartment blocks being built across the river, shabbily built, nicknamed "Khrushchevki." It takes years before sidewalks are paved, and the residents have to wade through mud, carrying dirt with them into their homes. Or the crew arrives to pave the street before the final thaw. When the ice melts, the asphalt bulges, splinters, and breaks. And in the spring, lovely mushrooms grow between the cracks in the pavement.

People are rude. "It's the only language they understand," Mama says. Many of my generation are heavy drinkers. Drink, or escape to the countryside where the air is bright and sharp: these are the only antidotes to the bleakness and drudgery of everyday life.

Mother is reluctant to talk about some things. She does verify that Papa was killed in battle at Poltava in 1941, but she doesn't know anything about his brothers and their families. (I will find Uncle Lazar on my next visit to Kiev. Uncle Yasha survived the war, died later; his son, my daredevil and best friend Cousin Vladimir, was killed at the front.) Tetya Valya still lives in Lvov with her son. I am glad Svetik survived the war. But most of his pals, and mine, did not.

My good friend, the gentle Shura Prudnik, committed suicide the spring before. I visit her sister Nadya, who tells me Shura's husband, an alcoholic, drove Shura to drink following their son's sudden death, and to suicide by his unfaithfulness. The day his mistress gave birth to his child, he was on his way to the hospital to welcome the newborn and was killed in a car accident, following Shura into the grave by a few weeks.

I ask Nadya about Aleksandr Platonov. "Oh-ho!" she flares up. "He's the one who made you leave Kiev and then abandoned you." I assure her it isn't so, that it was I who left him in Stalingrad because I wanted to return home. "He's a bigwig now," she tells me, "an assistant professor, academician. He was in Siberia for many years—in charge of the Lena River Fleet. He comes back and right away they give him a large apartment, and only him and his fat wife live there. He's got a car, too!" I detect envy in her voice. *There is much of that in Russia*, I reflect.

"Where does he live?"

"In the house next to us."

It takes all I have to keep my voice calm. "I'd like to see him." Nadya finds his phone number, and I telephone.

"You probably don't remember me. It's Zoya." I nearly add "Williams."

"Zoya! Where have you been? How I worried . . . I blamed myself. I thought you'd been killed . . . I tried to find you." Silence. Then: "When can I see you?"

And I thought he'd never ask.

We greet one another at the top of Vladimirskaya Hill, and I am a self-conscious girl of seventeen again. Aleksandr touches my arm and I blush, feeling electrified.

"Ekh, Zoya, Zoya." He sighs. "How I loved you. You were a beauty then—and you still are," he adds quickly, and I laugh. "Remember the first time you allowed me to kiss you?"

"I've never forgotten it. I've never forgotten you."

Aleksandr looks at his watch when I tell him I have only half an hour. He tells me he has a son the same age as Sylvia. I show him photographs of my children, and he looks at them for long moments. "They could have been mine," he says. "Whenever I was troubled, I blamed you for my un-happiness. If you hadn't left . . . Why did you leave me?"

"Why did you let me go? There were times I wished you hadn't let me leave Stalingrad."

"What are we to do?" he asks, knowing the answer as well as I do.

For us there are only profound, sweet, and painful memories. A last-ing love that could have meant a lifetime shared. If there had been no war.

Jim and I have only five days in Kiev, and they end too soon. On our last day, we wander through the stadium—now named for Khrushchev—that was to have opened on June 22, 1941. Instead, the opening ceremony took place some ten years later; the original ticketholders were invited to attend and were asked to come forward. But only a handful did. Thousands had lost their lives on the battlefields; the Nazis executed others; a total of 200,000 Kievans were killed in the war.

We sit above center field in silence, and I think of Shura, who was to have attended the opening of the stadium with me. I cannot rid myself of the feeling that if I had been there to comfort her she would be alive today.

I cannot help remembering the young men who were to play soccer at the opening. The entire team was wiped out during the occupation, killed by the Nazis because the Kievans won one and yet another match against them.

I can't help thinking that I might have been happy in Kiev had I not been uprooted by the war and transplanted to another soil. I feel like an uprooted tree—fortunately the kind of tree that survived its original trans-plant and was still young enough to grow among the giant sequoias of the marvelous country that adopted it. But how many people must there be who have never recovered from the shock of being transplanted, yet could never be happy again on their native soil?

I cry for all the Kievans who lost their lives in the war and for the Jews massacred at Babi Yar. I would have been one of them had I stayed. I cry for Papa, and I cry for all the uprooted people in the world.

That night Jim and I entertain the family in the hotel restaurant. After several toasts to peace—always peace—Cousin Valya's husband, Georgi Vasilyevich Bonkin, a retired defense attorney with a shock of silver-white hair, rises from his seat and speaks to us.

"This is the first time I have met you, Sophia, and the first time the family met you, Jim. Already you are in our hearts, and it is sad for us to part with you. A great distance will separate us. But I want you to know that I and everyone, the entire family, will feel close to you no matter where you are." His eyes are moist. "Please, Sophia and Jim, take our love and greetings to your country, our friendship and hope for growing understanding between our two great nations, the United States of America and the Soviet Union," he says, bringing tears to Jim's eyes and mine. "Let us drink to friendship and to enduring peace."

This is a farewell toast, I think, and I look long and hard at everyone so that I can imprint their faces in my mind and remember them forever.

But I will return when the chestnut trees are in bloom again.

POSTSCRIPT

My deeply satisfying association with the Bechtel Corporation, which began in San Francisco in 1955, spanned three decades. I worked as a draftsman, a piping designer, a supervising piping engineer—and I was a corporate wife. When Jim, a project enginner, was relocated to Edmonton, Alberta, Canada, in 1965, I was at his side. Later, during the construction phase of the colossal project—the surface mining of oil in the tar sands of Athabasca—I followed Jim into the wilderness of Fort McMurray.

My children, Sylvia and Guido, were both employed by Bechtel for a time. Sylvia soon turned to scriptwriting; her first film, *Golden Needles*, was released in 1974. Guido served one year in Vietnam. Immediately upon his discharge in 1968 he arrived in Edmonton, and Sylvia rushed from New York to celebrate his return with us. Both spent good times with Jim and me in Canada, and later also in London. Sylvia died in the spring of 2000. Guido graduated from university, established himself in a gratifying business, and married lovely Melody. They have two sons, Alexander and Michael, and six grandchildren.

Jim's promotion to manager of engineering at Bechtel International took him to London in 1969. I landed in London the day man landed on the moon.

During my six years abroad, I visited Kiev several times. I always stayed at the Hotel Dnipro and was at liberty to see anyone I wished without hurting my mother's sensibilities. In 1969, Tetya Valya came to Kiev to spend a day with me. We reminisced of bygone events and experiences, and later celebrated an emotional reunion with my father's family. Aunt Sonya, Uncle Yasha's widow, lived with her daughter, Maya. Maya married and had a son, Vladimir. Uncle Lazar and his wife Genya had a daughter, Lena, born after the war; she married and had a son, Boris. My cousins Maya and Lena are like sisters to me. When they immigrated to the United States in the 1980s, I felt blessed to have these bright, warm, and loving young families on American soil.

My mother died at home in March 1974. My Jim died in London in December 1974.

I returned to San Francisco and to work at Bechtel in 1975. Two years later I was transferred to the Bechtel Petrochemical Division office in Houston. During my career I was assigned to engineering and construction projects of numerous oil refineries and liquid natural gas plants at home and abroad, working in Arzew in Algeria on the Mediterranean Sea, in London, in Edmonton, and in Tokyo. I retired from Bechtel in 1985, live in Houston, and enjoy a busy life of traveling, writing, and trying to keep fit.

Four generations, from left to right, top row: Alexander; Michael; Ayden; and my son, Guy (Guido); center row: Grace, me, and Alexander Jr.; bottom row: Andrew, Sophia, and Emma.